Elements of Programming

Elements of Programming

Alexander Stepanov
Paul McJones

✦ Addison-Wesley

Upper Saddle River, NJ • Boston • Indianapolis • San Francisco
New York • Toronto • Montreal • London • Munich • Paris • Madrid
Capetown • Sydney • Tokyo • Singapore • Mexico City

The publisher offers excellent discounts on this book when ordered in quantity for bulk purchases or special sales, which may include electronic versions and/or custom covers and content particular to your business, training goals, marketing focus, and branding interests. For more information, please contact:

U.S. Corporate and Government Sales
(800) 382-3419
corpsales@pearsontechgroup.com

For sales outside the United States please contact:
International Sales
international@pearson.com

Visit us on the Web: www.informit.com/aw

Library of Congress Cataloging-in-Publication Data

Stepanov, Alexander A.
      Elements of programming/Alexander Stepanov, Paul McJones.
            p. cm.
      Includes bibliographical references and index.
      ISBN 0-321-63537-X (hardcover : alk. paper)
      1. Computer programming. 2. Computer algorithms.   I. McJones, Paul.   II. Title.
   QA76.6.S726 2009
   005.1–dc22   2009007604

ISBN-13: 978-0-321-63537-2
ISBN-10:   0-321-63537-X

Text printed in the United States on recycled paper at Edwards Brothers in Ann Arbor, Michigan.
Second printing, October 2009

Contents

Preface   *ix*

About the Authors   *xiii*

1 Foundations   1

   1.1   Categories of Ideas: Entity, Species, Genus   1

   1.2   Values   2

   1.3   Objects   4

   1.4   Procedures   6

   1.5   Regular Types   6

   1.6   Regular Procedures   8

   1.7   Concepts   10

   1.8   Conclusions   14

2 Transformations and Their Orbits   15

   2.1   Transformations   15

   2.2   Orbits   18

   2.3   Collision Point   21

   2.4   Measuring Orbit Sizes   27

   2.5   Actions   28

   2.6   Conclusions   29

3 Associative Operations   31

   3.1   Associativity   31

   3.2   Computing Powers   33

3.3   Program Transformations   35

3.4   Special-Case Procedures   39

3.5   Parameterizing Algorithms   42

3.6   Linear Recurrences   43

3.7   Accumulation Procedures   46

3.8   Conclusions   47

4 Linear Orderings   49

4.1   Classification of Relations   49

4.2   Total and Weak Orderings   51

4.3   Order Selection   52

4.4   Natural Total Ordering   61

4.5   Clusters of Derived Procedures   62

4.6   Extending Order-Selection Procedures   63

4.7   Conclusions   63

5 Ordered Algebraic Structures   65

5.1   Basic Algebraic Structures   65

5.2   Ordered Algebraic Structures   70

5.3   Remainder   71

5.4   Greatest Common Divisor   76

5.5   Generalizing gcd   79

5.6   Stein gcd   81

5.7   Quotient   81

5.8   Quotient and Remainder for Negative Quantities   83

5.9   Concepts and Their Models   85

5.10 Computer Integer Types   87

5.11 Conclusions   88

6 Iterators   89

6.1   Readability   89

6.2   Iterators   90

6.3   Ranges   92

6.4   Readable Ranges   95

6.5   Increasing Ranges   103
6.6   Forward Iterators   106
6.7   Indexed Iterators   110
6.8   Bidirectional Iterators   111
6.9   Random-Access Iterators   113
6.10 Conclusions   114

7 Coordinate Structures   115
7.1   Bifurcate Coordinates   115
7.2   Bidirectional Bifurcate Coordinates   119
7.3   Coordinate Structures   124
7.4   Isomorphism, Equivalence, and Ordering   124
7.5   Conclusions   131

8 Coordinates with Mutable Successors   133
8.1   Linked Iterators   133
8.2   Link Rearrangements   134
8.3   Applications of Link Rearrangements   140
8.4   Linked Bifurcate Coordinates   143
8.5   Conclusions   148

9 Copying   149
9.1   Writability   149
9.2   Position-Based Copying   151
9.3   Predicate-Based Copying   157
9.4   Swapping Ranges   164
9.5   Conclusions   168

10 Rearrangements   169
10.1 Permutations   169
10.2 Rearrangements   172
10.3 Reverse Algorithms   174
10.4 Rotate Algorithms   178
10.5 Algorithm Selection   186
10.6 Conclusions   189

11 Partition and Merging   191

  11.1   Partition   191

  11.2   Balanced Reduction   198

  11.3   Merging   202

  11.4   Conclusions   208

12 Composite Objects   209

  12.1   Simple Composite Objects   209

  12.2   Dynamic Sequences   216

  12.3   Underlying Type   222

  12.4   Conclusions   225

Afterword   227

Appendix A   Mathematical Notation   231

Appendix B   Programming Language   233

  B.1   Language Definition   233

  B.2   Macros and Trait Structures   240

Bibliography   243

Index   247

Preface

This book applies the deductive method to programming by affiliating programs with the abstract mathematical theories that enable them to work. Specification of these theories, algorithms written in terms of these theories, and theorems and lemmas describing their properties are presented together. The implementation of the algorithms in a real programming language is central to the book. While the specifications, which are addressed to human beings, should, and even must, combine rigor with appropriate informality, the code, which is addressed to the computer, must be absolutely precise even while being general.

As with other areas of science and engineering, the appropriate foundation of programming is the deductive method. It facilitates the decomposition of complex systems into components with mathematically specified behavior. That, in turn, is a necessary precondition for designing efficient, reliable, secure, and economical software.

The book is addressed to those who want a deeper understanding of programming, whether they are full-time software developers, or scientists and engineers for whom programming is an important part of their professional activity.

The book is intended to be read from beginning to end. Only by reading the code, proving the lemmas, and doing the exercises can readers gain understanding of the material. In addition, we suggest several projects, some open-ended. While the book is terse, a careful reader will eventually see the connections between its parts and the reasons for our choice of material. Discovering the architectural principles of the book should be the reader's goal.

We assume an ability to do elementary algebraic manipulations.[1] We also assume familiarity with the basic vocabulary of logic and set theory at the level of undergraduate courses on discrete mathematics; Appendix A summarizes the notation that we use. We provide definitions of a few concepts of abstract algebra when they are

---

1. For a refresher on elementary algebra, we recommend Chrystal [1904].

needed to specify algorithms. We assume programming maturity and understanding of computer architecture[2] and fundamental algorithms and data structures.[3]

We chose C++ because it combines powerful abstraction facilities with faithful representation of the underlying machine.[4] We use a small subset of the language and write requirements as structured comments. We hope that readers not already familiar with C++ are able to follow the book. Appendix B specifies the subset of the language used in the book.[5] Wherever there is a difference between mathematical notation and C++, the typesetting and the context determine whether the mathematical or C++ meaning applies. While many concepts and programs in the book have parallels in STL (the C++ Standard Template Library), the book departs from some of the STL design decisions. The book also ignores issues that a real library, such as STL, has to address: namespaces, visibility, inline directives, and so on.

Chapter 1 describes values, objects, types, procedures, and concepts. Chapters 2–5 describe algorithms on algebraic structures, such as semigroups and totally ordered sets. Chapters 6–11 describe algorithms on abstractions of memory. Chapter 12 describes objects containing other objects. The Afterword presents our reflections on the approach presented by the book.

Acknowledgments

We are grateful to Adobe Systems and its management for supporting the Foundations of Programming course and this book, which grew out of it. In particular, Greg Gilley initiated the course and suggested writing the book; Dave Story and then Bill Hensler provided unwavering support. Finally, the book would not have been possible without Sean Parent's enlightened management and continuous scrutiny of the code and the text. The ideas in the book stem from our close collaboration, spanning almost three decades, with Dave Musser. Bjarne Stroustrup deliberately evolved C++ to support these ideas. Both Dave and Bjarne were kind enough to come to San Jose and carefully review the preliminary draft. Sean Parent and Bjarne Stroustrup wrote the appendix defining the C++ subset used in the book. Jon Brandt reviewed multiple drafts of the book. John Wilkinson carefully read the final manuscript, providing innumerable valuable suggestions.

---

2. We recommend Patterson and Hennessy [2007].

3. For a selective but incisive introduction to algorithms and data structures, we recommend Tarjan [1983].

4. The standard reference is Stroustrup [2000].

5. The code in the book compiles and runs under Microsoft Visual C++ 9 and g++ 4. This code, together with a few trivial macros that enable it to compile, as well as unit tests, can be downloaded from www.elementsofprogramming.com.

The book has benefited significantly from the contributions of our editor, Peter Gordon, our project editor, Elizabeth Ryan, our copy editor, Evelyn Pyle, and the editorial reviewers: Matt Austern, Andrew Koenig, David Musser, Arch Robison, Jerry Schwarz, Jeremy Siek, and John Wilkinson.

We thank all the students who took the course at Adobe and an earlier course at SGI for their suggestions. We hope we succeeded in weaving the material from these courses into a coherent whole. We are grateful for comments from Dave Abrahams, Andrei Alexandrescu, Konstantine Arkoudas, John Banning, Hans Boehm, Angelo Borsotti, Jim Dehnert, John DeTreville, Boris Fomitchev, Kevlin Henney, Jussi Ketonen, Karl Malbrain, Mat Marcus, Larry Masinter, Dave Parent, Dmitry Polukhin, Jon Reid, Mark Ruzon, Geoff Scott, David Simons, Anna Stepanov, Tony Van Eerd, Walter Vannini, Tim Winkler, and Oleg Zabluda.

Finally, we are grateful to all the people who taught us through their writings or in person, and to the institutions that allowed us to deepen our understanding of programming.

About the Authors

Alexander Stepanov studied mathematics at Moscow State University from 1967 to 1972. He has been programming since 1972: first in the Soviet Union and, after emigrating in 1977, in the United States. He has programmed operating systems, programming tools, compilers, and libraries. His work on foundations of programming has been supported by GE, Brooklyn Polytechnic, AT&T, HP, SGI, and, since 2002, Adobe. In 1995 he received the *Dr. Dobb's Journal* Excellence in Programming Award for the design of the C++ Standard Template Library.

Paul McJones studied engineering mathematics at the University of California, Berkeley, from 1967 to 1971. He has been programming since 1967 in the areas of operating systems, programming environments, transaction processing systems, and enterprise and consumer applications. He has been employed by the University of California, IBM, Xerox, Tandem, DEC, and, since 2003, Adobe. In 1982 he and his coauthors received the ACM Programming Systems and Languages Paper Award for their paper "The Recovery Manager of the System R Database Manager."

Chapter 1
Foundations

*S*tarting *with a brief taxonomy of ideas, we introduce notions of* value, object, type, procedure, *and* concept *that represent different categories of ideas in the computer. A central notion of the book,* regularity, *is introduced and elaborated. When applied to procedures, regularity means that procedures return equal results for equal arguments. When applied to types, regularity means that types possess the equality operator and equality-preserving copy construction and assignment. Regularity enables us to apply equational reasoning (substituting equals for equals) to transform and optimize programs.*

1.1 Categories of Ideas: Entity, Species, Genus

In order to explain what objects, types, and other foundational computer notions are, it is useful to give an overview of some categories of ideas that correspond to these notions.

An *abstract entity* is an individual thing that is eternal and unchangeable, while a *concrete entity* is an individual thing that comes into and out of existence in space and time. An *attribute*—a correspondence between a concrete entity and an abstract entity—describes some property, measurement, or quality of the concrete entity. *Identity*, a primitive notion of our perception of reality, determines the sameness of a thing changing over time. Attributes of a concrete entity can change without affecting its identity. A *snapshot* of a concrete entity is a complete collection of its attributes at a particular point in time. Concrete entities are not only physical entities but also legal, financial, or political entities. Blue and 13 are examples of abstract entities. Socrates and the United States of America are examples of concrete entities. The color of Socrates' eyes and the number of U.S. states are examples of attributes.

An *abstract species* describes common properties of essentially equivalent abstract entities. Examples of abstract species are natural number and color. A *concrete species* describes the set of attributes of essentially equivalent concrete entities. Examples of concrete species are man and U.S. state.

A *function* is a rule that associates one or more abstract entities, called *arguments*, from corresponding species with an abstract entity, called the *result*, from another species. Examples of functions are the successor function, which associates each natural number with the one that immediately follows it, and the function that associates with two colors the result of blending them.

An *abstract genus* describes different abstract species that are similar in some respect. Examples of abstract genera are number and binary operator. A *concrete genus* describes different concrete species similar in some respect. Examples of concrete genera are mammal and biped.

An entity belongs to a single species, which provides the rules for its construction or existence. An entity can belong to several genera, each of which describes certain properties.

We show later in the chapter that objects and values represent entities, types represent species, and concepts represent genera.

1.2 Values

Unless we know the interpretation, the only things we see in a computer are 0s and 1s. A *datum* is a finite sequence of 0s and 1s.

A *value type* is a correspondence between a species (abstract or concrete) and a set of datums. A datum corresponding to a particular entity is called a *representation* of the entity; the entity is called the *interpretation* of the datum. We refer to a datum together with its interpretation as a *value*. Examples of values are integers represented in 32-bit two's complement big-endian format and rational numbers represented as a concatenation of two 32-bit sequences, interpreted as integer numerator and denominator, represented as two's complement big-endian values.

A datum is *well formed* with respect to a value type if and only if that datum represents an abstract entity. For example, every sequence of 32 bits is well formed when interpreted as a two's-complement integer; an IEEE 754 floating-point NaN (Not a Number) is not well formed when interpreted as a real number.

A value type is *properly partial* if its values represent a proper subset of the abstract entities in the corresponding species; otherwise it is *total*. For example, the type int is properly partial, while the type bool is total.

A value type is *uniquely represented* if and only if at most one value corresponds to each abstract entity. For example, a type representing a truth value as a byte that interprets zero as false and nonzero as true is not uniquely represented. A type representing an integer as a sign bit and an unsigned magnitude does not provide a unique representation of zero. A type representing an integer in two's complement is uniquely represented.

A value type is *ambiguous* if and only if a value of the type has more than one interpretation. The negation of ambiguous is *unambiguous*. For example, a type representing a calendar year over a period longer than a single century as two decimal digits is ambiguous.

Two values of a value type are *equal* if and only if they represent the same abstract entity. They are *representationally equal* if and only if their datums are identical sequences of 0s and 1s.

Lemma 1.1   If a value type is uniquely represented, equality implies representational equality.

Lemma 1.2   If a value type is not ambiguous, representational equality implies equality.

If a value type is uniquely represented, we implement equality by testing that both sequences of 0s and 1s are the same. Otherwise we must implement equality in such a way that preserves its consistency with the interpretations of its arguments. Nonunique representations are chosen when testing equality is done less frequently than operations generating new values and when it is possible to make generating new values faster at the cost of making equality slower. For example, two rational numbers represented as pairs of integers are equal if they reduce to the same lowest terms. Two finite sets represented as unsorted sequences are equal if, after sorting and eliminating duplicates, their corresponding elements are equal.

Sometimes, implementing true *behavioral* equality is too expensive or even impossible, as in the case for a type of encodings of computable functions. In these cases we must settle for the weaker *representational* equality: that two values are the same sequence of 0s and 1s.

Computers *implement* functions on abstract entities as functions on values. While values reside in memory, a properly implemented function on values does not depend on particular memory addresses: It implements a mapping from values to values.

A function defined on a value type is *regular* if and only if it respects equality: Substituting an equal value for an argument gives an equal result. Most numeric functions are regular. An example of a numeric function that is not regular is the function that returns the numerator of a rational number represented as a pair of integers, since $\frac{1}{2} = \frac{2}{4}$, but numerator$(\frac{1}{2}) \neq$ numerator$(\frac{2}{4})$. Regular functions allow *equational reasoning:* substituting equals for equals.

A nonregular function depends on the representation, not just the interpretation, of its argument. When designing the representation for a value type, two tasks go hand in hand: implementing equality and deciding which functions will be regular.

1.3 Objects

A *memory* is a set of words, each with an *address* and a *content*. The addresses are values of a fixed size, called the *address length*. The contents are values of another fixed size, called the *word length*. The content of an address is obtained by a *load* operation. The association of a content with an address is changed by a *store* operation. Examples of memories are bytes in main memory and blocks on a disk drive.

An *object* is a representation of a concrete entity as a value in memory. An object has a *state* that is a value of some value type. The state of an object is changeable. Given an object corresponding to a concrete entity, its state corresponds to a snapshot of that entity. An object owns a set of *resources*, such as memory words or records in a file, to hold its state.

While the value of an object is a contiguous sequence of 0s and 1s, the resources in which these 0s and 1s are stored are not necessarily contiguous. It is the interpretation that gives unity to an object. For example, two `doubles` may be interpreted as a single complex number even if they are not adjacent. The resources of an object might even be in different memories. This book, however, deals only with objects residing in a single memory with one address space. Every object has a unique *starting address*, from which all its resources can be reached.

An *object type* is a pattern for storing and modifying values in memory. Corresponding to every object type is a value type describing states of objects of that type. Every object belongs to an object type. An example of an object type is integers represented in 32-bit two's complement little-endian format aligned to a 4-byte address boundary.

Values and objects play complementary roles. Values are unchanging and are independent of any particular implementation in the computer. Objects are changeable and have computer-specific implementations. The state of an object at any point in time can be described by a value; this value could in principle be written down on paper (making a snapshot) or *serialized* and sent over a communication link.

Describing the states of objects in terms of values allows us to abstract from the particular implementations of the objects when discussing equality. Functional programming deals with values; imperative programming deals with objects.

We use values to represent entities. Since values are unchanging, they can represent abstract entities. Sequences of values can also represent sequences of snapshots of concrete entities. Objects hold values representing entities. Since objects are changeable, they can represent concrete entities by taking on a new value to represent a change in the entity. Objects can also represent abstract entities: staying constant or taking on different approximations to the abstract.

We use objects in the computer for the following three reasons.

1. Objects model changeable concrete entities, such as employee records in a payroll application.

2. Objects provide a powerful way to implement functions on values, such as a procedure implementing the square root of a floating-point number using an iterative algorithm.

3. Computers with memory constitute the only available realization of a universal computational device.

Some properties of value types carry through to object types. An object is *well formed* if and only if its state is well formed. An object type is *properly partial* if and only if its value type is properly partial; otherwise it is *total*. An object type is *uniquely represented* if and only if its value type is uniquely represented.

Since concrete entities have identities, objects representing them need a corresponding notion of identity. An *identity token* is a unique value expressing the identity of an object and is computed from the value of the object and the address of its resources. Examples of identity tokens are the address of the object, an index into an array where the object is stored, and an employee number in a personnel record. Testing equality of identity tokens corresponds to testing identity. During the lifetime of an application, a particular object could use different identity tokens as it moves either within a data structure or from one data structure to another.

Two objects of the same type are *equal* if and only if their states are equal. If two objects are equal, we say that one is a *copy* of the other. Making a change to an object does not affect any copy of it.

This book uses a programming language that has no way to describe values and value types as separate from objects and object types. So from this point on, when we refer to types without qualification, we mean object types.

1.4 Procedures

A *procedure* is a sequence of instructions that modifies the state of some objects; it may also construct or destroy objects.

The objects with which a procedure interacts can be divided into four kinds, corresponding to the intentions of the programmer.

1. *Input/output* consists of objects passed to/from a procedure directly or indirectly through its arguments or returned result.
2. *Local state* consists of objects created, destroyed, and usually modified during a single invocation of the procedure.
3. *Global state* consists of objects accessible to this and other procedures across multiple invocations.
4. *Own state* consists of objects accessible only to this procedure (and its affiliated procedures) but shared across multiple invocations.

An object is passed *directly* if it is passed as an argument or returned as the result and is passed *indirectly* if it is passed via a pointer or pointerlike object. An object is an *input* to a procedure if it is read, but not modified, by the procedure. An object is an *output* from a procedure if it is written, created, or destroyed by the procedure, but its initial state is not read by the procedure. An object is an *input/output* of a procedure if it is modified as well as read by the procedure.

A *computational basis* for a type is a finite set of procedures that enable the construction of any other procedure on the type. A basis is *efficient* if and only if any procedure implemented using it is as efficient as an equivalent procedure written in terms of an alternative basis. For example, a basis for unsigned k-bit integers providing only zero, equality, and the successor function is not efficient, since the complexity of addition in terms of successor is exponential in k.

A basis is *expressive* if and only if it allows compact and convenient definitions of procedures on the type. In particular, all the common mathematical operations need to be provided when they are appropriate. For example, subtraction could be implemented using negation and addition but should be included in an expressive basis. Similarly, negation could be implemented using subtraction and zero but should be included in an expressive basis.

1.5 Regular Types

There is a set of procedures whose inclusion in the computational basis of a type lets us place objects in data structures and use algorithms to copy objects from one data structure to another. We call types having such a basis *regular*, since their use guarantees regularity of behavior and, therefore, interoperability.[1] We derive the semantics of regular types from built-in types, such as `bool`, `int`, and, when restricted to well-formed values, `double`. A type is *regular* if and only if its basis includes equality, assignment, destructor, default constructor, copy constructor, total ordering,[2] and underlying type.[3]

Equality is a procedure that takes two objects of the same type and returns true if and only if the object states are equal. Inequality is always defined and returns the negation of equality. We use the following notation:

	Specifications	C++
Equality	$a = b$	`a == b`
Inequality	$a \neq b$	`a != b`

Assignment is a procedure that takes two objects of the same type and makes the first object equal to the second without modifying the second. The meaning of assignment does not depend on the initial value of the first object. We use the following notation:

	Specifications	C++
Assignment	$a \leftarrow b$	`a = b`

A *destructor* is a procedure causing the cessation of an object's existence. After a destructor has been called on an object, no procedure can be applied to it, and its former memory locations and resources may be reused for other purposes. The destructor is normally invoked implicitly. Global objects are destroyed when the application terminates, local objects are destroyed when the block in which they are declared is exited, and elements of a data structure are destroyed when the data structure is destroyed.

A *constructor* is a procedure transforming memory locations into an object. The possible behaviors range from doing nothing to establishing a complex object state.

An object is in a *partially formed* state if it can be assigned to or destroyed. For an object that is partially formed but not well formed, the effect of any procedure other than assignment (only on the left side) and destruction is not defined.

---

1. While regular types underlie the design of STL, they were first formally introduced in Dehnert and Stepanov [2000].
2. Strictly speaking, as becomes clear in Chapter 4, it could be either total ordering or default total ordering.
3. Underlying type is defined in Chapter 12.

Lemma 1.3   A well-formed object is partially formed.

A *default constructor* takes no arguments and leaves the object in a partially formed state. We use the following notation:

	C++
Local object of type T	T a;
Anonymous object of type T	T()

A *copy constructor* takes an additional argument of the same type and constructs a new object equal to it. We use the following notation:

	C++
Local copy of object b	T a = b;

1.6 Regular Procedures

A procedure is *regular* if and only if replacing its inputs with equal objects results in equal output objects. As with value types, when defining an object type we must make consistent choices in how to implement equality and which procedures on the type will be regular.

Exercise 1.1   Extend the notion of regularity to input/output objects of a procedure, that is, to objects that are modified as well as read.

While regularity is the default, there are reasons for nonregular behavior of procedures.

1. A procedure returns the address of an object; for example, the built-in function `addressof`.

2. A procedure returns a value determined by the state of the real world, such as the value of a clock or other device.

3. A procedure returns a value depending on own state; for example, a pseudorandom number generator.

4. A procedure returns a representation-dependent attribute of an object, such as the amount of reserved memory for a data structure.

A *functional procedure* is a regular procedure defined on regular types, with one or more direct inputs and a single output that is returned as the result of the procedure. The regularity of functional procedures allows two techniques for passing inputs. When the size of the parameter is small or if the procedure needs a copy it can mutate, we pass it *by value*, making a local copy. Otherwise we pass it *by constant reference*. A functional procedure can be implemented as a C++ function, function pointer, or function object.[4]

This is a functional procedure:

```
int plus_0(int a, int b)
{
    return a + b;
}
```

This is a semantically equivalent functional procedure:

```
int plus_1(const int& a, const int& b)
{
    return a + b;
}
```

This is semantically equivalent but is not a functional procedure, because its inputs and outputs are passed indirectly:

```
void plus_2(int* a, int* b, int* c)
{
    *c = *a + *b;
}
```

In plus_2, a and b are input objects, while c is an output object. The notion of a functional procedure is a syntactic rather than semantic property: In our terminology, plus_2 is regular but not functional.

The *definition space* for a functional procedure is that subset of values for its inputs to which it is intended to be applied. A functional procedure always terminates on input in its definition space; while it may terminate for input outside its definition space, it may not return a meaningful value.

---

4. C++ functions are not objects and cannot be passed as arguments; C++ function pointers and function objects are objects and can be passed as arguments.

A *homogeneous* functional procedure is one whose input objects are all the same type. The *domain* of a homogeneous functional procedure is the type of its inputs. Rather than defining the domain of a nonhomogeneous functional procedure as the direct product of its input types, we refer individually to the input types of a procedure.

The *codomain* for a functional procedure is the type of its output. The *result space* for a functional procedure is the set of all values from its codomain returned by the procedure for inputs from its definition space.

Consider the functional procedure

```
int square(int n) { return n * n; }
```

While its domain and codomain are int, its definition space is the set of integers whose square is representable in the type, and its result space is the set of square integers representable in the type.

> **Exercise 1.2**   Assuming that int is a 32-bit two's complement type, determine the exact definition and result space.

1.7 Concepts

A procedure using a type depends on syntactic, semantic, and complexity properties of the computational basis of the type. Syntactically it depends on the presence of certain literals and procedures with particular names and signatures. Its semantics depend on properties of these procedures. Its complexity depends on the time and space complexity of these procedures. A program remains correct if a type is replaced by a different type with the same properties. The utility of a software component, such as a library procedure or data structure, is increased by designing it not in terms of concrete types but in terms of requirements on types expressed as syntactic and semantic properties. We call a collection of requirements a *concept*. Types represent species; concepts represent genera.

In order to describe concepts, we need several mechanisms dealing with types: type attributes, type functions, and type constructors. A *type attribute* is a mapping from a type to a value describing some characteristic of the type. Examples of type attributes are the built-in type attribute sizeof(T) in C++, the alignment of an object of a type, and the number of members in a struct. If F is a functional procedure type, Arity(F) returns its number of inputs. A *type function* is a mapping from a type to an affiliated type. An example of a type function is: given "pointer to T," the type T. In some cases it is useful to define an *indexed* type function with an additional constant integer parameter; for example, a type function returning the type of the ith member of a structure type (counting from 0). If F is a functional procedure type, the type function Codomain(F) returns the type of the result. If F is a functional procedure type and $i <$ Arity(F), the indexed type function InputType(F, i) returns the type of the ith parameter (counting from 0).[5] A *type constructor* is a mechanism for creating a new type from one or more existing types. For example, `pointer(T)` is the built-in type constructor that takes a type T and returns the type "pointer to T"; `struct` is a built-in n-ary type constructor; a structure template is a user-defined n-ary type constructor.

If $\mathcal{T}$ is an n-ary type constructor, we usually denote its application to types $T_0, \ldots, T_{n-1}$ as $\mathcal{T}_{T_0,\ldots,T_{n-1}}$. An important example is pair, which, when applied to regular types T_0 and T_1, returns a `struct` type pair_{T_0, T_1} with a member m0 of type T_0 and a member m1 of type T_1. To ensure that the type pair_{T_0, T_1} is itself regular, equality, assignment, destructor, and constructors are defined through memberwise extensions of the corresponding operations on the types T_0 and T_1. The same technique is used for any tuple type, such as triple. In Chapter 12 we show the implementation of pair_{T_0, T_1} and describe how regularity is preserved by more complicated type constructors.

Somewhat more formally, a *concept* is a description of requirements on one or more types stated in terms of the existence and properties of procedures, type attributes, and type functions defined on the types. We say that a concept is *modeled by* specific types, or that the types *model* the concept, if the requirements are satisfied for these types. To assert that a concept $\mathcal{C}$ is modeled by types $T_0, \ldots, T_{n-1}$, we write $\mathcal{C}(T_0, \ldots, T_{n-1})$. Concept $\mathcal{C}'$ *refines* concept $\mathcal{C}$ if whenever $\mathcal{C}'$ is satisfied for a set of types, $\mathcal{C}$ is also satisfied for those types. We say that $\mathcal{C}$ *weakens* $\mathcal{C}'$ if $\mathcal{C}'$ refines $\mathcal{C}$.

A *type concept* is a concept defined on one type. For example, C++ defines the type concept *integral type*, which is refined by *unsigned integral type* and by *signed integral type*, while STL defines the type concept *sequence*. We use the primitive type concepts *Regular* and *FunctionalProcedure*, corresponding to the informal definitions we gave earlier.

---

5. Appendix B shows how to define type attributes and type functions in C++.

We define concepts formally by using standard mathematical notation. To define a concept $\mathcal{C}$, we write

$$\mathcal{C}(T_0, \ldots, T_{n-1}) \triangleq$$
$$\mathcal{E}_0$$
$$\wedge \; \mathcal{E}_1$$
$$\wedge \; \ldots$$
$$\wedge \; \mathcal{E}_{k-1}$$

where $\triangleq$ is read as "is equal to by definition," the T_i are formal type parameters, and the $\mathcal{E}_j$ are concept clauses, which take one of three forms:

1. Application of a previously defined concept, indicating a subset of the type parameters modeling it.

2. Signature of a type attribute, type function, or procedure that must exist for any types modeling the concept. A procedure signature takes the form $f : T \to T'$, where T is the domain and T' is the codomain. A type function signature takes the form $F : \mathcal{C} \to \mathcal{C}'$, where the domain and codomain are concepts.

3. Axiom expressed in terms of these type attributes, type functions, and procedures.

We sometimes include the definition of a type attribute, type function, or procedure following its signature in the second kind of concept clause. It takes the form $x \mapsto \mathcal{F}(x)$ for some expression $\mathcal{F}$. In a particular model, such a definition could be overridden with a different but consistent implementation.

For example, this concept describes a unary functional procedure:

$UnaryFunction(F) \triangleq$
    $FunctionalProcedure(F)$
  $\wedge \; \text{Arity}(F) = 1$

This concept describes a homogeneous functional procedure:

$HomogeneousFunction(F) \triangleq$
    $FunctionalProcedure(F)$
  $\wedge \; \text{Arity}(F) > 0$
  $\wedge \; (\forall i, j \in \mathbb{N})(i, j < \text{Arity}(F)) \Rightarrow (\text{InputType}(F, i) = \text{InputType}(F, j))$
  $\wedge \; \text{Domain} : HomogeneousFunction \to Regular$
      $F \mapsto \text{InputType}(F, 0)$

Observe that

$$(\forall F \in FunctionalProcedure)\ UnaryFunction(F) \Rightarrow HomogeneousFunction(F)$$

An *abstract* procedure is parameterized by types and constant values, with requirements on these parameters.[6] We use function templates and function object templates. The parameters follow the `template` keyword and are introduced by `typename` for types and `int` or another integral type for constant values. Requirements are specified via the `requires` clause, whose argument is an expression built up from constant values, concrete types, formal parameters, applications of type attributes and type functions, equality on values and types, concepts, and logical connectives.[7]

Here is an example of an abstract procedure:

```
template<typename Op>
    requires(BinaryOperation(Op))
Domain(Op) square(const Domain(Op)& x, Op op)
{
    return op(x, x);
}
```

The domain values could be large, so we pass them by constant reference. Operations tend to be small (e.g., a function pointer or small function object), so we pass them by value.

Concepts describe properties satisfied by all objects of a type, whereas *preconditions* describe properties of particular objects. For example, a procedure might require a parameter to be a prime number. The requirement for an integer type is specified by a concept, while primality is specified by a precondition. The type of a function pointer expresses only its signature, not its semantic properties. For example, a procedure might require a parameter to be a pointer to a function implementing an associative binary operation on integers. The requirement for a binary operation on integers is specified by a concept; associativity of a particular function is specified by a precondition.

---

6. Abstract procedures appeared, in substantially the form we use them, in 1930 in van der Waerden [1930], which was based on the lectures of Emmy Noether and Emil Artin. George Collins and David Musser used them in the context of computer algebra in the late 1960s and early 1970s. See, for example, Musser [1975].

7. See Appendix B for the full syntax of the `requires` clause.

To define a precondition for a family of types, we need to use mathematical notation, such as universal and existential quantifiers, implication, and so on. For example, to specify the primality of an integer, we define

property(N : *Integer*)
prime : N
$\quad n \mapsto (\forall u, v \in N)\, uv = n \Rightarrow (|u| = 1 \vee |v| = 1)$

where the first line introduces formal type parameters and the concepts they model, the second line names the property and gives its signature, and the third line gives the predicate establishing whether the property holds for a given argument.

To define regularity of a unary functional procedure, we write

property(F : *UnaryFunction*)
regular_unary_function : F
$\quad f \mapsto (\forall f' \in F)(\forall x, x' \in \text{Domain}(F))$
$\qquad (f = f' \wedge x = x') \Rightarrow (f(x) = f'(x'))$

The definition easily extends to n-ary functions: Application of equal functions to equal arguments gives equal results. By extension, we call an abstract function regular if all its instantiations are regular. In this book every procedural argument is a regular function unless otherwise stated; we omit the precondition stating this explicitly.

> **Project 1.1**   Extend the notions of equality, assignment, and copy construction to objects of distinct types. Think about the interpretations of the two types and axioms that connect cross-type procedures.

1.8 Conclusions

The commonsense view of reality humans share has a representation in the computer. By grounding the meanings of values and objects in their interpretations, we obtain a simple, coherent view. Design decisions, such as how to define equality, become straightforward when the correspondence to entities is taken into account.

Chapter 2

Transformations and Their Orbits

*T**his chapter defines a transformation as a unary regular function from a type to itself. Successive applications of a transformation starting from an initial value determine an orbit of this value. Depending only on the regularity of the transformation and the finiteness of the orbit, we implement an algorithm for determining orbit structures that can be used in different domains. For example, it could be used to detect a cycle in a linked list or to analyze a pseudorandom number generator. We derive an interface to the algorithm as a set of related procedures and definitions for their arguments and results. This analysis of an orbit-structure algorithm allows us to introduce our approach to programming in the simplest possible setting.*

2.1 Transformations

While there are functions from any sequence of types to any type, particular classes of signatures commonly occur. In this book we frequently use two such classes: *homogeneous predicates* and *operations*. Homogeneous predicates are of the form $T \times \cdots \times T \rightarrow$ bool; operations are functions of the form $T \times \cdots \times T \rightarrow T$. While there are n-ary predicates and n-ary operations, we encounter mostly unary and binary homogeneous predicates and unary and binary operations.

A *predicate* is a functional procedure returning a truth value:

Predicate(P) ≜
    FunctionalProcedure(P)
  ∧ Codomain(P) = bool

A homogeneous predicate is one that is also a homogeneous function:

HomogeneousPredicate(P) $\triangleq$
  Predicate(P)
  $\wedge$ *HomogeneousFunction*(P)

A *unary predicate* is a predicate taking one parameter:

UnaryPredicate(P) $\triangleq$
  Predicate(P)
  $\wedge$ *UnaryFunction*(P)

An *operation* is a homogeneous function whose codomain is equal to its domain:

Operation(Op) $\triangleq$
  HomogeneousFunction(Op)
  $\wedge$ Codomain(Op) = Domain(Op)

Examples of operations:

```
int abs(int x) {
    if (x < 0) return -x; else return x;
} // unary operation
```

```
double euclidean_norm(double x, double y) {
    return sqrt(x * x + y * y);
} // binary operation
```

```
double euclidean_norm(double x, double y, double z) {
    return sqrt(x * x + y * y + z * z);
} // ternary operation
```

Lemma 2.1   euclidean_norm(x, y, z) = euclidean_norm(euclidean_norm(x, y), z)

This lemma shows that the ternary version can be obtained from the binary version. For reasons of efficiency, expressiveness, and, possibly, accuracy, the ternary version is part of the computational basis for programs dealing with three-dimensional space.

A procedure is *partial* if its definition space is a subset of the direct product of the types of its inputs; it is *total* if its definition space is equal to the direct product. We follow standard mathematical usage, where partial function includes total function. We call partial procedures that are not total *nontotal*. Implementations of some total functions are nontotal on the computer because of the finiteness of the representation. For example, addition on signed 32-bit integers is nontotal.

A nontotal procedure is accompanied by a precondition specifying its definition space. To verify the correctness of a call of that procedure, we must determine that the arguments satisfy the precondition. Sometimes, a partial procedure is passed as a parameter to an algorithm that needs to determine at runtime the definition space of the procedural parameter. To deal with such cases, we define a *definition-space predicate* with the same inputs as the procedure; the predicate returns true if and only if the inputs are within the definition space of the procedure. Before a nontotal procedure is called, either its precondition must be satisfied, or the call must be guarded by a call of its definition-space predicate.

Exercise 2.1   Implement a definition-space predicate for addition on 32-bit signed integers.

This chapter deals with unary operations, which we call *transformations:*

$Transformation(F) \triangleq$
$\quad\quad Operation(F)$
$\quad \wedge \ UnaryFunction(F)$
$\quad \wedge \ \text{DistanceType} : Transformation \rightarrow Integer$

We discuss DistanceType in the next section.

Transformations are self-composable: $f(x)$, $f(f(x))$, $f(f(f(x)))$, and so on. The definition space of $f(f(x))$ is the intersection of the definition space and result space of f. This ability to self-compose, together with the ability to test for equality, allows us to define interesting algorithms.

When f is a transformation, we define its powers as follows:

$$f^n(x) = \begin{cases} x & \text{if } n = 0, \\ f^{n-1}(f(x)) & \text{if } n > 0 \end{cases}$$

To implement an algorithm to compute $f^n(x)$, we need to specify the requirement for an integer type. We study various concepts describing integers in Chapter 5. For now we rely on the intuitive understanding of integers. Their models include signed and unsigned integral types, as well as arbitrary-precision integers, with these operations and literals:

	Specifications	C++
Sum	$+$	+
Difference	$-$	-
Product	$\cdot$	*
Quotient	$/$	/
Remainder	mod	%
Zero	0	I(0)
One	1	I(1)
Two	2	I(2)

where I is an integer type.

That leads to the following algorithm:

```
template<typename F, typename N>
    requires(Transformation(F) && Integer(N))
Domain(F) power_unary(Domain(F) x, N n, F f)
{
    // Precondition: n ≥ 0 ∧ (∀i ∈ N)0 < i ≤ n ⇒ fⁱ(x) is defined
    while (n != N(0)) {
        n = n - N(1);
        x = f(x);
    }
    return x;
}
```

2.2 Orbits

To understand the global behavior of a transformation, we examine the structure of its *orbits*: elements reachable from a starting element by repeated applications of the transformation. y is *reachable* from x under a transformation f if for some $n \geq 0$, $y = f^n(x)$. x is *cyclic* under f if for some $n \geq 1$, $x = f^n(x)$. x is *terminal* under f if and only if x is not in the definition space of f. The *orbit* of x under a transformation f is the set of all elements reachable from x under f.

Lemma 2.2   An orbit does not contain both a cyclic and a terminal element.

Lemma 2.3   An orbit contains at most one terminal element.

If y is reachable from x under f, the *distance* from x to y is the least number of transformation steps from x to y. Obviously, distance is not always defined.

Given a transformation type F, DistanceType(F) is an integer type large enough to encode the maximum number of steps by any transformation $f \in F$ from one element of T = Domain(F) to another. If type T occupies k bits, there can be as many as 2^k values but only $2^k - 1$ steps between distinct values. Thus if T is a fixed-size type, an integral type of the same size is a valid distance type for any transformation on T. (Instead of using the distance type, we allow the use of any integer type in power_unary, since the extra generality does not appear to hurt there.) It is often the case that all transformation types over a domain have the same distance type. In this case the type function DistanceType is defined for the domain type and defines the corresponding type function for the transformation types.

The existence of DistanceType leads to the following procedure:

```
template<typename F>
    requires(Transformation(F))
DistanceType(F) distance(Domain(F) x, Domain(F) y, F f)
{
    // Precondition: y is reachable from x under f
    typedef DistanceType(F) N;
    N n(0);
    while (x != y) {
        x = f(x);
        n = n + N(1);
    }
    return n;
}
```

Orbits have different shapes. An orbit of x under a transformation is

infinite	if it has no cyclic or terminal elements
terminating	if it has a terminal element
circular	if x is cyclic
ρ-shaped	if x is not cyclic, but its orbit contains a cyclic element

An orbit of x is *finite* if it is not infinite. Figure 2.1 illustrates the various cases.

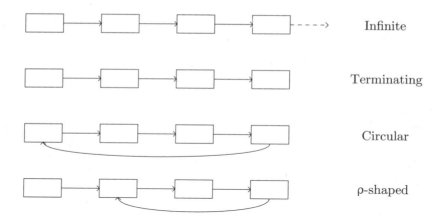

Figure 2.1 Orbit Shapes.

The *orbit cycle* is the set of cyclic elements in the orbit and is empty for infinite and terminating orbits. The *orbit handle*, the complement of the orbit cycle with respect to the orbit, is empty for a circular orbit. The *connection point* is the first cyclic element, and is the first element of a circular orbit and the first element after the handle for a ρ-shaped orbit. The *orbit size* o of an orbit is the number of distinct elements in it. The *handle size* h of an orbit is the number of elements in the orbit handle. The *cycle size* c of an orbit is the number of elements in the orbit cycle.

Lemma 2.4 $o = h + c$

Lemma 2.5   The distance from any point in an orbit to a point in a cycle of that orbit is always defined.

Lemma 2.6   If x and y are distinct points in a cycle of size c,

$$c = \text{distance}(x, y, f) + \text{distance}(y, x, f)$$

Lemma 2.7   If x and y are points in a cycle of size c, the distance from x to y satisfies

$$0 \le \text{distance}(x, y, f) < c$$

2.3 Collision Point

If we observe the behavior of a transformation, without access to its definition, we cannot determine whether a particular orbit is infinite: It might terminate or cycle back at any point. If we know that an orbit is finite, we can use an algorithm to determine the shape of the orbit. Therefore there is an implicit precondition of orbit finiteness for all the algorithms in this chapter.

There is, of course, a naive algorithm that stores every element visited and checks at every step whether the new element has been previously encountered. Even if we could use hashing to speed up the search, such an algorithm still would require linear storage and would not be practical in many applications. However, there is an algorithm that requires only a constant amount of storage.

The following analogy helps to understand the algorithm. If a fast car and a slow one start along a path, the fast one will catch up with the slow one if and only if there is a cycle. If there is no cycle, the fast one will reach the end of the path before the slow one. If there is a cycle, by the time the slow one enters the cycle, the fast one will already be there and will catch up eventually. Carrying our intuition from the continuous domain to the discrete domain requires care to avoid the fast one skipping past the slow one.[1]

The discrete version of the algorithm is based on looking for a point where fast meets slow. The *collision point* of a transformation f and a starting point x is the unique y such that

$$y = f^n(x) = f^{2n+1}(x)$$

and $n \geq 0$ is the smallest integer satisfying this condition. This definition leads to an algorithm for determining the orbit structure that needs one comparison of fast and slow per iteration. To handle partial transformations, we pass a definition-space predicate to the algorithm:

```
template<typename F, typename P>
    requires(Transformation(F) && UnaryPredicate(P) &&
        Domain(F) == Domain(P))
Domain(F) collision_point(const Domain(F)& x, F f, P p)
{
    // Precondition: p(x) ⇔ f(x) is defined
    if (!p(x)) return x;
```

---

1. Knuth [1997, page 7] attributes this algorithm to Robert W. Floyd.

```
    Domain(F) slow = x;           // slow = f^0(x)
    Domain(F) fast = f(x);        // fast = f^1(x)
                                  // n ← 0 (completed iterations)
    while (fast != slow) {        // slow = f^n(x) ∧ fast = f^{2n+1}(x)
        slow = f(slow);           // slow = f^{n+1}(x) ∧ fast = f^{2n+1}(x)
        if (!p(fast)) return fast;
        fast = f(fast);           // slow = f^{n+1}(x) ∧ fast = f^{2n+2}(x)
        if (!p(fast)) return fast;
        fast = f(fast);           // slow = f^{n+1}(x) ∧ fast = f^{2n+3}(x)
                                  // n ← n + 1
    }
    return fast;                  // slow = f^n(x) ∧ fast = f^{2n+1}(x)
    // Postcondition: return value is terminal point or collision point
}
```

We establish the correctness of collision_point in three stages: (1) verifying that it never applies f to an argument outside the definition space; (2) verifying that if it terminates, the postcondition is satisfied; and (3) verifying that it always terminates.

While f is a partial function, its use by the procedure is well defined, since the movement of fast is guarded by a call of p. The movement of slow is unguarded, because by the regularity of f, slow traverses the same orbit as fast, so f is always defined when applied to slow.

The annotations show that if, after $n \geq 0$ iterations, fast becomes equal to slow, then fast $= f^{2n+1}(x)$ and slow $= f^n(x)$. Moreover, n is the smallest such integer, since we checked the condition for every $i < n$.

If there is no cycle, p will eventually return false because of finiteness. If there is a cycle, slow will eventually reach the connection point (the first element in the cycle). Consider the distance d from fast to slow at the top of the loop when slow first enters the cycle: $0 \leq d < c$. If $d = 0$, the procedure terminates. Otherwise the distance from fast to slow decreases by 1 on each iteration. Therefore the procedure always terminates; when it terminates, slow has moved a total of $h + d$ steps.

The following procedure determines whether an orbit is terminating:

```
template<typename F, typename P>
    requires(Transformation(F) && UnaryPredicate(P) &&
        Domain(F) == Domain(P))
bool terminating(const Domain(F)& x, F f, P p)
```

```
{
    // Precondition: p(x) ⟺ f(x) is defined
    return !p(collision_point(x, f, p));
}
```

Sometimes we know either that the transformation is total or that the orbit is nonterminating for a particular starting element. For these situations it is useful to have a specialized version of collision_point:

```
template<typename F>
    requires(Transformation(F))
Domain(F)
collision_point_nonterminating_orbit(const Domain(F)& x, F f)
{
    Domain(F) slow = x;          // slow = f⁰(x)
    Domain(F) fast = f(x);       // fast = f¹(x)
                                 // n ← 0 (completed iterations)
    while (fast != slow) {       // slow = fⁿ(x) ∧ fast = f²ⁿ⁺¹(x)
        slow = f(slow);          // slow = fⁿ⁺¹(x) ∧ fast = f²ⁿ⁺¹(x)
        fast = f(fast);          // slow = fⁿ⁺¹(x) ∧ fast = f²ⁿ⁺²(x)
        fast = f(fast);          // slow = fⁿ⁺¹(x) ∧ fast = f²ⁿ⁺³(x)
                                 // n ← n + 1
    }
    return fast;                 // slow = fⁿ(x) ∧ fast = f²ⁿ⁺¹(x)
    // Postcondition: return value is collision point
}
```

In order to determine the cycle structure—handle size, connection point, and cycle size—we need to analyze the position of the collision point.

When the procedure returns the collision point

$$f^n(x) = f^{2n+1}(x)$$

n is the number of steps taken by slow, and $2n + 1$ is the number of steps taken by fast.

$$n = h + d$$

where h is the handle size and $0 \le d < c$ is the number of steps taken by slow inside the cycle. The number of steps taken by fast is

$$2n + 1 = h + d + qc$$

where $q > 0$ is the number of full cycles completed by fast when it collides with slow. Since $n = h + d$,

$$2(h + d) + 1 = h + d + qc$$

Simplifying gives

$$qc = h + d + 1$$

Let us represent h modulo c:

$$h = mc + r$$

with $0 \le r < c$. Substitution gives

$$qc = mc + r + d + 1$$

or

$$d = (q - m)c - r - 1$$

$0 \le d < c$ implies

$$q - m = 1$$

so

$$d = c - r - 1$$

and $r + 1$ steps are needed to complete the cycle.

Therefore the distance from the collision point to the connection point is

$$e = r + 1$$

In the case of a circular orbit $h = 0$, $r = 0$, and the distance from the collision point to the beginning of the orbit is

$$e = 1$$

Circularity, therefore, can be checked with the following procedures:

```
template<typename F>
    requires(Transformation(F))
bool circular_nonterminating_orbit(const Domain(F)& x, F f)
{
    return x == f(collision_point_nonterminating_orbit(x, f));
}

template<typename F, typename P>
    requires(Transformation(F) && UnaryPredicate(P) &&
        Domain(F) == Domain(P))
bool circular(const Domain(F)& x, F f, P p)
{
    // Precondition: p(x) ⇔ f(x) is defined
    Domain(F) y = collision_point(x, f, p);
    return p(y) && x == f(y);
}
```

We still don't know the handle size h and the cycle size c. Determining the latter is simple once the collision point is known: Traverse the cycle and count the steps.

To see how to determine h, let us look at the position of the collision point:

$$f^{h+d}(x) = f^{h+c-r-1}(x) = f^{mc+r+c-r-1}(x) = f^{(m+1)c-1}(x)$$

Taking $h + 1$ steps from the collision point gets us to the point $f^{(m+1)c+h}(x)$, which equals $f^h(x)$, since $(m + 1)c$ corresponds to going around the cycle $m + 1$ times. If we simultaneously take h steps from x and $h + 1$ steps from the collision point, we meet at the connection point. In other words, the orbits of x and 1 step past the collision point converge in exactly h steps, which leads to the following sequence of algorithms:

```
template<typename F>
    requires(Transformation(F))
Domain(F) convergent_point(Domain(F) x0, Domain(F) x1, F f)
{
    while (x0 != x1) {
```

```
        x0 = f(x0);
        x1 = f(x1);
    }
    return x0;
}


template<typename F>
    requires(Transformation(F))
Domain(F)
connection_point_nonterminating_orbit(const Domain(F)& x, F f)
{
    return convergent_point(
        x,
        f(collision_point_nonterminating_orbit(x, f)),
        f);
}


template<typename F, typename P>
    requires(Transformation(F) && UnaryPredicate(P) &&
        Domain(F) == Domain(P))
Domain(F) connection_point(const Domain(F)& x, F f, P p)
{
    // Precondition: p(x) ⟺ f(x) is defined
    Domain(F) y = collision_point(x, f, p);
    if (!p(y)) return y;
    return convergent_point(x, f(y), f);
}
```

Lemma 2.8   If the orbits of two elements intersect, they have the same cyclic elements.

Exercise 2.2   Design an algorithm that determines, given a transformation and its definition-space predicate, whether the orbits of two elements intersect.

Exercise 2.3   For convergent_point to work, it must be called with elements whose distances to the convergent point are equal. Implement an algorithm convergent_point_guarded for use when that is not known to be the case, but there is an element in common to the orbits of both.

2.4 Measuring Orbit Sizes

The natural type to use for the sizes o, h, and c of an orbit on type T would be an integer count type large enough to count all the distinct values of type T. If a type T occupies k bits, there can be as many as 2^k values, so a count type occupying k bits could not represent all the counts from 0 to 2^k. There is a way to represent these sizes by using distance type.

An orbit could potentially contain all values of a type, in which case o might not fit in the distance type. Depending on the shape of such an orbit, h and c would not fit either. However, for a ρ-shaped orbit, both h and c fit. In all cases each of these fits: o − 1 (the maximum distance in the orbit), h − 1 (the maximum distance in the handle), and c − 1 (the maximum distance in the cycle). That allows us to implement procedures returning a triple representing the complete structure of an orbit, where the members of the triple are as follows:

Case	m0	m1	m2
Terminating	h − 1	0	terminal element
Circular	0	c − 1	x
ρ-shaped	h	c − 1	connection point

```
template<typename F>
    requires(Transformation(F))
triple<DistanceType(F), DistanceType(F), Domain(F)>
orbit_structure_nonterminating_orbit(const Domain(F)& x, F f)
{
    typedef DistanceType(F) N;
    Domain(F) y = connection_point_nonterminating_orbit(x, f);
    return triple<N, N, Domain(F)>(distance(x, y, f),
                                   distance(f(y), y, f),
                                   y);
}

template<typename F, typename P>
    requires(Transformation(F) &&
        UnaryPredicate(P) && Domain(F) == Domain(P))
triple<DistanceType(F), DistanceType(F), Domain(F)>
orbit_structure(const Domain(F)& x, F f, P p)
{
    // Precondition: p(x) ⇔ f(x) is defined
```

```
typedef DistanceType(F) N;
Domain(F) y = connection_point(x, f, p);
N m = distance(x, y, f);
N n(0);
if (p(y)) n = distance(f(y), y, f);
// Terminating: m = h − 1 ∧ n = 0
// Otherwise: m = h ∧ n = c − 1
return triple<N, N, Domain(F)>(m, n, y);
}
```

Exercise 2.4 Derive formulas for the count of different operations (f, p, equality) for the algorithms in this chapter.

Exercise 2.5 Use orbit_structure_nonterminating_orbit to determine the average handle size and cycle size of the pseudorandom number generators on your platform for various seeds.

2.5 Actions

Algorithms often use a transformation f in a statement like

```
x = f(x);
```

Changing the state of an object by applying a transformation to it defines an *action* on the object. There is a duality between transformations and the corresponding actions: An action is definable in terms of a transformation, and vice versa:

```
void a(T& x) { x = f(x); }    // action from transformation
```

and

```
T f(T x) { a(x); return x; } // transformation from action
```

Despite this duality, independent implementations are sometimes more efficient, in which case both action and transformation need to be provided. For example, if a transformation is defined on a large object and modifies only part of its overall state, the action could be considerably faster.

Exercise 2.6 Rewrite all the algorithms in this chapter in terms of actions.

Project 2.1   Another way to detect a cycle is to repeatedly test a single advancing element for equality with a stored element while replacing the stored element at ever-increasing intervals. This and other ideas are described in Sedgewick, et al. [1979], Brent [1980], and Levy [1982]. Implement other algorithms for orbit analysis, compare their performance for different applications, and develop a set of recommendations for selecting the appropriate algorithm.

2.6 Conclusions

Abstraction allowed us to define abstract procedures that can be used in different domains. Regularity of types and functions is essential to make the algorithms work: fast and slow follow the same orbit because of regularity. Developing nomenclature is essential (e.g., orbit kinds and sizes). Affiliated types, such as distance type, need to be precisely defined.

Chapter 3
Associative Operations

T*his chapter discusses associative binary operations. Associativity allows regroup-ing the adjacent operations. This ability to regroup leads to an efficient algorithm for computing powers of the binary operation. Regularity enables a variety of program transformations to optimize the algorithm. We then use the algorithm to compute linear recurrences, such as Fibonacci numbers, in logarithmic time.*

3.1 Associativity

A binary operation is an operation with two arguments:

BinaryOperation(Op) $\triangleq$
    Operation(Op)
  $\land$ Arity(Op) = 2

The binary operations of addition and multiplication are central to mathematics. Many more are used, such as min, max, conjunction, disjunction, set union, set intersection, and so on. All these operations are *associative:*

property(Op : *BinaryOperation*)
associative : Op
    op $\mapsto$ ($\forall a, b, c \in$ Domain(op)) op(op(a, b), c) = op(a, op(b, c))

There are, of course, nonassociative binary operations, such as subtraction and division.

When a particular associative binary operation op is clear from the context, we often use implied multiplicative notation by writing ab instead of op(a, b). Because of associativity, we do not need to parenthesize an expression involving two or more applications of op, because all the groupings are equivalent: $(\cdots(a_0 a_1)\cdots)$ $a_{n-1} = \cdots = a_0(\cdots(a_{n-2}a_{n-1})\cdots) = a_0 a_1 \cdots a_{n-1}$. When $a_0 = a_1 = \cdots = a_{n-1} = a$, we write a^n: the nth *power* of a.

Lemma 3.1 $a^n a^m = a^m a^n = a^{n+m}$ (powers of the same element commute)

Lemma 3.2 $(a^n)^m = a^{nm}$

It is not, however, always true that $(ab)^n = a^n b^n$. This condition holds only when the operation is commutative.

If f and g are transformations on the same domain, their *composition*, $g \circ f$, is a transformation mapping x to $g(f(x))$.

Lemma 3.3   The binary operation of composition is associative.

If we choose some element a of the domain of an associative operation op and consider the expression $op(a, x)$ as a unary operation with formal parameter x, we can think of a as the transformation "multiplication by a." This justifies the use of the same notation for powers of a transformation, f^n, and powers of an element under an associative binary operation, a^n. This duality allows us to use an algorithm from the previous chapter to prove an interesting theorem about powers of an associative operation. An element x has *finite order* under an associative operation if there exist integers $0 < n < m$ such that $x^n = x^m$. An element x is an *idempotent element* under an associative operation if $x = x^2$.

Theorem 3.1   An element of finite order has an idempotent power (Frobenius [1895]).

Proof: Assume that x is an element of finite order under an associative operation op. Let $g(z) = op(x, z)$. Since x is an element of finite order, its orbit under g has a cycle. By its postcondition,

$$\text{collision\_point}(x, g) = g^n(x) = g^{2n+1}(x)$$

for some $n \geq 0$. Thus

$$g^n(x) = x^{n+1}$$
$$g^{2n+1}(x) = x^{2n+2} = x^{2(n+1)} = (x^{n+1})^2$$

and x^{n+1} is the idempotent power of x.

Lemma 3.4   collision_point_nonterminating_orbit can be used in the proof.

3.2 **Computing Powers**

An algorithm to compute a^n for an associative operation op will take a, n, and op as parameters. The type of a is the domain of op; n must be of an integer type. Without the assumption of associativity, two algorithms compute power from left to right and right to left, respectively:

```
template<typename I, typename Op>
    requires(Integer(I) && BinaryOperation(Op))
Domain(Op) power_left_associated(Domain(Op) a, I n, Op op)
{
    // Precondition: n > 0
    if (n == I(1)) return a;
    return op(power_left_associated(a, n - I(1), op), a);
}


template<typename I, typename Op>
    requires(Integer(I) && BinaryOperation(Op))
Domain(Op) power_right_associated(Domain(Op) a, I n, Op op)
{
    // Precondition: n > 0
    if (n == I(1)) return a;
    return op(a, power_right_associated(a, n - I(1), op));
}
```

The algorithms perform $n - 1$ operations. They return different results for a nonassociative operation. Consider, for example, raising 1 to the 3rd power with the operation of subtraction.

When both a and n are integers, and if the operation is multiplication, both algorithms give us exponentiation; if the operation is addition, both give us multiplication. The ancient Egyptians discovered a faster multiplication algorithm that can be generalized to computing powers of any associative operation.[1]

Since associativity allows us to freely regroup operations, we have

$$a^n = \begin{cases} a & \text{if } n = 1 \\ (a^2)^{n/2} & \text{if } n \text{ is even} \\ (a^2)^{n/2}a & \text{if } n \text{ is odd} \end{cases}$$

---

1. The original is in Robins and Shute [1987, pages 16–17]; the papyrus is from around 1650 BC but its scribe noted that it was a copy of another papyrus from around 1850 BC.

which corresponds to

```
template<typename I, typename Op>
    requires(Integer(I) && BinaryOperation(Op))
Domain(Op) power_0(Domain(Op) a, I n, Op op)
{
    // Precondition: associative(op) ∧ n > 0
    if (n == I(1)) return a;
    if (n % I(2) == I(0))
        return power_0(op(a, a), n / I(2), op);
    return op(power_0(op(a, a), n / I(2), op), a);
}
```

Let us count the number of operations performed by power_0 for an exponent of n. The number of recursive calls is $\lfloor \log_2 n \rfloor$. Let v be the number of 1s in the binary representation of n. Each recursive call performs an operation to square a. Also, $v - 1$ of the calls perform an extra operation. So the number of operations is

$$\lfloor \log_2 n \rfloor + (v - 1) \le 2 \lfloor \log_2 n \rfloor$$

For $n = 15$, $\lfloor \log_2 n \rfloor = 3$ and the number of 1s is four, so the formula gives six operations. A different grouping gives $a^{15} = (a^3)^5$, where a^3 takes two operations and a^5 takes three operations, for a total of five. There are also faster groupings for other exponents, such as $23, 27, 39$, and 43.[2]

Since power_left_associated does $n - 1$ operations and power_0 does at most $2\lfloor \log_2 n \rfloor$ operations, it might appear that for very large n, power_0 will always be much faster. This is not always the case. For example, if the operation is multiplication of univariate polynomials with arbitrary-precision integer coefficients, power_left_associated is faster.[3] Even for this simple algorithm, we do not know how to precisely specify the complexity requirements that determine which of the two is better.

The ability of power_0 to handle very large exponents, say 10^{300}, makes it crucial for cryptography.[4]

---

2. For a comprehensive discussion of minimal-operation exponentiation, see Knuth [1997, pages 465–481].

3. See McCarthy [1986].

4. See the work on RSA by Rivest, et al. [1978].

3.3 Program Transformations

power_0 is a satisfactory implementation of the algorithm and is appropriate when the cost of performing the operation is considerably larger than the overhead of the function calls caused by recursion. In this section we derive the iterative algorithm that performs the same number of operations as power_0, using a sequence of program transformations that can be used in many contexts.[5] For the rest of the book, we only show final or almost-final versions.

power_0 contains two identical recursive calls. While only one is executed in a given invocation, it is possible to reduce the code size via *common-subexpression elimination:*

```
template<typename I, typename Op>
    requires(Integer(I) && BinaryOperation(Op))
Domain(Op) power_1(Domain(Op) a, I n, Op op)
{
    // Precondition: associative(op) ∧ n > 0
    if (n == I(1)) return a;
    Domain(Op) r = power_1(op(a, a), n / I(2), op);
    if (n % I(2) != I(0)) r = op(r, a);
    return r;
}
```

Our goal is to eliminate the recursive call. A first step is to transform the procedure to *tail-recursive form*, where the procedure's execution ends with the recursive call. One of the techniques that allows this transformation is *accumulation-variable introduction*, where the accumulation variable carries the accumulated result between recursive calls:

```
template<typename I, typename Op>
    requires(Integer(I) && BinaryOperation(Op))
Domain(Op) power_accumulate_0(Domain(Op) r, Domain(Op) a, I n,
                              Op op)
```

_____

5. Compilers perform similar transformations only for built-in types when the semantics and complexity of the operations are known. The concept of regularity is an assertion by the creator of a type that programmers and compilers can safely perform such transformations.

```
{
    // Precondition: associative(op) ∧ n ≥ 0
    if (n == I(0)) return r;
    if (n % I(2) != I(0)) r = op(r, a);
    return power_accumulate_0(r, op(a, a), n / I(2), op);
}
```

If r_0, a_0, and n_0 are the original values of r, a, and n, this invariant holds at every recursive call: $ra^n = r_0 a_0^{n_0}$. As an additional benefit, this version computes not just power but also power multiplied by a coefficient. It also handles zero as the value of the exponent. However, power_accumulate_0 does an unnecessary squaring when going from 1 to 0. That can be eliminated by adding an extra case:

```
template<typename I, typename Op>
    requires(Integer(I) && BinaryOperation(Op))
Domain(Op) power_accumulate_1(Domain(Op) r, Domain(Op) a, I n,
                             Op op)
{
    // Precondition: associative(op) ∧ n ≥ 0
    if (n == I(0)) return r;
    if (n == I(1)) return op(r, a);
    if (n % I(2) != I(0)) r = op(r, a);
    return power_accumulate_1(r, op(a, a), n / I(2), op);
}
```

Adding the extra case results in a duplicated subexpression and in three tests that are not independent. Analyzing the dependencies between the tests and ordering the tests based on expected frequency gives

```
template<typename I, typename Op>
    requires(Integer(I) && BinaryOperation(Op))
Domain(Op) power_accumulate_2(Domain(Op) r, Domain(Op) a, I n,
                             Op op)
{
    // Precondition: associative(op) ∧ n ≥ 0
    if (n % I(2) != I(0)) {
        r = op(r, a);
        if (n == I(1)) return r;
    } else if (n == I(0)) return r;
    return power_accumulate_2(r, op(a, a), n / I(2), op);
}
```

A *strict tail-recursive* procedure is one in which all the tail-recursive calls are done with the formal parameters of the procedure being the corresponding arguments:

```
template<typename I, typename Op>
    requires(Integer(I) && BinaryOperation(Op))
Domain(Op) power_accumulate_3(Domain(Op) r, Domain(Op) a, I n,
                             Op op)
{
    // Precondition: associative(op) ∧ n ≥ 0
    if (n % I(2) != I(0)) {
        r = op(r, a);
        if (n == I(1)) return r;
    } else if (n == I(0)) return r;
    a = op(a, a);
    n = n / I(2);
    return power_accumulate_3(r, a, n, op);
}
```

A strict tail-recursive procedure can be transformed to an iterative procedure by replacing each recursive call with a `goto` to the beginning of the procedure or by using an equivalent iterative construct:

```
template<typename I, typename Op>
    requires(Integer(I) && BinaryOperation(Op))
Domain(Op) power_accumulate_4(Domain(Op) r, Domain(Op) a, I n,
                             Op op)
{
    // Precondition: associative(op) ∧ n ≥ 0
    while (true) {
        if (n % I(2) != I(0)) {
            r = op(r, a);
            if (n == I(1)) return r;
        } else if (n == I(0)) return r;
        a = op(a, a);
        n = n / I(2);
    }
}
```

The recursion invariant becomes the *loop invariant*.

If $n > 0$ initially, it would pass through 1 before becoming 0. We take advantage of this by eliminating the test for 0 and strengthening the precondition:

```
template<typename I, typename Op>
    requires(Integer(I) && BinaryOperation(Op))
Domain(Op) power_accumulate_positive_0(Domain(Op) r,
                                       Domain(Op) a, I n,
                                       Op op)
{
    // Precondition: associative(op) ∧ n > 0
    while (true) {
        if (n % I(2) != I(0)) {
            r = op(r, a);
            if (n == I(1)) return r;
        }
        a = op(a, a);
        n = n / I(2);
    }
}
```

This is useful when it is known that $n > 0$. While developing a component, we often discover new interfaces.

Now we relax the precondition again:

```
template<typename I, typename Op>
    requires(Integer(I) && BinaryOperation(Op))
Domain(Op) power_accumulate_5(Domain(Op) r, Domain(Op) a, I n,
                              Op op)
{
    // Precondition: associative(op) ∧ n ≥ 0
    if (n == I(0)) return r;
    return power_accumulate_positive_0(r, a, n, op);
}
```

We can implement power from power_accumulate by using a simple identity:

$$a^n = a a^{n-1}$$

The transformation is *accumulation-variable elimination:*

```
template<typename I, typename Op>
    requires(Integer(I) && BinaryOperation(Op))
Domain(Op) power_2(Domain(Op) a, I n, Op op)
{
    // Precondition: associative(op) ∧ n > 0
    return power_accumulate_5(a, a, n - I(1), op);
}
```

This algorithm performs more operations than necessary. For example, when n is 16, it performs seven operations where only four are needed. When n is odd, this algorithm is fine. Therefore we can avoid the problem by repeated squaring of a and halving the exponent until it becomes odd:

```
template<typename I, typename Op>
    requires(Integer(I) && BinaryOperation(Op))
Domain(Op) power_3(Domain(Op) a, I n, Op op)
{
    // Precondition: associative(op) ∧ n > 0
    while (n % I(2) == I(0)) {
        a = op(a, a);
        n = n / I(2);
    }
    n = n / I(2);
    if (n == I(0)) return a;
    return power_accumulate_positive_0(a, op(a, a), n, op);
}
```

Exercise 3.1   Convince yourself that the last three lines of code are correct.

3.4 Special-Case Procedures

In the final versions we used these operations:

```
n / I(2)
n % I(2) == I(0)
n % I(2) != I(0)
n == I(0)
n == I(1)
```

Both / and % are expensive. We can use shifts and masks on non-negative values of both signed and unsigned integers.

It is frequently useful to identify commonly occuring expressions involving procedures and constants of a type by defining *special-case* procedures. Often these special cases can be implemented more efficiently than the general case and, therefore, belong to the computational basis of the type. For built-in types, there may exist machine instructions for the special cases. For user-defined types, there are often even more significant opportunities for optimizing special cases. For example, division of two arbitrary polynomials is more difficult than division of a polynomial by x. Similarly, division of two Gaussian integers (numbers of the form $a + bi$ where a and b are integers and $i = \sqrt{-1}$) is more difficult than division of a Gaussian integer by $1 + i$.

Any integer type must provide the following special-case procedures:

$Integer(I) \triangleq$

    successor : $I \to I$
        $n \mapsto n + 1$
  $\wedge$ predecessor : $I \to I$
        $n \mapsto n - 1$
  $\wedge$ twice : $I \to I$
        $n \mapsto n + n$
  $\wedge$ half_nonnegative : $I \to I$
        $n \mapsto \lfloor n/2 \rfloor$, where $n \geq 0$
  $\wedge$ binary_scale_down_nonnegative : $I \times I \to I$
        $(n, k) \mapsto \lfloor n/2^k \rfloor$, where $n, k \geq 0$
  $\wedge$ binary_scale_up_nonnegative : $I \times I \to I$
        $(n, k) \mapsto 2^k n$, where $n, k \geq 0$
  $\wedge$ positive : $I \to$ bool
        $n \mapsto n > 0$
  $\wedge$ negative : $I \to$ bool
        $n \mapsto n < 0$
  $\wedge$ zero : $I \to$ bool
        $n \mapsto n = 0$
  $\wedge$ one : $I \to$ bool
        $n \mapsto n = 1$
  $\wedge$ even : $I \to$ bool
        $n \mapsto (n \bmod 2) = 0$
  $\wedge$ odd : $I \to$ bool
        $n \mapsto (n \bmod 2) \neq 0$

Exercise 3.2 Implement these procedures for C++ integral types.

Now we can give the final implementations of the power procedures by using the special-case procedures:

```
template<typename I, typename Op>
    requires(Integer(I) && BinaryOperation(Op))
Domain(Op) power_accumulate_positive(Domain(Op) r,
                                     Domain(Op) a, I n,
                                     Op op)
{
    // Precondition: associative(op) ∧ positive(n)
    while (true) {
      if (odd(n)) {
          r = op(r, a);
          if (one(n)) return r;
      }
      a = op(a, a);
      n = half_nonnegative(n);
    }
}
template<typename I, typename Op>
    requires(Integer(I) && BinaryOperation(Op))
Domain(Op) power_accumulate(Domain(Op) r, Domain(Op) a, I n,
                            Op op)
{
    // Precondition: associative(op) ∧ ¬negative(n)
    if (zero(n)) return r;
    return power_accumulate_positive(r, a, n, op);
}
template<typename I, typename Op>
    requires(Integer(I) && BinaryOperation(Op))
Domain(Op) power(Domain(Op) a, I n, Op op)
{
    // Precondition: associative(op) ∧ positive(n)
    while (even(n)) {
        a = op(a, a);
        n = half_nonnegative(n);
    }
```

```
    n = half_nonnegative(n);
    if (zero(n)) return a;
    return power_accumulate_positive(a, op(a, a), n, op);
}
```

Since we know that $a^{n+m} = a^n a^m$, a^0 must evaluate to the identity element for the operation op. We can extend power to zero exponents by passing the identity element as another parameter:[6]

```
template<typename I, typename Op>
    requires(Integer(I) && BinaryOperation(Op))
Domain(Op) power(Domain(Op) a, I n, Op op, Domain(Op) id)
{
    // Precondition: associative(op) ∧ ¬negative(n)
    if (zero(n)) return id;
    return power(a, n, op);
}
```

Project 3.1   Floating-point multiplication and addition are not associative, so they may give different results when they are used as the operation for power and power_left_associated; establish whether power or power_left_ associated gives a more accurate result for raising a floating-point number to an integral power.

3.5 Parameterizing Algorithms

In power we use two different techniques for providing operations for the abstract algorithm.

1. The associative operation is passed as a parameter. This allows power to be used with different operations on the same type, such as multiplication modulo n.

2. The operations on the exponent are provided as part of the computational basis for the exponent type. We do not choose, for example, to pass half_nonnegative as a parameter to power, because we do not know of a case in which there are competing implementations of half_nonnegative on the same type.

---

6. Another technique involves defining a function identity_element such that identity_element(op) returns the identity element for op.

In general, we pass an operation as a parameter when an algorithm could be used with different operations on the same type. When a procedure is defined with an operation as a parameter, a suitable default should be specified whenever possible. For example, the natural default for the operation passed to power is multiplication.

Using an operator symbol or a procedure name with the same semantics on different types is called *overloading*, and we say that the operator symbol or procedure name is *overloaded* on the type. For example, + is used on natural numbers, integers, rationals, polynomials, and matrices. In mathematics + is always used for an associative and commutative operation, so using + for string concatenation would be inconsistent. Similarly, when both + and × are present, × must distribute over +. In power, half_nonnegative is overloaded on the exponent type.

When we instantiate an abstract procedure, such as collision_point or power, we create overloaded procedures. When actual type parameters satisfy the requirements, the instances of the abstract procedure have the same semantics.

3.6 Linear Recurrences

A *linear recurrence function of order* k is a function f such that

$$f(y_0, \ldots, y_{k-1}) = \sum_{i=0}^{k-1} a_i y_i$$

where coefficients $a_0, a_{k-1} \neq 0$. A sequence $\{x_0, x_1, \cdots\}$ is a *linear recurrence sequence of order* k if there is a linear recurrence function of order k—say, f—and

$$(\forall n \geq k)\, x_n = f(x_{n-1}, \ldots, x_{n-k})$$

Note that indices of x decrease. Given k *initial values* $x_0, \ldots, x_{k-1}$ and a linear recurrence function of order k, we can generate a linear recurrence sequence via a straightforward iterative algorithm. This algorithm requires $n - k + 1$ applications of the function to compute x_n, for $n \geq k$. As we will see, we can compute x_n in $O(\log_2 n)$ steps, using power.[7] If $f(y_0, \ldots, y_{k-1}) = \sum_{i=0}^{k-1} a_i y_i$ is a linear recurrence

---

7. The first $O(\log n)$ algorithm for linear recurrences is due to Miller and Brown [1966].

function of order k, we can view f as performing vector inner product:[8]

$$\begin{bmatrix} a_0 & \cdots & a_{k-1} \end{bmatrix} \begin{bmatrix} y_0 \\ \vdots \\ y_{k-1} \end{bmatrix}$$

If we extend the vector of coefficients to the *companion matrix* with 1s on its subdiagonal, we can simultaneously compute the new value x_n and shift the old values $x_{n-1}, \ldots, x_{x-k+1}$ to the correct positions for the next iteration:

$$\begin{bmatrix} a_0 & a_1 & a_2 & \cdots & a_{k-2} & a_{k-1} \\ 1 & 0 & 0 & \cdots & 0 & 0 \\ 0 & 1 & 0 & \cdots & 0 & 0 \\ \vdots & \vdots & \vdots & & \vdots & \vdots \\ 0 & 0 & 0 & \cdots & 1 & 0 \end{bmatrix} \begin{bmatrix} x_{n-1} \\ x_{n-2} \\ x_{n-3} \\ \vdots \\ x_{n-k} \end{bmatrix} = \begin{bmatrix} x_n \\ x_{n-1} \\ x_{n-2} \\ \vdots \\ x_{n-k+1} \end{bmatrix}$$

By the associativity of matrix multiplication, it follows that we can obtain x_n by multiplying the vector of the k initial values by the companion matrix raised to the power $n - k + 1$:

$$\begin{bmatrix} x_n \\ x_{n-1} \\ x_{n-2} \\ \vdots \\ x_{n-k+1} \end{bmatrix} = \begin{bmatrix} a_0 & a_1 & a_2 & \cdots & a_{k-2} & a_{k-1} \\ 1 & 0 & 0 & \cdots & 0 & 0 \\ 0 & 1 & 0 & \cdots & 0 & 0 \\ \vdots & \vdots & \vdots & & \vdots & \vdots \\ 0 & 0 & 0 & \cdots & 1 & 0 \end{bmatrix}^{n-k+1} \begin{bmatrix} x_{k-1} \\ x_{k-2} \\ x_{k-3} \\ \vdots \\ x_0 \end{bmatrix}$$

Using power allows us to find x_n with at most $2 \log_2(n - k + 1)$ matrix multiplication operations. A straightforward matrix multiplication algorithm requires k^3 multiplications and $k^3 - k^2$ additions of coefficients. Therefore the computation of x_n requires no more than $2k^3 \log_2(n-k+1)$ multiplications and $2(k^3 - k^2) \log_2(n-k+1)$ additions of the coefficients. Recall that k is the order of the linear recurrence and is a constant.[9]

We never defined the domain of the elements of a linear recurrence sequence. It could be integers, rationals, reals, or complex numbers: The only requirements are

---

8. For a review of linear algebra, see Kwak and Hong [2004]. They discuss linear recurrences starting on page 214.

9. Fiduccia [1985] shows how the constant factor can be reduced via modular polynomial multiplication.

the existence of associative and commutative addition, associative multiplication, and distributivity of multiplication over addition.[10]

The sequence f_i generated by the linear recurrence function

$$\text{fib}(y_0, y_1) = y_0 + y_1$$

of order 2 with initial values $f_0 = 0$ and $f_1 = 1$ is called the Fibonacci sequence.[11] It is straightforward to compute the nth Fibonacci number f_n by using power with 2×2 matrix multiplication. We use the Fibonacci sequence to illustrate how the k^3 multiplications can be reduced for this particular case. Let

$$F = \begin{bmatrix} 1 & 1 \\ 1 & 0 \end{bmatrix}$$

be the companion matrix for the linear recurrence generating the Fibonacci sequence. We can show by induction that

$$F^n = \begin{bmatrix} f_{n+1} & f_n \\ f_n & f_{n-1} \end{bmatrix}$$

Indeed:

$$F^1 = \begin{bmatrix} f_2 & f_1 \\ f_1 & f_0 \end{bmatrix} = \begin{bmatrix} 1 & 1 \\ 1 & 0 \end{bmatrix}$$

$$F^{n+1} = FF^n$$

$$= \begin{bmatrix} 1 & 1 \\ 1 & 0 \end{bmatrix} \begin{bmatrix} f_{n+1} & f_n \\ f_n & f_{n-1} \end{bmatrix}$$

$$= \begin{bmatrix} f_{n+1} + f_n & f_n + f_{n-1} \\ f_{n+1} & f_n \end{bmatrix} = \begin{bmatrix} f_{n+2} & f_{n+1} \\ f_{n+1} & f_n \end{bmatrix}$$

This allows us to express the matrix product of F^m and F^n as

$$F^m F^n = \begin{bmatrix} f_{m+1} & f_m \\ f_m & f_{m-1} \end{bmatrix} \begin{bmatrix} f_{n+1} & f_n \\ f_n & f_{n-1} \end{bmatrix}$$

$$= \begin{bmatrix} f_{m+1}f_{n+1} + f_m f_n & f_{m+1}f_n + f_m f_{n-1} \\ f_m f_{n+1} + f_{m-1} f_n & f_m f_n + f_{m-1} f_{n-1} \end{bmatrix}$$

---

10. It could be any type that models semiring, which we define in Chapter 5.

11. Leonardo Pisano, *Liber Abaci*, first edition, 1202. For an English translation, see Sigler [2002]. The sequence appears on page 404.

We can represent the matrix F^n with a pair corresponding to its bottom row, (f_n, f_{n-1}), since the top row could be computed as $(f_{n-1} + f_n, f_n)$, which leads to the following code:

```
template<typename I>
    requires(Integer(I))
pair<I, I> fibonacci_matrix_multiply(const pair<I, I>& x,
                                     const pair<I, I>& y)
{
    return pair<I, I>(
        x.m0 * (y.m1 + y.m0) + x.m1 * y.m0,
        x.m0 * y.m0 + x.m1 * y.m1);
}
```

This procedure performs only four multiplications instead of the eight required for general 2×2 matrix multiplication. Since the first element of the bottom row of F^n is f_n, the following procedure computes f_n:

```
template<typename I>
    requires(Integer(I))
I fibonacci(I n)
{
    // Precondition: n ≥ 0
    if (n == I(0)) return I(0);
    return power(pair<I, I>(I(1), I(0)),
                 n,
                 fibonacci_matrix_multiply<I>).m0;
}
```

3.7 Accumulation Procedures

The previous chapter defined an action as a dual to a transformation. There is a dual procedure for a binary operation when it is used in a statement like

```
x = op(x, y);
```

Changing the state of an object by combining it with another object via a binary operation defines an *accumulation procedure* on the object. An accumulation procedure is definable in terms of a binary operation, and vice versa:

```
void op_accumulate(T& x, const T& y) { x = op(x, y); }
    // accumulation procedure from binary operation
```

and

```
T op(T x, const T& y) { op_accumulate(x, y); return x; }
    // binary operation from accumulation procedure
```

As with actions, sometimes independent implementations are more efficient, in which case both operation and accumulation procedures need to be provided.

Exercise 3.3   Rewrite all the algorithms in this chapter in terms of accumulation procedures.

Project 3.2   Create a library for the generation of linear recurrence sequences based on the results of Miller and Brown [1966] and Fiduccia [1985].

3.8 Conclusions

Algorithms are *abstract* when they can be used with different models satisfying the same requirements, such as associativity. Code optimization depends on equational reasoning; unless types are known to be regular, few optimizations can be performed. Special-case procedures can make code more efficient and even more abstract. The combination of mathematics and abstract algorithms leads to surprising algorithms, such as logarithmic time generation of the nth element of a linear recurrence.

Chapter 4
Linear Orderings

T*his chapter describes properties of binary relations, such as transitivity and symmetry. In particular, we introduce total and weak linear orderings. We introduce the concept of stability of functions based on linear ordering: preserving order present in the arguments for equivalent elements. We generalize* min *and* max *to order-selection functions, such as the median of three elements, and introduce a technique for managing their implementation complexity through reduction to constrained subproblems.*

4.1 Classification of Relations

A *relation* is a predicate taking two parameters of the same type:

$Relation(Op) \triangleq$
    $Predicate(Op)$
  $\wedge\ HomogeneousFunction(Op)$
  $\wedge\ \mathsf{Arity}(Op) = 2$

A relation is *transitive* if, whenever it holds between a and b, and between b and c, it holds between a and c:

property$(\mathsf{R} : Relation)$
transitive : R
    $r \mapsto (\forall a, b, c \in \mathsf{Domain}(\mathsf{R}))\ (r(a, b) \wedge r(b, c) \Rightarrow r(a, c))$

Examples of transitive relations are equality, equality of the first member of a pair, reachability in an orbit, and divisibility.

A relation is *strict* if it never holds between an element and itself; a relation is *reflexive* if it always holds between an element and itself:

property(R : *Relation*)
strict : R
  $r \mapsto (\forall a \in \mathrm{Domain}(R)) \neg r(a, a)$

property(R : *Relation*)
reflexive : R
  $r \mapsto (\forall a \in \mathrm{Domain}(R)) \, r(a, a)$

All the previous examples of transitive relations are reflexive; proper factor is strict.

Exercise 4.1   Give an example of a relation that is neither strict nor reflexive.

A relation is *symmetric* if, whenever it holds in one direction, it holds in the other; a relation is *asymmetric* if it never holds in both directions:

property(R : *Relation*)
symmetric : R
  $r \mapsto (\forall a, b \in \mathrm{Domain}(R)) \, (r(a, b) \Rightarrow r(b, a))$

property(R : *Relation*)
asymmetric : R
  $r \mapsto (\forall a, b \in \mathrm{Domain}(R)) \, (r(a, b) \Rightarrow \neg r(b, a))$

An example of a symmetric transitive relation is "sibling"; an example of an asymmetric transitive relation is "ancestor."

Exercise 4.2   Give an example of a symmetric relation that is not transitive.

Exercise 4.3   Give an example of a symmetric relation that is not reflexive.

Given a relation $r(a, b)$, there are *derived relations* with the same domain:

$$\mathrm{complement}_r(a, b) \quad \Leftrightarrow \quad \neg r(a, b)$$
$$\mathrm{converse}_r(a, b) \quad \Leftrightarrow \quad r(b, a)$$
$$\mathrm{complement\_of\_converse}_r(a, b) \quad \Leftrightarrow \quad \neg r(b, a)$$

Given a symmetric relation, the only interesting derivable relation is the complement, because the converse is equivalent to the original relation.

A relation is an *equivalence* if it is transitive, reflexive, and symmetric:

property(R : *Relation*)
equivalence : R
  r ↦ transitive(r) ∧ reflexive(r) ∧ symmetric(r)

Examples of equivalence relations are equality, geometric congruence, and integer congruence modulo n.

> **Lemma 4.1**   If r is an equivalence relation, $a = b \Rightarrow r(a, b)$.

An equivalence relation partitions its domain into a set of *equivalence classes:* subsets containing all elements equivalent to a given element. We can often implement an equivalence relation by defining a *key function*, a function that returns a unique value for all the elements in each equivalence class. Applying equality to the results of the key function determines equivalence:

property(F : *UnaryFunction*, R : *Relation*)
  requires(Domain(F) = Domain(R))
key_function : F × R
  $(f, r) \mapsto (\forall a, b \in$ Domain(F)$) (r(a, b) \Leftrightarrow f(a) = f(b))$

> **Lemma 4.2**   key_function(f, r) ⇒ equivalence(r)

4.2 Total and Weak Orderings

A relation is a *total ordering* if it is transitive and obeys the *trichotomy law*, whereby for every pair of elements, exactly one of the following holds: the relation, its converse, or equality:

property(R : *Relation*)
total_ordering : R
  r ↦ transitive(r) ∧
    $(\forall a, b \in$ Domain(R)$)$ exactly one of the following holds:
      $r(a, b), r(b, a),$ or $a = b$

A relation is a *weak ordering* if it is transitive and there is an equivalence relation on the same domain such that the original relation obeys the *weak-trichotomy law*, whereby for every pair of elements, exactly one of the following holds: the relation, its converse, or the equivalence:

property(R : *Relation*, E : *Relation*) **requires**(Domain(R) = Domain(E))
weak_ordering : R
    r ↦ transitive(r) ∧ (∃e ∈ E) equivalence(e) ∧
        (∀a, b ∈ Domain(R)) exactly one of the following holds:
           r(a, b), r(b, a), or e(a, b)

Given a relation r, the relation $\neg r(a, b) \wedge \neg r(b, a)$ is called the *symmetric complement* of r.

Lemma 4.3 The symmetric complement of a weak ordering is an equivalence relation.

Examples of a weak ordering are pairs ordered by their first members and employees ordered by salary.

Lemma 4.4 A total ordering is a weak ordering.

Lemma 4.5 A weak ordering is asymmetric.

Lemma 4.6 A weak ordering is strict.

A key function f on a set T, together with a total ordering r on the codomain of f, define a weak ordering $\tilde{r}(x, y) \Leftrightarrow r(f(x), f(y))$.

We refer to total and weak orderings as *linear* orderings because of their respective trichotomy laws.

4.3 Order Selection

Given a weak ordering r and two objects a and b from r's domain, it makes sense to ask which is the minimum. It is obvious how to define the minimum when r or its converse holds between a and b but is not so when they are equivalent. A similar problem arises if we ask which is the maximum.

A property for dealing with this problem is known as *stability*. Informally, an algorithm is *stable* if it respects the original order of equivalent objects. So if we think of minimum and maximum as selecting, respectively, the smallest and second smallest from a list of two arguments, stability requires that when called with equivalent elements, minimum should return the first and maximum the second.[1]

---

1. In later chapters we extend the notion of stability to other categories of algorithms.

We can generalize minimum and maximum to (j, k)-order selection, where $k > 0$ indicates the number of arguments, and $0 \leq j < k$ indicates that the jth smallest is to be selected. To formalize our notion of stability, assume that each of the k arguments is associated with a unique natural number called its *stability index*. Given the original weak ordering r, we define the *strengthened* relation $\hat{r}$ on (object, stability index) pairs:

$$\hat{r}((a, i_a), (b, i_b)) \Leftrightarrow r(a, b) \vee (\neg r(b, a) \wedge i_a < i_b)$$

If we implement an order-selection algorithm in terms of $\hat{r}$, there are no ambiguous cases caused by equivalent arguments. The natural default for the stability index of an argument is its ordinal position in the argument list.

While the strengthened relation $\hat{r}$ gives us a powerful tool for reasoning about stability, it is straightforward to define simple order-selection procedures without making the stability indices explicit. This implementation of minimum returns a when a and b are equivalent, satisfying our definition of stability:[2]

```
template<typename R>
    requires(Relation(R))
const Domain(R)& select_0_2(const Domain(R)& a,
                            const Domain(R)& b, R r)
{
    // Precondition: weak_ordering(r)
    if (r(b, a)) return b;
    return a;
}
```

Similarly, this implementation of maximum returns b when a and b are equivalent, again satisfying our definition of stability:[3]

```
template<typename R>
    requires(Relation(R))
const Domain(R)& select_1_2(const Domain(R)& a,
                            const Domain(R)& b, R r)
{
    // Precondition: weak_ordering(r)
```

---

2. We explain our naming convention later in this section.
3. STL incorrectly requires that max(a, b) returns a when a and b are equivalent.

```
    if (r(b, a)) return a;
    return b;
}
```

For the remainder of this chapter, the precondition weak_ordering(r) is implied.

While it is useful to have other order-selection procedures for k arguments, the difficulty of writing such an order-selection procedure grows quickly with k, and there are many different procedures we might have a need for. A technique we call *reduction to constrained subproblems* addresses both issues. We develop a family of procedures that assume a certain amount of information about the relative ordering of their arguments.

Naming these procedures systematically is essential. Each name begins with select_j_k, where $0 \le j < k$, to indicate selection of the jth largest of k arguments. We append a sequence of letters to indicate a precondition on the ordering of parameters, expressed as increasing chains. For example, a suffix of _ab means that the first two parameters are in order, and _abd means that the first, second, and fourth parameters are in order. More than one such suffix appears when there are preconditions on different chains of parameters.

For example, it is straightforward to implement minimum and maximum for three elements:

```
template<typename R>
    requires(Relation(R))
const Domain(R)& select_0_3(const Domain(R)& a,
                            const Domain(R)& b,
                            const Domain(R)& c, R r)
{
    return select_0_2(select_0_2(a, b, r), c, r);
}


template<typename R>
    requires(Relation(R))
const Domain(R)& select_2_3(const Domain(R)& a,
                            const Domain(R)& b,
                            const Domain(R)& c, R r)
{
    return select_1_2(select_1_2(a, b, r), c, r);
}
```

It is easy to find the median of three elements if we know that the first two elements are in increasing order:

```
template<typename R>
    requires(Relation(R))
const Domain(R)& select_1_3_ab(const Domain(R)& a,
                               const Domain(R)& b,
                               const Domain(R)& c, R r)
{
    if (!r(c, b)) return b;      // a, b, c are sorted
    return select_1_2(a, c, r);  // b is not the median
}
```

Establishing the precondition for select_1_3_ab requires only one comparison. Because the parameters are passed by constant reference, no data movement takes place:

```
template<typename R>
    requires(Relation(R))
const Domain(R)& select_1_3(const Domain(R)& a,
                            const Domain(R)& b,
                            const Domain(R)& c, R r)
{
    if (r(b, a)) return select_1_3_ab(b, a, c, r);
    return              select_1_3_ab(a, b, c, r);
}
```

In the worst case, select_1_3 does three comparisons. The function does two comparisons only when c is the maximum of a, b, c, and since it happens in one-third of the cases, the average number of comparisons is $2\frac{2}{3}$, assuming a uniform distribution of inputs.

Finding the second smallest of n elements requires at least $n + \lceil \log_2 n \rceil - 2$ comparisons.[4] In particular, finding the second of four requires four comparisons.

It is easy to select the second of four if we know that the first pair of arguments and the second pair of arguments are each in increasing order:

---

4. This result was conjectured by Jozef Schreier and proved by Sergei Kislitsyn [Knuth, 1998, Theorem S, page 209].

```
template<typename R>
    requires(Relation(R))
const Domain(R)& select_1_4_ab_cd(const Domain(R)& a,
                                  const Domain(R)& b,
                                  const Domain(R)& c,
                                  const Domain(R)& d, R r) {
    if (r(c, a)) return select_0_2(a, d, r);
    return               select_0_2(b, c, r);
}
```

The precondition for select_1_4_ab_cd can be established with one comparison if we already know that the first pair of arguments are in increasing order:

```
template<typename R>
    requires(Relation(R))
const Domain(R)& select_1_4_ab(const Domain(R)& a,
                               const Domain(R)& b,
                               const Domain(R)& c,
                               const Domain(R)& d, R r) {
    if (r(d, c)) return select_1_4_ab_cd(a, b, d, c, r);
    return               select_1_4_ab_cd(a, b, c, d, r);
}
```

The precondition for select_1_4_ab can be established with one comparison:

```
template<typename R>
    requires(Relation(R))
const Domain(R)& select_1_4(const Domain(R)& a,
                            const Domain(R)& b,
                            const Domain(R)& c,
                            const Domain(R)& d, R r) {
    if (r(b, a)) return select_1_4_ab(b, a, c, d, r);
    return               select_1_4_ab(a, b, c, d, r);
}
```

Exercise 4.4 Implement select_2_4.

Maintaining stability of order-selection networks up through order 4 has not been too difficult. But with order 5, situations arise in which the procedure

corresponding to a constrained subproblem is called with arguments out of order from the original caller, which violates stability. A systematic way to deal with
such situations is to pass the stability indices along with the actual parameters and
to use the strengthened relation r̂. We avoid extra runtime cost by using integer
template parameters.

   We name the stability indices ia, ib, ... , corresponding to the parameters a,
b, and so on. The strengthened relation r̂ is obtained by using the function object
template compare_strict_or_reflexive, which takes a bool template parameter that, if
true, means that the stability indices of its arguments are in increasing order:

```
template<bool strict, typename R>
    requires(Relation(R))
struct compare_strict_or_reflexive;
```

   When we construct an instance of compare_strict_or_reflexive, we supply the appropriate Boolean template argument:

```
template<int ia, int ib, typename R>
    requires(Relation(R))
const Domain(R)& select_0_2(const Domain(R)& a,
                           const Domain(R)& b, R r)
{
    compare_strict_or_reflexive<(ia < ib), R> cmp;
    if (cmp(b, a, r)) return b;
    return a;
}
```

   We specialize compare_strict_or_reflexive for the two cases: (1) stability indices in
increasing order, in which case we use the original strict relation r; and (2) decreasing
order, in which case we use the corresponding reflexive version of r:

```
template<typename R>
    requires(Relation(R))
struct compare_strict_or_reflexive<true, R> // strict
{
    bool operator()(const Domain(R)& a,
                   const Domain(R)& b, R r)
    {
        return r(a, b);
    }
};
```

```
template<typename R>
    requires(Relation(R))
struct compare_strict_or_reflexive<false, R> // reflexive
{
    bool operator()(const Domain(R)& a,
                    const Domain(R)& b, R r)
    {
        return !r(b, a); // complement_of_converse_r(a, b)
    }
};
```

When an order-selection procedure with stability indices calls another such procedure, the stability indices corresponding to the parameters, in the same order as they appear in the call, are passed:

```
template<int ia, int ib, int ic, int id, typename R>
    requires(Relation(R))
const Domain(R)& select_1_4_ab_cd(const Domain(R)& a,
                                  const Domain(R)& b,
                                  const Domain(R)& c,
                                  const Domain(R)& d, R r)
{
    compare_strict_or_reflexive<(ia < ic), R> cmp;
    if (cmp(c, a, r)) return
        select_0_2<ia,id>(a, d, r);
    return
        select_0_2<ib,ic>(b, c, r);
}

template<int ia, int ib, int ic, int id, typename R>
    requires(Relation(R))
const Domain(R)& select_1_4_ab(const Domain(R)& a,
                               const Domain(R)& b,
                               const Domain(R)& c,
                               const Domain(R)& d, R r)
{
    compare_strict_or_reflexive<(ic < id), R> cmp;
    if (cmp(d, c, r)) return
        select_1_4_ab_cd<ia,ib,id,ic>(a, b, d, c, r);
```

```
    return
        select_1_4_ab_cd<ia,ib,ic,id>(a, b, c, d, r);
}


template<int ia, int ib, int ic, int id, typename R>
    requires(Relation(R))
const Domain(R)& select_1_4(const Domain(R)& a,
                            const Domain(R)& b,
                            const Domain(R)& c,
                            const Domain(R)& d, R r)
{
    compare_strict_or_reflexive<(ia < ib), R> cmp;
    if (cmp(b, a, r)) return
        select_1_4_ab<ib,ia,ic,id>(b, a, c, d, r);
    return
        select_1_4_ab<ia,ib,ic,id>(a, b, c, d, r);
}
```

Now we are ready to implement order 5 selections:

```
template<int ia, int ib, int ic, int id, int ie, typename R>
    requires(Relation(R))
const Domain(R)& select_2_5_ab_cd(const Domain(R)& a,
                                  const Domain(R)& b,
                                  const Domain(R)& c,
                                  const Domain(R)& d,
                                  const Domain(R)& e, R r)
{
    compare_strict_or_reflexive<(ia < ic), R> cmp;
    if (cmp(c, a, r)) return
        select_1_4_ab<ia,ib,id,ie>(a, b, d, e, r);
    return
        select_1_4_ab<ic,id,ib,ie>(c, d, b, e, r);
}


template<int ia, int ib, int ic, int id, int ie, typename R>
    requires(Relation(R))
```

```
const Domain(R)& select_2_5_ab(const Domain(R)& a,
                               const Domain(R)& b,
                               const Domain(R)& c,
                               const Domain(R)& d,
                               const Domain(R)& e, R r)
{
    compare_strict_or_reflexive<(ic < id), R> cmp;
    if (cmp(d, c, r)) return
        select_2_5_ab_cd<ia,ib,id,ic,ie>(
                          a, b, d, c, e, r);
    return
        select_2_5_ab_cd<ia,ib,ic,id,ie>(
                          a, b, c, d, e, r);
}


template<int ia, int ib, int ic, int id, int ie, typename R>
    requires(Relation(R))
const Domain(R)& select_2_5(const Domain(R)& a,
                            const Domain(R)& b,
                            const Domain(R)& c,
                            const Domain(R)& d,
                            const Domain(R)& e, R r)
{
    compare_strict_or_reflexive<(ia < ib), R> cmp;
    if (cmp(b, a, r)) return
        select_2_5_ab<ib,ia,ic,id,ie>(b, a, c, d, e, r);
    return
        select_2_5_ab<ia,ib,ic,id,ie>(a, b, c, d, e, r);
}
```

Lemma 4.7   select_2_5 performs six comparisons.

Exercise 4.5   Find an algorithm for median of 5 that does slightly fewer comparisons on average.

We can wrap an order-selection procedure with an outer procedure that supplies, as the stability indices, any strictly increasing series of integer constants; by convention, we use successive integers starting with 0:

```
template<typename R>
    requires(Relation(R))
const Domain(R)& median_5(const Domain(R)& a,
                          const Domain(R)& b,
                          const Domain(R)& c,
                          const Domain(R)& d,
                          const Domain(R)& e, R r)
{
    return select_2_5<0,1,2,3,4>(a, b, c, d, e, r);
}
```

Exercise 4.6   Prove the stability of every order-selection procedure in this section.

Exercise 4.7   Verify the correctness and stability of every order-selection procedure in this section by exhaustive testing.

Project 4.1   Design a set of necessary and sufficient conditions preserving stability under composition of order-selection procedures.

Project 4.2   Create a library of minimum-comparison procedures for stable sorting and merging.[5] Minimize not only the number of comparisons but also the number of data movements.

4.4 Natural Total Ordering

There is a unique equality on a type because equality of values of the type means that those values represent the same entity. Often there is no unique natural total ordering on a type. For a concrete species, there are often many total and weak orderings, without any of them playing a special role. For an abstract species, there may be one special total ordering that respects its fundamental operations. Such an ordering is called the *natural total ordering* and is denoted by the symbol $<$, as follows:

---

5. See Knuth [1998, Section 5.3: Optimum Sorting].

$TotallyOrdered(\mathsf{T}) \triangleq$
  $Regular(\mathsf{T})$
  $\wedge\ <: \mathsf{T} \times \mathsf{T} \rightarrow \mathsf{bool}$
  $\wedge\ \mathsf{total\_ordering}(<)$

For example, the natural total ordering on integers respects fundamental operations:

$$a < \mathsf{successor}(a)$$
$$a < b \Rightarrow \mathsf{successor}(a) < \mathsf{successor}(b)$$
$$a < b \Rightarrow a + c < b + c$$
$$a < b \wedge 0 < c \Rightarrow ca < cb$$

Sometimes, a type does not have a natural total ordering. For example, complex numbers and employee records do not have natural total orderings. We require regular types to provide a *default total ordering* (sometimes abbreviated to *default ordering*) to enable logarithmic searching. An example of default total ordering where no natural total ordering exists is lexicographical ordering for complex numbers. When the natural total ordering exists, it coincides with the default ordering. We use the following notation:

	Specifications	C++
Default ordering for T	less_T	`less<T>`

4.5 Clusters of Derived Procedures

Some procedures naturally come in clusters. If some procedures in a cluster are defined, the definitions of the others naturally follow. The complement of equality, inequality, is defined whenever equality is defined; the operators = and $\neq$ must be defined consistently. For every totally ordered type, all four operators $<$, $>$, $\leq$, and $\geq$ must be defined together in such a way that the following hold:

$$a > b \Leftrightarrow b < a$$
$$a \leq b \Leftrightarrow \neg(b < a)$$
$$a \geq b \Leftrightarrow \neg(a < b)$$

4.6 Extending Order-Selection Procedures

The order-selection procedures in this chapter do not return an object that can be mutated, because they work with constant references. It is useful and straightforward to have versions that return a mutable object, so that they could be used on the left side of an assignment or as the mutable argument to an action or accumulation procedure. An overloaded mutable version of an order-selection procedure is implemented by removing from the nonmutable version the const from each parameter type and the result type. For example, our version of select_0_2 is supplemented with

```
template<typename R>
    requires(Relation(R))
Domain(R)& select_0_2(Domain(R)& a, Domain(R)& b, R r)
{
    if (r(b, a)) return b;
    return a;
}
```

In addition, a library should provide versions for totally ordered types (with <), since it is a common case. This means that there are four versions of each procedure.

The trichotomy and weak-trichotomy laws satisfied by total and weak ordering suggest that instead of a two-valued relation, we could use a three-valued comparison procedure, since, in some situations, this would avoid an additional procedure call.

Exercise 4.8 Rewrite the algorithms in this chapter using three-valued comparison.

4.7 Conclusions

The axioms of total and weak ordering provide the interface to connect specific orderings with general-purpose algorithms. Systematic solutions to small problems lead to easy decomposition of large problems. There are clusters of procedures with interrelated semantics.

Chapter 5

Ordered Algebraic Structures

T*his chapter presents a hierarchy of concepts from abstract algebra, starting with semigroups and ending with rings and modules. We then combine algebraic concepts with the notion of total ordering. When ordered algebraic structures are* Archimedean, *we can define an efficient algorithm for finding quotient and remainder. Quotient and remainder in turn lead to a generalized version of Euclid's algorithm for the greatest common divisor. We briefly treat concept-related logical notions, such as consistency and independence. We conclude with a discussion of computer integer arithmetic.*

5.1 Basic Algebraic Structures

An element is called an *identity element* of a binary operation if, when combined with any other element as the first or second argument, the operation returns the other element:

> **property**(T : *Regular*, Op : *BinaryOperation*)
>   **requires**(T = Domain(Op))
> identity_element : T × Op
>   (e, op) $\mapsto$ ($\forall a \in$ T) op(a, e) = op(e, a) = a

> **Lemma 5.1**   An identity element is unique:

$$\text{identity\_element}(e, op) \land \text{identity\_element}(e', op) \Rightarrow e = e'$$

The empty string is the identity element of string concatenation. The matrix $\left(\begin{smallmatrix} 1 & 0 \\ 0 & 1 \end{smallmatrix}\right)$ is the multiplicative identity of 2 × 2 matrices, while $\left(\begin{smallmatrix} 0 & 0 \\ 0 & 0 \end{smallmatrix}\right)$ is their additive identity.

A transformation is called an *inverse operation* of a binary operation if an element and its transformation, when combined in either order, give the identity element:

property(F : *Transformation*, T : *Regular*, Op : *BinaryOperation*)
   requires(Domain(F) = T = Domain(Op))
 inverse_operation : F × T × Op
    $(inv, e, op) \mapsto (\forall a \in T)\ op(a, inv(a)) = op(inv(a), a) = e$

Lemma 5.2 n^3 is the multiplicative inverse modulo 5 of a positive integer $n \neq 0$.

A binary operation is *commutative* if its result is the same when its arguments are interchanged:

property(Op : *BinaryOperation*)
 commutative : Op
    $op \mapsto (\forall a, b \in Domain(Op))\ op(a, b) = op(b, a)$

Composition of transformations is associative but not commutative.

A set with an associative operation is called a *semigroup*. Since, as we remarked in Chapter 3, + is always used to denote an associative, commutative operation, a type with + is called an *additive semigroup:*

AdditiveSemigroup(T) ≜
    Regular(T)
 ∧ + : T × T → T
 ∧ associative(+)
 ∧ commutative(+)

Multiplication is sometimes not commutative. Consider, for example, matrix multiplication.

MultiplicativeSemigroup(T) ≜
    Regular(T)
 ∧ · : T × T → T
 ∧ associative(·)

We use the following notation:

	Specifications	C++
Multiplication	·	*

A semigroup with an identity element is called a *monoid*. The additive identity element is denoted by 0, which leads to the definition of an *additive monoid:*

AdditiveMonoid(T) ≜
    AdditiveSemigroup(T)
   ∧ 0 ∈ T
   ∧ identity_element(0, +)

We use the following notation:

	Specifications	C++
Additive identity	0	T(0).

Non-negative reals are an additive monoid, as are matrices with natural numbers as their coefficients.

The multiplicative identity element is denoted by 1, which leads to the definition of a *multiplicative monoid:*

MultiplicativeMonoid(T) ≜
    MultiplicativeSemigroup(T)
   ∧ 1 ∈ T
   ∧ identity_element(1, ·)

We use the following notation:

	Specifications	C++
Multiplicative identity	1	T(1)

Matrices with integer coefficients are a multiplicative monoid.

A monoid with an inverse operation is called a *group*. If an additive monoid has an inverse, it is denoted by unary −, and there is a derived operation called *subtraction*, denoted by binary −. That leads to the definition of an *additive group:*

AdditiveGroup(T) ≜
    AdditiveMonoid(T)
   ∧ − : T → T
   ∧ inverse_operation(unary −, 0, +)
   ∧ − : T × T → T
        (a, b) ↦ a + (−b)

Matrices with integer coefficients are an additive group.

Lemma 5.3   In an additive group, $-0 = 0$.

Just as there is a concept of additive group, there is a corresponding concept of *multiplicative group*. In this concept the inverse is called *multiplicative inverse*, and there is a derived operation called *division*, denoted by binary $/$:

MultiplicativeGroup(T) $\triangleq$
    MultiplicativeMonoid(T)
  $\land$ multiplicative_inverse : T $\to$ T
  $\land$ inverse_operation(multiplicative_inverse, 1, $\cdot$)
  $\land$ $/$: T $\times$ T $\to$ T
      $(a, b) \mapsto a \cdot$ multiplicative_inverse(b)

  multiplicative_inverse(x) is written as x^{-1}.

The set $\{\cos\theta + i\sin\theta\}$ of complex numbers on the unit circle is a commutative multiplicative group. A unimodular group $GL_n(\mathbb{Z})$ ($n \times n$ matrices with integer coefficients with determinant equal to ± 1) is a noncommutative multiplicative group.

Two concepts can be combined on the same type with the help of axioms connecting their operations. When both $+$ and $\cdot$ are present on a type, they are interrelated with axioms defining a *semiring*:

Semiring(T) $\triangleq$
    AdditiveMonoid(T)
  $\land$ *MultiplicativeMonoid*(T)
  $\land$ $0 \neq 1$
  $\land$ $(\forall a \in T)\, 0 \cdot a = a \cdot 0 = 0$
  $\land$ $(\forall a, b, c \in T)$
       $a \cdot (b + c) = a \cdot b + a \cdot c$
      $\land$ $(b + c) \cdot a = b \cdot a + c \cdot a$

The axiom about multiplication by 0 is called the *annihilation property*. The final axiom connecting $+$ and $\cdot$ is called *distributivity*.

Matrices with non-negative integer coefficients constitute a semiring.

CommutativeSemiring(T) $\triangleq$
    Semiring(T)
  $\land$ commutative($\cdot$)

Non-negative integers constitute a commutative semiring.

Ring(T) ≜
    AdditiveGroup(T)
  ∧ *Semiring*(T)

Matrices with integer coefficients constitute a ring.

CommutativeRing(T) ≜
    AdditiveGroup(T)
  ∧ *CommutativeSemiring*(T)

Integers constitute a commutative ring; polynomials with integer coefficients constitute a commutative ring.

A *relational concept* is a concept defined on two types. *Semimodule* is a relational concept that connects an additive monoid and a commutative semiring:

Semimodule(T, S) ≜
    AdditiveMonoid(T)
  ∧ *CommutativeSemiring*(S)
  ∧ · : S × T → T
  ∧ ($\forall \alpha, \beta \in$ S)($\forall$a, b $\in$ T)

$$\alpha \cdot (\beta \cdot a) = (\alpha \cdot \beta) \cdot a$$
$$(\alpha + \beta) \cdot a = \alpha \cdot a + \beta \cdot a$$
$$\alpha \cdot (a + b) = \alpha \cdot a + \alpha \cdot b$$
$$1 \cdot a = a$$

If *Semimodule*(T, S), we say that T is a semimodule *over* S. We borrow terminology from vector spaces and call elements of T *vectors* and elements of S *scalars*. For example, polynomials with non-negative integer coefficients constitute a semimodule over non-negative integers.

Theorem 5.1 *AdditiveMonoid*(T) ⇒ *Semimodule*(T, $\mathbb{N}$), where scalar multiplication is defined as $n \cdot x = \underbrace{x + \cdots + x}_{n \text{ times}}$.

Proof: It follows trivially from the definition of scalar multiplication together with associativity and commutativity of the monoid operation. For example,

$$n \cdot a + n \cdot b = (a + \cdots + a) + (b + \cdots + b)$$
$$= (a + b) + \cdots + (a + b)$$
$$= n \cdot (a + b)$$

Using power from Chapter 3 allows us to implement multiplication by an integer in $\log_2 n$ steps.

Strengthening the requirements by replacing the additive monoid with an additive group and replacing the semiring with a ring transforms a semimodule into a module:

$Module(\mathsf{T}, \mathsf{S}) \triangleq$
$\qquad Semimodule(\mathsf{T}, \mathsf{S})$
$\quad \wedge\ AdditiveGroup(\mathsf{T})$
$\quad \wedge\ Ring(\mathsf{S})$

Lemma 5.4   Every additive group is a module over integers with an appropriately defined scalar multiplication.

Computer types are often partial models of concepts. A model is called *partial* when the operations satisfy the axioms where they are defined but are not everywhere defined. For example, the result of concatenation of strings may not be representable, because of memory limitations, but concatenation is associative whenever it is defined.

5.2 Ordered Algebraic Structures

When a total ordering is defined on the elements of a structure in such a way that the ordering is consistent with the structure's algebraic properties, it is the *natural total ordering* for the structure:

$OrderedAdditiveSemigroup(\mathsf{T}) \triangleq$
$\qquad AdditiveSemigroup(\mathsf{T})$
$\quad \wedge\ TotallyOrdered(\mathsf{T})$
$\quad \wedge\ (\forall a, b, c \in \mathsf{T})\, a < b \Rightarrow a + c < b + c$

$OrderedAdditiveMonoid(\mathsf{T}) \triangleq$
$\qquad OrderedAdditiveSemigroup(\mathsf{T})$
$\quad \wedge\ AdditiveMonoid(\mathsf{T})$

$OrderedAdditiveGroup(\mathsf{T}) \triangleq$
$\qquad OrderedAdditiveMonoid(\mathsf{T})$
$\quad \wedge\ AdditiveGroup(\mathsf{T})$

Lemma 5.5   In an ordered additive semigroup, $a < b \wedge c < d \Rightarrow a + c < b + d$.

Lemma 5.6   In an ordered additive monoid viewed as a semimodule over natural numbers, $a > 0 \wedge n > 0 \Rightarrow na > 0$.

Lemma 5.7   In an ordered additive group, $a < b \Rightarrow -b < -a$.

Total ordering and negation allow us to define absolute value:

```
template<typename T>
    requires(OrderedAdditiveGroup(T))
T abs(const T& a)
{
    if (a < T(0)) return -a;
    else          return  a;
}
```

The following lemma captures an important property of abs.

Lemma 5.8   In an ordered additive group, $a < 0 \Rightarrow 0 < -a$.

We use the notation $|a|$ for the absolute value of a. Absolute value satisfies the following properties.

Lemma 5.9
$$|a - b| = |b - a|$$
$$|a + b| \leq |a| + |b|$$
$$|a - b| \geq |a| - |b|$$
$$|a| = 0 \Rightarrow a = 0$$
$$a \neq 0 \Rightarrow |a| > 0$$

5.3 Remainder

We saw that repeated addition in an additive monoid induces multiplication by an integer. In an additive group, this algorithm can be inverted, obtaining division by repeated subtraction on elements of the form $a = nb$, where b divides a. To extend this to division with remainder for an arbitrary pair of elements, we need ordering. The ordering allows the algorithm to terminate when it is no longer possible to subtract. As we shall see, it also enables an algorithm to take a logarithmic number of steps. The subtraction operation does not need to be defined everywhere; it is sufficient to have a partial subtraction called *cancellation*, where $a - b$ is only defined when b does not exceed a:

$CancellableMonoid(\mathsf{T}) \triangleq$
  $OrderedAdditiveMonoid(\mathsf{T})$
  $\wedge\ - : \mathsf{T} \times \mathsf{T} \rightarrow \mathsf{T}$
  $\wedge\ (\forall a, b \in \mathsf{T})\ b \leq a \Rightarrow a - b \text{ is defined} \wedge (a - b) + b = a$

We write the axiom as $(a - b) + b = a$ instead of $(a + b) - b = a$ to avoid overflow in partial models of *CancellableMonoid*:

```
template<typename T>
    requires(CancellableMonoid(T))
T slow_remainder(T a, T b)
{
    // Precondition: a ≥ 0 ∧ b > 0
    while (b <= a) a = a - b;
    return a;
}
```

The concept *CancellableMonoid* is not strong enough to prove termination of slow_remainder. For example, slow_remainder does not always terminate for polynomials with integer coefficients, ordered lexicographically.

Exercise 5.1   Give an example of two polynomials with integer coefficients for which the algorithm does not terminate.

To ensure that the algorithm terminates, we need another property, called the *Axiom of Archimedes:*[1]

$ArchimedeanMonoid(\mathsf{T}) \triangleq$
  $CancellableMonoid(\mathsf{T})$
  $\wedge\ (\forall a, b \in \mathsf{T})\ (a \geq 0 \wedge b > 0) \Rightarrow \mathsf{slow\_remainder}(a, b) \text{ terminates}$
  $\wedge\ \mathsf{QuotientType} : ArchimedeanMonoid \rightarrow Integer$

---

1. " . . . the excess by which the greater of (two) unequal areas exceeds the less can, by being added to itself, be made to exceed any given finite area." See Heath [1912, page 234].

Observe that termination of an algorithm is a legitimate axiom; in this case it is equivalent to

$$(\exists n \in \mathsf{QuotientType}(T)) \; a - n \cdot b < b$$

While the Axiom of Archimedes is usually given as "there exists an integer n such that $a < n \cdot b$," our version works with partial Archimedean monoids where $n \cdot b$ might overflow. The type function $\mathsf{QuotientType}$ returns a type large enough to represent the number of iterations performed by slow_remainder.

Lemma 5.10 The following are Archimedean monoids: integers, rational numbers, binary fractions $\{\frac{n}{2^k}\}$, ternary fractions $\{\frac{n}{3^k}\}$, and real numbers.

We can trivially adapt the code of slow_remainder to return the quotient:

```
template<typename T>
    requires(ArchimedeanMonoid(T))
QuotientType(T) slow_quotient(T a, T b)
{
    // Precondition: a ≥ 0 ∧ b > 0
    QuotientType(T) n(0);
    while (b <= a) {
        a = a - b;
        n = successor(n);
    }
    return n;
}
```

Repeated doubling leads to the logarithmic-complexity power algorithm. A related algorithm is possible for remainder.[2] Let us derive an expression for the remainder u from dividing a by b in terms of the remainder v from dividing a by $2b$:

$$a = n(2b) + v$$

Since the remainder v must be less than the divisor $2b$, it follows that

$$u = \begin{cases} v & \text{if } v < b \\ v - b & \text{if } v \geq b \end{cases}$$

---

2. The Egyptians used this algorithm to do division with remainder, as they used the power algorithm to do multiplication. See Robins and Shute [1987, page 18].

That leads to the following recursive procedure:

```
template<typename T>
    requires(ArchimedeanMonoid(T))
T remainder_recursive(T a, T b)
{
    // Precondition: a ≥ b > 0
    if (a - b >= b) {
        a = remainder_recursive(a, b + b);
        if (a < b) return a;
    }
    return a - b;
}
```

Testing $a - b \geq b$ rather than $a \geq b + b$ avoids overflow of $b + b$:

```
template<typename T>
    requires(ArchimedeanMonoid(T))
T remainder_nonnegative(T a, T b)
{
    // Precondition: a ≥ 0 ∧ b > 0
    if (a < b) return a;
    return remainder_recursive(a, b);
}
```

Exercise 5.2 Analyze the complexity of remainder_nonnegative.

Floyd and Knuth [1990] give a constant-space algorithm for remainder on Archimedean monoids that performs about 31% more operations than remainder_nonnegative, but when we can divide by 2 an algorithm exists that does not increase the operation count.[3] This is likely to be possible in many situations. For example, while the general k-section of an angle by ruler and compass cannot be done, the bisection is trivial.

$HalvableMonoid(\mathsf{T}) \triangleq$
    $ArchimedeanMonoid(\mathsf{T})$
$\wedge$ half : $\mathsf{T} \to \mathsf{T}$
$\wedge \; (\forall a, b \in \mathsf{T})\,(b > 0 \wedge a = b + b) \Rightarrow \mathrm{half}(a) = b$

Observe that half needs to be defined only for "even" elements.

---

3. Dijkstra [1972, page 13] attributes this algorithm to N. G. de Bruijn.

```
template<typename T>
    requires(HalvableMonoid(T))
T remainder_nonnegative_iterative(T a, T b)
{
    // Precondition: a ≥ 0 ∧ b > 0
    if (a < b) return a;
    T c = largest_doubling(a, b);
    a = a - c;
    while (c != b) {
        c = half(c);
        if (c <= a) a = a - c;
    }
    return a;
}
```

where largest_doubling is defined by the following procedure:

```
template<typename T>
    requires(ArchimedeanMonoid(T))
T largest_doubling(T a, T b)
{
    // Precondition: a ≥ b > 0
    while (b <= a - b) b = b + b;
    return b;
}
```

The correctness of remainder_nonnegative_iterative depends on the following lemma.

Lemma 5.11 The result of doubling a positive element of a halvable monoid k times may be halved k times.

We would only need remainder_nonnegative if we had an Archimedean monoid that was not halvable. The examples we gave—line segments in Euclidean geometry, rational numbers, binary and ternary fractions—are all halvable.

Project 5.1 Are there useful models of Archimedean monoids that are not halvable monoids?

5.4 Greatest Common Divisor

For $a \geq 0$ and $b > 0$ in an Archimedean monoid T, we define *divisibility* as follows:

$$b \text{ divides } a \Leftrightarrow (\exists n \in \mathsf{QuotientType}(T))\ a = nb$$

Lemma 5.12   In an Archimedean monoid T with positive x, a, b:

- b divides $a \Leftrightarrow \mathsf{remainder\_nonnegative}(a, b) = 0$
- b divides $a \Rightarrow b \leq a$
- $a > b \wedge x$ divides $a \wedge x$ divides $b \Rightarrow x$ divides $(a - b)$
- x divides $a \wedge x$ divides $b \Rightarrow x$ divides $\mathsf{remainder\_nonnegative}(a, b)$

The *greatest common divisor* of a and b, denoted by $\gcd(a, b)$, is a divisor of a and b that is divisible by any other common divisor of a and b.[4]

Lemma 5.13   In an Archimedean monoid, the following hold for positive x, a, b:

- gcd is commutative
- gcd is associative
- x divides $a \wedge x$ divides $b \Rightarrow x \leq \gcd(a, b)$
- $\gcd(a, b)$ is unique
- $\gcd(a, a) = a$
- $a > b \Rightarrow \gcd(a, b) = \gcd(a - b, b)$

The previous lemmas immediately imply that if the following algorithm terminates, it returns the gcd of its arguments:[5]

```
template<typename T>
    requires(ArchimedeanMonoid(T))
T subtractive_gcd_nonzero(T a, T b)
{
```

---

4. While this definition works for Archimedean monoids, it does not depend on ordering and can be extended to other structures with divisibility relations, such as rings.

5. It is known as Euclid's algorithm [Heath, 1925, pages 14–22].

```
// Precondition: a > 0 ∧ b > 0
while (true) {
    if (b < a)        a = a - b;
    else if (a < b) b = b - a;
    else              return a;
}
}
```

Lemma 5.14   It always terminates for integers and rationals.

There are types for which it does not always terminate. In particular, it does not always terminate for real numbers; specifically, it does not terminate for input of $\sqrt{2}$ and 1. The proof of this fact depends on the following two lemmas:

Lemma 5.15 $\gcd(\frac{a}{\gcd(a,\,b)}, \frac{b}{\gcd(a,\,b)}) = 1$

Lemma 5.16   If the square of an integer n is even, n is even.

Theorem 5.2   subtractive_gcd_nonzero($\sqrt{2}$, 1) does not terminate.

Proof: Suppose that subtractive_gcd_nonzero($\sqrt{2}$, 1) terminates, returning d. Let $m = \frac{\sqrt{2}}{d}$ and $n = \frac{1}{d}$; by Lemma 5.15, m and n have no common factors greater than 1. $\frac{m}{n} = \frac{\sqrt{2}}{1} = \sqrt{2}$, so $m^2 = 2n^2$; m is even; for some integer u, $m = 2u$. $4u^2 = 2n^2$, so $n^2 = 2u^2$; n is even. Both m and n are divisible by 2; a contradiction.[6]

A *Euclidean* monoid is an Archimedean monoid where subtractive_gcd_nonzero always terminates:

EuclideanMonoid(T) ≜
   ArchimedeanMonoid(T)
   ∧ (∀a, b ∈ T) (a > 0 ∧ b > 0) ⇒ subtractive_gcd_nonzero(a, b) terminates

Lemma 5.17   Every Archimedean monoid with a smallest positive element is Euclidean.

---

6. The incommensurability of the side and the diagonal of a square was one of the first mathematical proofs discovered by the Greeks. Aristotle refers to it in *Prior Analytics* I. 23 as the canonical example of proof by contradiction (*reductio ad absurdum*).

Lemma 5.18   The rational numbers are a Euclidean monoid.

It is straightforward to extend subtractive_gcd_nonzero to the case in which one of its arguments is zero, since any $b \neq 0$ divides the zero of the monoid:

```
template<typename T>
    requires(EuclideanMonoid(T))
T subtractive_gcd(T a, T b)
{
    // Precondition: a ≥ 0 ∧ b ≥ 0 ∧ ¬(a = 0 ∧ b = 0)
    while (true) {
        if (b == T(0)) return a;
        while (b <= a) a = a - b;
        if (a == T(0)) return b;
        while (a <= b) b = b - a;
    }
}
```

Each of the inner while statements in subtractive_gcd is equivalent to a call of slow_remainder. By using our logarithmic remainder algorithm, we speed up the case when a and b are very different in magnitude while relying only on primitive subtraction on type T:

```
template<typename T>
    requires(EuclideanMonoid(T))
T fast_subtractive_gcd(T a, T b)
{
    // Precondition: a ≥ 0 ∧ b ≥ 0 ∧ ¬(a = 0 ∧ b = 0)
    while (true) {
        if (b == T(0)) return a;
        a = remainder_nonnegative(a, b);
        if (a == T(0)) return b;
        b = remainder_nonnegative(b, a);
    }
}
```

The concept of Euclidean monoid gives us an abstract setting for the original Euclid algorithm, which was based on repeated subtraction.

5.5   Generalizing gcd

We can use fast_subtractive_gcd with integers because they constitute a Euclidean monoid. For integers, we could also use the same algorithm with the built-in remainder instead of remainder_nonnegative. Furthermore, the algorithm works for certain non-Archimedean domains, provided that they possess a suitable remainder function. For example, the standard long-division algorithm easily extends from decimal integers to polynomials over reals.[7] Using such a remainder, we can compute the gcd of two polynomials.

Abstract algebra introduces the notion of a Euclidean ring (also known as a Euclidean domain) to accommodate such uses of the Euclid algorithm.[8] However, the requirements of semiring suffice:

$EuclideanSemiring(\mathsf{T}) \triangleq$

$\quad CommutativeSemiring(\mathsf{T})$

$\land$ NormType : $EuclideanSemiring \rightarrow Integer$

$\land$ w : $\mathsf{T} \rightarrow$ NormType(T)

$\land$ $(\forall a \in \mathsf{T})\, w(a) \geq 0$

$\land$ $(\forall a \in \mathsf{T})\, w(a) = 0 \Leftrightarrow a = 0$

$\land$ $(\forall a, b \in \mathsf{T})\, b \neq 0 \Rightarrow w(a \cdot b) \geq w(a)$

$\land$ remainder : $\mathsf{T} \times \mathsf{T} \rightarrow \mathsf{T}$

$\land$ quotient : $\mathsf{T} \times \mathsf{T} \rightarrow \mathsf{T}$

$\land$ $(\forall a, b \in \mathsf{T})\, b \neq 0 \Rightarrow a = quotient(a, b) \cdot b + remainder(a, b)$

$\land$ $(\forall a, b \in \mathsf{T})\, b \neq 0 \Rightarrow w(remainder(a, b)) < w(b)$

w is called the *Euclidean function*.

Lemma 5.19   In a Euclidean semiring, $a \cdot b = 0 \Rightarrow a = 0 \lor b = 0$.

```
template<typename T>
    requires(EuclideanSemiring(T))
T gcd(T a, T b)
{
    // Precondition: ¬(a = 0 ∧ b = 0)
    while (true) {
        if (b == T(0)) return a;
```

---

7. See Chrystal [1904, Chapter 5].
8. See van der Waerden [1930, Chapter 3, Section 18].

```
        a = remainder(a, b);
        if (a == T(0)) return b;
        b = remainder(b, a);
    }
}
```

Observe that instead of using remainder_nonnegative, we use the remainder function defined by the type. The fact that w decreases with every application of remainder ensures termination.

Lemma 5.20   gcd terminates on a Euclidean semiring.

In a Euclidean semiring, quotient returns an element of the semiring. This precludes its use in the original setting of Euclid: determining the common measure of any two commensurable quantities. For example, $\gcd(\frac{1}{2}, \frac{3}{4}) = \frac{1}{4}$. We can unify the original setting and the modern setting with the concept *Euclidean semimodule*, which allows quotient to return a different type and takes the termination of gcd as an axiom:

$EuclideanSemimodule(\mathsf{T}, \mathsf{S}) \triangleq$
    $Semimodule(\mathsf{T}, \mathsf{S})$
    $\wedge$ remainder : $\mathsf{T} \times \mathsf{T} \to \mathsf{T}$
    $\wedge$ quotient : $\mathsf{T} \times \mathsf{T} \to \mathsf{S}$
    $\wedge$ $(\forall a, b \in \mathsf{T})\, b \neq 0 \Rightarrow a = \text{quotient}(a, b) \cdot b + \text{remainder}(a, b)$
    $\wedge$ $(\forall a, b \in \mathsf{T})\, (a \neq 0 \vee b \neq 0) \Rightarrow \gcd(a, b)$ terminates

where gcd is defined as

```
template<typename T, typename S>
    requires(EuclideanSemimodule(T, S))
T gcd(T a, T b)
{
    // Precondition: ¬(a = 0 ∧ b = 0)
    while (true) {
        if (b == T(0)) return a;
        a = remainder(a, b);
        if (a == T(0)) return b;
        b = remainder(b, a);
    }
}
```

Since every commutative semiring is a semimodule over itself, this algorithm can be used even when quotient returns the same type, as with polynomials over reals.

5.6 Stein gcd

In 1961 Josef Stein discovered a new gcd algorithm for integers that is frequently faster than Euclid's algorithm [Stein, 1967]. His algorithm depends on these two familiar properties:

$$\gcd(a, b) = \gcd(b, a)$$
$$\gcd(a, a) = a$$

together with these additional properties that for all $a > b > 0$:

$$\gcd(2a, 2b) = 2 \gcd(a, b)$$
$$\gcd(2a, 2b + 1) = \gcd(a, 2b + 1)$$
$$\gcd(2a + 1, 2b) = \gcd(2a + 1, b)$$
$$\gcd(2a + 1, 2b + 1) = \gcd(2b + 1, a - b)$$

Exercise 5.3   Implement Stein gcd for integers, and prove its termination.

While it might appear that Stein gcd depends on the binary representation of integers, the intuition that 2 is the smallest prime integer allows generalizing it to other domains by using smallest primes in these domains; for example, the monomial x for polynomials[9] or $1 + i$ for Gaussian integers.[10] Stein gcd could be used in rings that are not Euclidean.[11]

Project 5.2   Find the correct general setting for Stein gcd.

5.7 Quotient

The derivation of fast quotient and remainder exactly parallels our earlier derivation of fast remainder. We derive an expression for the quotient m and remainder u from dividing a by b in terms of the quotient n and remainder v from dividing a by $2b$:

$$a = n(2b) + v$$

---

9. See Knuth [1997, Exercise 4.6.1.6 (page 435) and Solution (page 673)].
10. See Weilert [2000].
11. See Agarwal and Frandsen [2004].

Since the remainder v must be less than the divisor $2b$, it follows that

$$u = \begin{cases} v & \text{if } v < b \\ v - b & \text{if } v \geq b \end{cases}$$

and

$$m = \begin{cases} 2n & \text{if } v < b \\ 2n + 1 & \text{if } v \geq b \end{cases}$$

This leads to the following code:

```
template<typename T>
    requires(ArchimedeanMonoid(T))
pair<QuotientType(T), T>
quotient_remainder_nonnegative(T a, T b)
{
    // Precondition: a ≥ 0 ∧ b > 0
    typedef QuotientType(T) N;
    if (a < b) return pair<N, T>(N(0), a);
    if (a - b < b) return pair<N, T>(N(1), a - b);
    pair<N, T> q = quotient_remainder_nonnegative(a, b + b);
    N m = twice(q.m0);
    a = q.m1;
    if (a < b) return pair<N, T>(m, a);
    else        return pair<N, T>(successor(m), a - b);
}
```

When "halving" is available, we obtain the following:

```
template<typename T>
    requires(HalvableMonoid(T))
pair<QuotientType(T), T>
quotient_remainder_nonnegative_iterative(T a, T b)
{
    // Precondition: a ≥ 0 ∧ b > 0
    typedef QuotientType(T) N;
    if (a < b) return pair<N, T>(N(0), a);
    T c = largest_doubling(a, b);
    a = a - c;
    N n(1);
    while (c != b) {
```

```
        n = twice(n);
        c = half(c);
        if (c <= a) {
            a = a - c;
            n = successor(n);
        }
    }
    return pair<N, T>(n, a);
}
```

5.8 Quotient and Remainder for Negative Quantities

The definition of quotient and remainder used by many computer processors and programming languages handles negative quantities incorrectly. An extension of our definitions for an Archimedean monoid to an Archimedean group T must satisfy these properties, where $b \neq 0$:

$$a = \text{quotient}(a, b) \cdot b + \text{remainder}(a, b)$$

$$|\text{remainder}(a, b)| < |b|$$

$$\text{remainder}(a + b, b) = \text{remainder}(a - b, b) = \text{remainder}(a, b)$$

The final property is equivalent to the classical mathematical definition of congruence.[12] While books on number theory usually assume $b > 0$, we can consistently extend remainder to $b < 0$. These requirements are not satisfied by implementations that truncate quotient toward zero, thus violating our third requirement.[13] In addition to violating the third requirement, truncation is an inferior way of rounding because it sends twice as many values to zero as to any other integer, thus leading to a nonuniform distribution.

Given a remainder procedure rem and a quotient-remainder procedure quo_rem satisfying our three requirements for non-negative inputs, we can write adapter procedures that give correct results for positive or negative inputs. These adapter procedures will work on an *Archimedean group*:

$ArchimedeanGroup(\text{T}) \triangleq$
  $ArchimedeanMonoid(\text{T})$
  $\wedge\ AdditiveGroup(\text{T})$

---

12. "If two numbers a and b have the same remainder r relative to the same modulus k they will be called *congruent* relative to the modulus k (following Gauss)" [Dirichlet, 1863].

13. For an excellent discussion of quotient and remainder, see Boute [1992]. Boute identifies the two acceptable extensions as E and F; we follow Knuth in preferring what Boute calls F.

```
template<typename Op>
    requires(BinaryOperation(Op) &&
        ArchimedeanGroup(Domain(Op)))
Domain(Op) remainder(Domain(Op) a, Domain(Op) b, Op rem)
{
    // Precondition: b ≠ 0
    typedef Domain(Op) T;
    T r;
    if (a < T(0))
        if (b < T(0)) {
            r = -rem(-a, -b);
        } else {
            r =  rem(-a,  b); if (r != T(0)) r = b - r;
        }
    else
        if (b < T(0)) {
            r =  rem(a, -b);  if (r != T(0)) r = b + r;
        } else {
            r =  rem(a,  b);
        }
    return r;
}

template<typename F>
    requires(HomogeneousFunction(F) && Arity(F) == 2 &&
        ArchimedeanGroup(Domain(F)) &&
        Codomain(F) == pair<QuotientType(Domain(F)),
                             Domain(F)>)
pair<QuotientType(Domain(F)), Domain(F)>
quotient_remainder(Domain(F) a, Domain(F) b, F quo_rem)
{
    // Precondition: b ≠ 0
    typedef Domain(F) T;
    pair<QuotientType(T), T> q_r;
    if (a < T(0)) {
        if (b < T(0)) {
            q_r = quo_rem(-a, -b); q_r.m1 = -q_r.m1;
        } else {
```

```
            q_r = quo_rem(-a,  b);
            if (q_r.m1 != T(0)) {
                q_r.m1 = b - q_r.m1; q_r.m0 = successor(q_r.m0);
            }
            q_r.m0 = -q_r.m0;
        }
    } else {
        if (b < T(0)) {
            q_r = quo_rem( a, -b);
            if (q_r.m1 != T(0)) {
                q_r.m1 = b + q_r.m1; q_r.m0 = successor(q_r.m0);
            }
            q_r.m0 = -q_r.m0;
        }
        else
            q_r = quo_rem( a,  b);
    }
    return q_r;
}
```

Lemma 5.21 remainder and quotient_remainder satisfy our requirements when their functional parameters satisfy the requirements for positive arguments.

5.9 Concepts and Their Models

We have been using integer types since Chapter 2 without formally defining the concept. Building on the ordered algebraic structures defined earlier in this chapter, we can formalize our treatment of integers. First, we define *discrete Archimedean semiring:*

$DiscreteArchimedeanSemiring(T) \triangleq$
  $CommutativeSemiring(T)$
  $\wedge \; ArchimedeanMonoid(T)$
  $\wedge \; (\forall a, b, c \in T)\, a < b \wedge 0 < c \Rightarrow a \cdot c < b \cdot c$
  $\wedge \; \neg(\exists a \in T)\, 0 < a < 1$

Discreteness refers to the last property: There is no element between 0 and 1.

A discrete Archimedean semiring might have negative elements. The related concept that does not have negative elements is

NonnegativeDiscreteArchimedeanSemiring(T) $\triangleq$
  DiscreteArchimedeanSemiring(T)
  $\wedge\ (\forall a \in$ T$)\, 0 \leq a$

A discrete Archimedean semiring lacks additive inverses; the related concept with additive inverses is

DiscreteArchimedeanRing(T) $\triangleq$
  DiscreteArchimedeanSemiring(T)
  $\wedge$ *AdditiveGroup*(T)

Two types T and T' are *isomorphic* if it is possible to write conversion functions from T to T' and from T' to T that preserve the procedures and their axioms.

A concept is *univalent* if any types satisfying it are isomorphic. The concept *NonnegativeDiscreteArchimedeanSemiring* is univalent; types satisfying it are isomorphic to $\mathbb{N}$, the natural numbers.[14] *DiscreteArchimedeanRing* is univalent; types satisfying it are isomorphic to $\mathbb{Z}$, the integers. As we have seen here, adding axioms reduces the number of models of a concept, so that one quickly reaches the point of univalency.

This chapter proceeds deductively, from more general to more specific concepts, by adding more operations and axioms. The deductive approach statically presents a taxonomy of concepts and affiliated theorems and algorithms. The actual process of discovery proceeds inductively, starting with concrete models, such as integers or reals, and then removing operations and axioms to find the weakest concept to which interesting algorithms apply.

When we define a concept, the independence and consistency of its axioms must be verified, and its usefulness must be demonstrated.

A proposition is *independent* from a set of axioms if there is a model in which all the axioms are true, but the proposition is false. For example, associativity and commutativity are independent: String concatenation is associative but not commutative, while the average of two values ($\frac{x+y}{2}$) is commutative but not associative. A proposition is *dependent* or *provable* from a set of axioms if it can be derived from them.

---

14. We follow Peano [1908, page 27] and include 0 in the natural numbers.

A concept is *consistent* if it has a model. Continuing our example, addition of natural numbers is associative and commutative. A concept is *inconsistent* if both a proposition and its negation can be derived from its axioms. In other words, to demonstrate consistency, we construct a model; to demonstrate inconsistency, we derive a contradiction.

A concept is *useful* if there are useful algorithms for which this is the most abstract setting. For example, parallel out-of-order reduction applies to any associative, commutative operation.

5.10   Computer Integer Types

Computer instruction sets typically provide partial representations of natural numbers and integers. For example, a *bounded unsigned binary integer type*, U_n, where $n = 8, 16, 32, 64, \dots$, is an unsigned integer type capable of representing a value in the interval $[0, 2^n)$; a *bounded signed binary integer type*, S_n, where $n = 8, 16, 32, 64, \dots$, is a signed integer type capable of representing a value in the interval $[-2^{n-1}, 2^{n-1})$. Although these types are bounded, typical computer instructions provide total operations on them because the results are encoded as a tuple of bounded values.

Instructions on bounded unsigned types with signatures like these usually exist:

$$\text{sum\_extended} : U_n \times U_n \times U_1 \to U_1 \times U_n$$

$$\text{difference\_extended} : U_n \times U_n \times U_1 \to U_1 \times U_n$$

$$\text{product\_extended} : U_n \times U_n \to U_{2n}$$

$$\text{quotient\_remainder\_extended} : U_{2n} \times U_n \to U_n \times U_n$$

Observe that U_{2n} can be represented as $U_n \times U_n$ (a pair of U_n). Programming languages that provide full access to these hardware operations make it possible to write efficient and abstract software components involving integer types.

> **Project 5.3**   Design a family of concepts for bounded unsigned and signed binary integers. A study of the instruction sets for modern computer architectures shows the functionality that should be encompassed. A good abstraction of these instruction sets is provided by MMIX [Knuth, 2005].

5.11 Conclusions

We can combine algorithms and mathematical structures into a seamless whole by describing algorithms in abstract terms and adjusting theories to fit algorithmic requirements. The mathematics and algorithms in this chapter are abstract restatements of results that are more than two thousand years old.

Chapter 6

Iterators

*T*his chapter introduces the concept of iterator: *an interface between algorithms and sequential data structures. A hierarchy of iterator concepts corresponds to different kinds of sequential traversals: single-pass forward, multipass forward, bidirectional, and random access.*[1] *We investigate a variety of interfaces to common algorithms, such as linear and binary search. Bounded and counted ranges provide a flexible way of defining interfaces for variations of a sequential algorithm.*

6.1 Readability

Every object has an address: an integer index into computer memory. Addresses allow us to access or modify an object. In addition, they allow us to create a wide variety of data structures, many of which rely on the fact that addresses are effectively integers and allow integer-like operations.

Iterators are a family of concepts that abstract different aspects of addresses, allowing us to write algorithms that work not only with addresses but also with any addresslike objects satisfying the minimal set of requirements. In Chapter 7 we introduce an even broader conceptual family: *coordinate structures*.

There are two kinds of operations on iterators: accessing values or traversal. There are three kinds of access: reading, writing, or both reading and writing. There are four kinds of linear traversal: single-pass forward (an input stream), multipass forward (a singly linked list), bidirectional (a doubly linked list), and random access (an array).

---

1. Our treatment of iterators is a further refinement of the one in Stepanov and Lee [1995] but differs from it in several aspects.

This chapter studies the first kind of access: readability, that is, the ability to obtain the value of the object denoted by another. A type T is *readable* if a unary function source defined on it returns an object of type ValueType(T):

Readable(T) ≜
    Regular(T)
  ∧ ValueType : *Readable* → *Regular*
  ∧ source : T ⇸ ValueType(T)

source is only used in contexts in which a value is needed; its result can be passed to a procedure by value or by constant reference.

There may be objects of a readable type on which source is not defined; source does not have to be total. The concept does not provide a definition-space predicate to determine whether source is defined for a particular object. For example, given a pointer to a type T, it is impossible to determine whether it points to a validly constructed object. Validity of the use of source in an algorithm must be derivable from preconditions.

Accessing data by calling source on an object of a readable type is as fast as any other way of accessing this data. In particular, for an object of a readable type with value type T residing in main memory, we expect the cost of source to be approximately equal to the cost of dereferencing an ordinary pointer to T. As with ordinary pointers, there could be nonuniformity owing to the memory hierarchy. In other words, there is no need to store pointers instead of iterators to speed up an algorithm.

It is useful to extend source to types whose objects don't point to other objects. We do this by having source return its argument when applied to an object of such a type. This allows a program to specify its requirement for a value of type T in such a way that the requirement can be satisfied by a value of type T, a pointer to type T, or, in general, any readable type with a value type of T. Therefore we assume that unless otherwise defined, ValueType(T) = T and that source returns the object to which it is applied.

6.2 Iterators

Traversal requires the ability to generate new iterators. As we saw in Chapter 2, one way to generate new values of a type is with a transformation. While transformations are regular, some one-pass algorithms do not require regularity of traversal, and some models, such as input streams, do not provide regularity of traversal. Thus the weakest iterator concept requires only the *pseudotransformation*[2] successor and the type function DistanceType:

Iterator(T) $\triangleq$
    Regular(T)
    $\wedge$ DistanceType : *Iterator* $\rightarrow$ *Integer*
    $\wedge$ successor : T $\rightarrow$ T
    $\wedge$ successor is not necessarily regular

DistanceType returns an integer type large enough to measure any sequence of applications of successor allowable for the type. Since regularity is assumed by default, we must explicitly state that it is not a requirement for successor.

As with source on readable types, successor does not have to be total; there may be objects of an iterator type on which successor is not defined. The concept does not provide a definition-space predicate to determine whether successor is defined for a particular object. For example, a pointer into an array contains no information indicating how many times it could be incremented. Validity of the use of successor in an algorithm must be derivable from preconditions.

The following defines the action corresponding to successor:

```
template<typename I>
    requires(Iterator(I))
void increment(I& x)
{
    // Precondition: successor(x) is defined
    x = successor(x);
}
```

Many important algorithms, such as linear search and copying, are *single-pass;* that is, they apply successor to the value of each iterator once. Therefore they can be used with input streams, and that is why we drop the requirement for successor to be regular: i = j does not imply successor(i) = successor(j) even when successor is defined. Furthermore, after successor(i) is called, i and any iterator equal to it may no longer be well formed. They remain partially formed and can be destroyed or assigned to; successor, source, and = should not be applied to them.

---

2. A pseudotransformation has the signature of a transformation but is not regular.

Note that successor(i) = successor(j) does not imply that i = j. Consider, for example, two null-terminating singly linked lists.

An iterator provides as fast a linear traversal through an entire collection of data as any other way of traversing that data.

In order for an integer type to model *Iterator*, it must have a distance type. An unsigned integer type is its own distance type; for any bounded signed binary integer type S_n, its distance type is the corresponding unsigned type U_n.

6.3 Ranges

When f is an object of an iterator type and n is an object of the corresponding distance type, we want to be able to define algorithms operating on a *weak range* $[\![f, n)\!]$ of n iterators beginning with f, using code of the form

```
while (!zero(n)) { n = predecessor(n); ... f = successor(f); }
```

This property enables such an iteration:

property(I : *Iterator*)
weak_range : I × DistanceType(I)
   $(f, n) \mapsto (\forall i \in \text{DistanceType}(I))$
        $(0 \leq i \leq n) \Rightarrow \text{successor}^i(f)$ is defined

Lemma 6.1 $0 \leq j \leq i \wedge \text{weak\_range}(f, i) \Rightarrow \text{weak\_range}(f, j)$

In a weak range, we can advance up to its size:

```
template<typename I>
    requires(Iterator(I))
I operator+(I f, DistanceType(I) n)
{
    // Precondition: n ≥ 0 ∧ weak_range(f, n)
    while (!zero(n)) {
        n = predecessor(n);
        f = successor(f);
    }
    return f;
}
```

The addition of the following axiom ensures that there are no cycles in the range:

property(I : *Iterator*, N : *Integer*)
counted_range : I × N
  (f, n) ↦ weak_range(f, n) ∧
      (∀i, j ∈ N) (0 ≤ i < j ≤ n) ⇒
          successor^i(f) ≠ successor^j(f)

When f and l are objects of an iterator type, we want to be able to define algorithms working on a *bounded range* [f, l) of iterators beginning with f and limited by l, using code of the form

```
while (f != l) { ... f = successor(f); }
```

This property enables such an iteration:

property(I : *Iterator*)
bounded_range : I × I
  (f, l) ↦ (∃k ∈ DistanceType(I)) counted_range(f, k) ∧ successor^k(f) = l

The structure of iteration using a bounded range terminates the first time l is encountered; therefore, unlike a weak range, it cannot have cycles.

In a bounded range, we can implement[3] a partial subtraction on iterators:

```
template<typename I>
    requires(Iterator(I))
DistanceType(I) operator-(I l, I f)
{
    // Precondition: bounded_range(f, l)
    DistanceType(I) n(0);
    while (f != l) {
        n = successor(n);
        f = successor(f);
    }
    return n;
}
```

---

3. Notice the similarity to **distance** from Chapter 2.

Because successor may not be regular, subtraction should be used only in preconditions or in situations in which we only want to compute the size of a bounded range.

Our definitions of $+$ and $-$ between iterators and integers are not inconsistent with mathematical usage, where $+$ and $-$ are always defined on the same type. As in mathematics, both $+$ between iterators and integers and $-$ between iterators are defined inductively in terms of successor. The standard inductive definition of addition on natural numbers uses the successor function:[4]

$$a + 0 = a$$

$$a + \text{successor}(b) = \text{successor}(a + b)$$

Our iterative definition of $f + n$ for iterators is equivalent even though f and n are of different types. As with natural numbers, a variant of associativity is provable by induction.

Lemma 6.2 $(f + n) + m = f + (n + m)$

In preconditions we need to specify membership within a range. We borrow conventions from intervals (see Appendix A) to introduce *half-open* and *closed* ranges. We use variations of the notation for weak or counted ranges and for bounded ranges.

A *half-open weak* or *counted* range $[\![f, n)\!)$, where $n \geq 0$ is an integer, denotes the sequence of iterators $\{\text{successor}^k(f) \mid 0 \leq k < n\}$. A *closed weak* or *counted* range $[\![f, n]\!]$, where $n \geq 0$ is an integer, denotes the sequence of iterators $\{\text{successor}^k(f) \mid 0 \leq k \leq n\}$.

A *half-open* bounded range $[f, l)$ is equivalent to the half-open counted range $[\![f, l - f)\!)$. A *closed* bounded range $[f, l]$ is equivalent to the closed counted range $[\![f, l - f]\!]$.

The *size* of a range is the number of iterators in the sequence it denotes.

Lemma 6.3   successor is defined for every iterator in a half-open range and for every iterator except the last in a closed range.

If r is a range and i is an iterator, we say that $i \in r$ if i is a member of the corresponding set of iterators.

---

4. First introduced in Grassmann [1861]; Grassmann's definition was popularized in Peano [1908].

Lemma 6.4   If $i \in [f, l)$, both $[f, i)$ and $[i, l)$ are bounded ranges.

Empty half-open ranges are specified by $[\![i, 0)\!]$ or $[i, i)$ for some iterator i. There are no empty closed ranges.

Lemma 6.5 $i \notin [\![i, 0)\!] \wedge i \notin [i, i)$

Lemma 6.6   Empty ranges have neither first nor last elements.

It is useful to describe an empty sequence of iterators starting at a particular iterator. For example, binary search looks for the sequence of iterators whose values are equal to a given value. This sequence is empty if there are no such values but is positioned where they would appear if inserted.

An iterator l is called the *limit* of a half-open bounded range $[f, l)$. An iterator $f + n$ is the limit of a half-open weak range $[\![f, n)\!]$. Observe that an empty range has a limit even though it does not have a first or last element.

Lemma 6.7   The size of a half-open weak range $[\![f, n)\!]$ is n. The size of a closed weak range $[\![f, n]\!]$ is $n + 1$. The size of a half-open bounded range $[f, l)$ is $l - f$. The size of a closed bounded range $[f, l]$ is $(l - f) + 1$.

If i and j are iterators in a counted or bounded range, we define the relation $i \prec j$ to mean that $i \neq j \wedge \mathsf{bounded\_range}(i, j)$: in other words, that one or more applications of successor leads from i to j. The relation $\prec$ ("precedes") and the corresponding reflexive relation $\preceq$ ("precedes or equal") are used in specifications, such as preconditions and postconditions of algorithms. For many pairs of values of an iterator type, $\prec$ is not defined, so there is often no effective way to write code implementing $\prec$. For example, there is no efficient way to determine whether one node precedes another in a linked structure; the nodes might not even be linked together.

6.4 Readable Ranges

A range of iterators from a type modeling *Readable* and *Iterator* is *readable* if source is defined on all the iterators in the range:

property(I : *Readable*)
  requires(Iterator(I))
readable_bounded_range : I × I
    $(f, l) \mapsto \mathsf{bounded\_range}(f, l) \wedge (\forall i \in [f, l)) \, \mathsf{source}(i)$ is defined

Observe that source need not be defined on the limit of the range. Also, since an iterator may no longer be well-formed after successor is applied, it is not guaranteed that source can be applied to an iterator after its successor has been obtained. readable_weak_range and readable_counted_range are defined similarly.

Given a readable range, we could apply a procedure to each value in the range:

```
template<typename I, typename Proc>
    requires(Readable(I) && Iterator(I) &&
        Procedure(Proc) && Arity(Proc) == 1 &&
        ValueType(I) == InputType(Proc, 0))
Proc for_each(I f, I l, Proc proc)
{
    // Precondition: readable_bounded_range(f, l)
    while (f != l) {
        proc(source(f));
        f = successor(f);
    }
    return proc;
}
```

We return the procedure because it could have accumulated useful information during the traversal.[5]

We implement linear search with the following procedure:

```
template<typename I>
    requires(Readable(I) && Iterator(I))
I find(I f, I l, const ValueType(I)& x)
{
    // Precondition: readable_bounded_range(f, l)
    while (f != l && source(f) != x) f = successor(f);
    return f;
}
```

Either the returned iterator is equal to the limit of the range, or its value is equal to x. Returning the limit indicates failure of the search. Since there are $n + 1$ outcomes for a search of a range of size n, the limit serves a useful purpose here

---

5. A function object can be used in this way.

and in many other algorithms. A search involving find can be restarted by advancing past the returned iterator and then calling find again.

Changing the comparison with x to use equality instead of inequality gives us find_not.

We can generalize from searching for an equal value to searching for the first value satisfying a unary predicate:

```
template<typename I, typename P>
    requires(Readable(I) && Iterator(I) &&
        UnaryPredicate(P) && ValueType(I) == Domain(P))
I find_if(I f, I l, P p)
{
    // Precondition: readable_bounded_range(f, l)
    while (f != l && !p(source(f))) f = successor(f);
    return f;
}
```

Applying the predicate instead of its complement gives us find_if_not.

Exercise 6.1   Use find_if and find_if_not to implement quantifier functions all, none, not_all, and some, each taking a bounded range and a predicate.

The find and quantifier functions let us search for values satisfying a condition; we can also count the number of satisfying values:

```
template<typename I, typename P, typename J>
    requires(Readable(I) && Iterator(I) &&
        UnaryPredicate(P) && Iterator(J) &&
        ValueType(I) == Domain(P))
J count_if(I f, I l, P p, J j)
{
    // Precondition: readable_bounded_range(f, l)
    while (f != l) {
        if (p(source(f))) j = successor(j);
        f = successor(f);
    }
    return j;
}
```

Passing j explicitly is useful when adding an integer to j takes linear time. The type J could be any integer or iterator type, including I.

Exercise 6.2 Implement count_if by passing an appropriate function object to for_each and extracting the accumulation result from the returned function object.

The natural default is to start the count from zero and use the distance type of the iterators:

```
template<typename I, typename P>
    requires(Readable(I) && Iterator(I) &&
        UnaryPredicate(P) && ValueType(I) == Domain(P))
DistanceType(I) count_if(I f, I l, P p) {
    // Precondition: readable_bounded_range(f, l)
    return count_if(f, l, p, DistanceType(I)(0));
}
```

Replacing the predicate with an equality test gives us count; negating the tests gives us count_not and count_if_not.

The notation $\sum_{i=0}^{n} a_i$ for the sum of the a_i is frequently generalized to other binary operations; for example, $\prod_{i=0}^{n} a_i$ is used for products and $\bigwedge_{i=0}^{n} a_i$ for conjunctions. In each case, the operation is associative, which means that the grouping is not important. Kenneth Iverson unified this notation in the programming language APL with the *reduction operator* /, which takes a binary operation and a sequence and reduces the elements into a single result.[6] For example, +/1 2 3 equals 6.

Iverson does not restrict reduction to associative operations. We extend Iverson's reduction to work on iterator ranges but restrict it to *partially associative* operations: If an operation is defined between adjacent elements, it can be reassociated:

property(Op : *BinaryOperation*)
partially_associative : Op
   op $\mapsto$ ($\forall a, b, c \in$ Domain(op))
            If op(a, b) and op(b, c) are defined,
            op(op(a, b), c) and op(a, op(b, c))) are defined
            and are equal.

As an example of an operation that is partially associative but not associative, consider concatenation of two ranges $[f_0, l_0)$ and $[f_1, l_1)$, which is defined only when $l_0 = f_1$.

---

6. See Iverson [1962].

We allow a unary function to be applied to each iterator before the binary operation is performed, obtaining a_i from i. Since an arbitrary partially associative operation might not have an identity, we provide a version of reduction requiring a nonempty range:

```
template<typename I, typename Op, typename F>
    requires(Iterator(I) && BinaryOperation(Op) &&
        UnaryFunction(F) &&
        I == Domain(F) && Codomain(F) == Domain(Op))
Domain(Op) reduce_nonempty(I f, I l, Op op, F fun)
{
    // Precondition: bounded_range(f, l) ∧ f ≠ l
    // Precondition: partially_associative(op)
    // Precondition: (∀x ∈ [f, l)) fun(x) is defined
    Domain(Op) r = fun(f);
    f = successor(f);
    while (f != l) {
        r = op(r, fun(f));
        f = successor(f);
    }
    return r;
}
```

The natural default for fun is source. An identity element can be passed in to be returned on an empty range:

```
template<typename I, typename Op, typename F>
    requires(Iterator(I) && BinaryOperation(Op) &&
        UnaryFunction(F) &&
        I == Domain(F) && Codomain(F) == Domain(Op))
Domain(Op) reduce(I f, I l, Op op, F fun, const Domain(Op)& z)
{
    // Precondition: bounded_range(f, l)
    // Precondition: partially_associative(op)
    // Precondition: (∀x ∈ [f, l)) fun(x) is defined
    if (f == l) return z;
    return reduce_nonempty(f, l, op, fun);
}
```

When operations involving the identity element are slow or require extra logic to implement, the following procedure is useful:

```
template<typename I, typename Op, typename F>
    requires(Iterator(I) && BinaryOperation(Op) &&
        UnaryFunction(F) &&
        I == Domain(F) && Codomain(F) == Domain(Op))
Domain(Op) reduce_nonzeroes(I f, I l,
                            Op op, F fun, const Domain(Op)& z)
{
    // Precondition: bounded_range(f, l)
    // Precondition: partially_associative(op)
    // Precondition: (∀x ∈ [f, l)) fun(x) is defined
    Domain(Op) x;
    do {
        if (f == l) return z;
        x = fun(f);
        f = successor(f);
    } while (x == z);
    while (f != l) {
        Domain(Op) y = fun(f);
        if (y != z) x = op(x, y);
        f = successor(f);
    }
    return x;
}
```

Algorithms taking a bounded range have a corresponding version taking a weak or counted range; more information, however, needs to be returned:

```
template<typename I, typename Proc>
    requires(Readable(I) && Iterator(I) &&
        Procedure(Proc) && Arity(Proc) == 1 &&
        ValueType(I) == InputType(Proc, 0))
pair<Proc, I> for_each_n(I f, DistanceType(I) n, Proc proc)
{
    // Precondition: readable_weak_range(f, n)
    while (!zero(n)) {
        n = predecessor(n);
        proc(source(f));
```

```
        f = successor(f);
    }
    return pair<Proc, I>(proc, f);
}
```

The final value of the iterator must be returned because the lack of regularity of successor means that it could not be recomputed. Even for iterators where successor is regular, recomputing it could take time linear in the size of the range.

```
template<typename I>
    requires(Readable(I) && Iterator(I))
pair<I, DistanceType(I)> find_n(I f, DistanceType(I) n,
                                const ValueType(I)& x)
{
    // Precondition: weak_range(f, n)
    while (!zero(n) && source(f) != x) {
        n = predecessor(n);
        f = successor(f);
    }
    return pair<I, DistanceType(I)>(f, n);
}
```

find_n returns the final value of the iterator and the count because both are needed to restart a search.

Exercise 6.3 Implement variations taking a weak range instead of a bounded range of all the versions of find, quantifiers, count, and reduce.

We can eliminate one of the two tests in the loop of find_if when we are assured that an element in the range satisfies the predicate; such an element is called a *sentinel*:

```
template<typename I, typename P>
    requires(Readable(I) && Iterator(I) &&
        UnaryPredicate(P) && ValueType(I) == Domain(P))
I find_if_unguarded(I f, P p) {
    // Precondition: (∃l) readable_bounded_range(f, l) ∧ some(f, l, p)
    while (!p(source(f))) f = successor(f);
    return f;
    // Postcondition: p(source(f))
}
```

Applying the predicate instead of its complement gives find_if_not_unguarded.

Given two ranges with the same value type and a relation on that value type, we can search for a mismatched pair of values:

```
template<typename I0, typename I1, typename R>
    requires(Readable(I0) && Iterator(I0) &&
        Readable(I1) && Iterator(I1) && Relation(R) &&
        ValueType(I0) == ValueType(I1) &&
        ValueType(I0) == Domain(R))
pair<I0, I1> find_mismatch(I0 f0, I0 l0, I1 f1, I1 l1, R r)
{
    // Precondition: readable_bounded_range(f0, l0)
    // Precondition: readable_bounded_range(f1, l1)
    while (f0 != l0 && f1 != l1 && r(source(f0), source(f1))) {
        f0 = successor(f0);
        f1 = successor(f1);
    }
    return pair<I0, I1>(f0, f1);
}
```

Exercise 6.4   State the postcondition for find_mismatch, and explain why the final values of both iterators are returned.

The natural default for the relation in find_mismatch is the equality on the value type.

Exercise 6.5   Design variations of find_mismatch for all four combinations of counted and bounded ranges.

Sometimes, it is important to find a mismatch not between ranges but between adjacent elements of the same range:

```
template<typename I, typename R>
    requires(Readable(I) && Iterator(I) &&
        Relation(R) && ValueType(I) == Domain(R))
```

```
I find_adjacent_mismatch(I f, I l, R r)
{
    // Precondition: readable_bounded_range(f, l)
    if (f == l) return l;
    ValueType(I) x = source(f);
    f = successor(f);
    while (f != l && r(x, source(f))) {
        x = source(f);
        f = successor(f);
    }
    return f;
}
```

We must copy the previous value because we cannot apply source to an iterator after successor has been applied to it. The weak requirements of *Iterator* also imply that returning the first iterator in the mismatched pair may return a value that is not well formed.

6.5 Increasing Ranges

Given a relation on the value type of some iterator, a range over that iterator type is called *relation preserving* if the relation holds for every adjacent pair of values in the range. In other words, find_adjacent_mismatch will return the limit when called with this range and relation:

```
template<typename I, typename R>
    requires(Readable(I) && Iterator(I) &&
        Relation(R) && ValueType(I) == Domain(R))
bool relation_preserving(I f, I l, R r)
{
    // Precondition: readable_bounded_range(f, l)
    return l == find_adjacent_mismatch(f, l, r);
}
```

Given a weak ordering r, we say that a range is r-*increasing* if it is relation preserving with respect to the complement of the converse of r. Given a weak ordering r, we say that a range is *strictly* r-*increasing* if it is relation preserving with respect to r.[7] It is straightforward to implement a test for a strictly increasing range:

```
template<typename I, typename R>
    requires(Readable(I) && Iterator(I) &&
        Relation(R) && ValueType(I) == Domain(R))
bool strictly_increasing_range(I f, I l, R r)
{
    // Precondition: readable_bounded_range(f, l) ∧ weak_ordering(r)
    return relation_preserving(f, l, r);
}
```

With the help of a function object, we can implement a test for an increasing range:

```
template<typename R>
    requires(Relation(R))
struct complement_of_converse
{
    typedef Domain(R) T;
    R r;
    complement_of_converse(const R& r) : r(r) { }
    bool operator()(const T& a, const T& b)
    {
        return !r(b, a);
    }
};
```

```
template<typename I, typename R>
    requires(Readable(I) && Iterator(I) &&
        Relation(R) && ValueType(I) == Domain(R))
bool increasing_range(I f, I l, R r)
{
    // Precondition: readable_bounded_range(f, l) ∧ weak_ordering(r)
```

---

7. Some authors use nondecreasing and increasing instead of increasing and strictly increasing, respectively.

```
    return relation_preserving(
        f, l,
        complement_of_converse<R>(r));
}
```

Defining   strictly_increasing_counted_range   and   increasing_counted_range   is straightforward.

Given a predicate p on the value type of some iterator, a range over that iterator type is called p-*partitioned* if any values of the range satisfying the predicate follow every value of the range not satisfying the predicate. A test that shows whether a range is p-partitioned is straightforward:

```
template<typename I, typename P>
    requires(Readable(I) && Iterator(I) &&
        UnaryPredicate(P) && ValueType(I) == Domain(P))
bool partitioned(I f, I l, P p)
{
    // Precondition: readable_bounded_range(f, l)
    return l == find_if_not(find_if(f, l, p), l, p);
}
```

The iterator returned by the call of find_if is called the *partition point;* it is the first iterator, if any, whose value satisfies the predicate.

Exercise 6.6   Implement the predicate partitioned_n, which tests whether a counted range is p-partitioned.

Linear search must invoke source after each application of successor because a failed test provides no information about the value of any other iterator in the range. However, the uniformity of a partitioned range gives us more information.

Lemma 6.8   If p is a predicate and [f, l) is a p-partitioned range:

$$(\forall m \in [f, l) \neg p(\text{source}(m)) \Rightarrow (\forall j \in [f, m]) \neg p(\text{source}(j))$$
$$(\forall m \in [f, l) \ p(\text{source}(m)) \Rightarrow (\forall j \in [m, l)) \ p(\text{source}(j))$$

This suggests a bisection algorithm for finding the partition point: Assuming a uniform distribution, testing the midpoint of the range reduces the search space by a factor of 2. However, such an algorithm may need to traverse an already traversed subrange, which requires the regularity of successor.

6.6 Forward Iterators

Making successor regular allows us to pass through the same range more than once and to maintain more than one iterator into the range:

ForwardIterator(T) ≜
    Iterator(T)
  ∧ regular_unary_function(successor)

Note that *Iterator* and *ForwardIterator* differ only by an axiom; there are no new operations. In addition to successor, all the other functional procedures defined on refinements of the forward iterator concept introduced later in the chapter are regular. The regularity of successor allows us to implement find_adjacent_mismatch without saving the value before advancing:

```
template<typename I, typename R>
    requires(Readable(I) && ForwardIterator(I) &&
        Relation(R) && ValueType(I) == Domain(R))
I find_adjacent_mismatch_forward(I f, I l, R r)
{
    // Precondition: readable_bounded_range(f, l)
    if (f == l) return l;
    I t;
    do {
        t = f;
        f = successor(f);
    } while (f != l && r(source(t), source(f)));
    return f;
}
```

Note that t points to the first element of this mismatched pair and could also be returned.

In Chapter 10 we show how to use *concept dispatch* to overload versions of an algorithm written for different iterator concepts. Suffixes such as _forward allow us to disambiguate the different versions.

The regularity of successor also allows us to implement the bisection algorithm for finding the partition point:

```
template<typename I, typename P>
    requires(Readable(I) && ForwardIterator(I) &&
        UnaryPredicate(P) && ValueType(I) == Domain(P))
```

```
I partition_point_n(I f, DistanceType(I) n, P p)
{
    // Precondition: readable_counted_range(f, n) ∧ partitioned_n(f, n, p)
    while (!zero(n)) {
        DistanceType(I) h = half_nonnegative(n);
        I m = f + h;
        if (p(source(m))) {
            n = h;
        } else {
            n = n - successor(h); f = successor(m);
        }
    }
    return f;
}
```

Lemma 6.9   partition_point_n returns the partition point of the p-partitioned range $[[f, n)\!)$.

Finding the partition point in a bounded range by bisection[8] requires first finding the size of the range:

```
template<typename I, typename P>
    requires(Readable(I) && ForwardIterator(I) &&
        UnaryPredicate(P) && ValueType(I) == Domain(P))
I partition_point(I f, I l, P p)
{
    // Precondition: readable_bounded_range(f, l) ∧ partitioned(f, l, p)
    return partition_point_n(f, l - f, p);
}
```

The definition of partition point immediately leads to binary search algorithms on an r-increasing range for a weak ordering r. Any value a, whether or not it appears in the increasing range, determines two iterators in the range called *lower bound* and *upper bound*. Informally, a lower bound is the first position where a

---

8. The bisection technique dates back at least as far as the proof of the Intermediate Value Theorem in Bolzano [1817] and, independently, in Cauchy [1821]. While Bolzano and Cauchy used the technique for the most general case of continuous functions, Lagrange [1795] had previously used it to solve a particular problem of approximating a root of a polynomial. The first description of bisection for searching was John W. Mauchly's lecture "Sorting and collating" [Mauchly, 1946].

value equivalent to a could occur in the increasing sequence. Similarly, an upper bound is the successor of the last position where a value equivalent to a could occur. Therefore elements equivalent to a appear only in the half-open range from lower bound to upper bound. For example, assuming total ordering, a sequence with lower bound l and upper bound u for the value a looks like this:

$$\underbrace{x_0, x_1, \ldots, x_{l-1},}_{x_i < a} \underbrace{x_l, \ldots, x_{u-1},}_{x_i = a} \underbrace{x_u, x_{u+1}, \ldots, x_{n-1}}_{x_i > a}$$

Note that any of the three regions may be empty.

Lemma 6.10   In an increasing range $[f, l)$, for any value a of the value type of the range, the range is partitioned by the following two predicates:

$$\text{lower\_bound}_a(x) \Leftrightarrow \neg r(x, a)$$
$$\text{upper\_bound}_a(x) \Leftrightarrow r(a, x)$$

That allows us to formally define lower bound and upper bound as the partition points of the corresponding predicates.

Lemma 6.11   The lower-bound iterator precedes or equals the upper-bound iterator.

Implementing a function object corresponding to the predicate leads immediately to an algorithm for determining the lower bound:

```
template<typename R>
    requires(Relation(R))
struct lower_bound_predicate
{
    typedef Domain(R) T;
    const T& a;
    R r;
    lower_bound_predicate(const T& a, R r) : a(a), r(r) { }
    bool operator()(const T& x) { return !r(x, a); }
};


template<typename I, typename R>
    requires(Readable(I) && ForwardIterator(I) &&
```

```
                  Relation(R) && ValueType(I) == Domain(R))
I lower_bound_n(I f, DistanceType(I) n,
                  const ValueType(I)& a, R r)
{
    // Precondition: weak_ordering(r) ∧ increasing_counted_range(f, n, r)
    lower_bound_predicate<R> p(a, r);
    return partition_point_n(f, n, p);
}
```

Similarly, for the upper bound:

```
template<typename R>
    requires(Relation(R))
struct upper_bound_predicate
{
    typedef Domain(R) T;
    const T& a;
    R r;
    upper_bound_predicate(const T& a, R r) : a(a), r(r) { }
    bool operator()(const T& x) { return r(a, x); }
};
```

```
template<typename I, typename R>
    requires(Readable(I) && ForwardIterator(I) &&
        Relation(R) && ValueType(I) == Domain(R))
I upper_bound_n(I f, DistanceType(I) n,
                  const ValueType(I)& a, R r)
{
    // Precondition: weak_ordering(r) ∧ increasing_counted_range(f, n, r)
    upper_bound_predicate<R> p(a, r);
    return partition_point_n(f, n, p);
}
```

Exercise 6.7   Implement a procedure that returns both lower and upper bounds and does fewer comparisons than the sum of the comparisons that would be done by calling both lower_bound_n and upper_bound_n.[9]

---

9. A similar STL function is called equal_range.

Applying the predicate in the middle of the range ensures the optimal worst-case number of predicate applications in the partition-point algorithm. Any other choice would be defeated by an adversary who ensures that the larger subrange contains the partition point. Prior knowledge of the expected position of the partition point would lead to probing at that point.

partition_point_n applies the predicate $\lfloor \log_2 n \rfloor + 1$ times, since the length of the range is reduced by a factor of 2 at each step. The algorithm performs a logarithmic number of iterator/integer additions.

Lemma 6.12 For a forward iterator, the total number of successor operations performed by the algorithm is less than or equal to the size of the range.

partition_point also calculates $l - f$, which, for forward iterators, adds another n calls of successor. It is worthwhile to use it on forward iterators, such as linked lists, whenever the predicate application is more expensive than calling successor.

Lemma 6.13 Assuming that the expected distance to the partition point is equal to half the size of the range, partition_point is faster than find_if on finding the partition point for forward iterators whenever

$$\text{cost}_{\text{successor}} < \left(1 - 2\frac{\log_2 n}{n} \right) \text{cost}_{\text{predicate}}$$

6.7 Indexed Iterators

In order for partition_point, lower_bound, and upper_bound to dominate linear search, we need to ensure that adding an integer to an iterator and subtracting an iterator from an iterator are fast:

$IndexedIterator(T) \triangleq$
    $ForwardIterator(T)$
    $\wedge\ + : T \times \text{DistanceType}(T) \to T$
    $\wedge\ - : T \times T \to \text{DistanceType}(T)$
    $\wedge\ +$ takes constant time
    $\wedge\ -$ takes constant time

The operations $+$ and $-$, which were defined for *Iterator* in terms of successor, are now required to be primitive and fast: This concept differs from *ForwardIterator* only by strengthening complexity requirements. We expect the cost of $+$ and $-$ on indexed iterators to be essentially identical to the cost of successor.

6.8 Bidirectional Iterators

There are situations in which indexing is not possible, but we have the ability to go backward:

$BidirectionalIterator(T) \triangleq$
$\quad ForwardIterator(T)$
$\quad \wedge$ predecessor $: T \rightarrow T$
$\quad \wedge$ predecessor takes constant time
$\quad \wedge (\forall i \in T)$ successor(i) is defined $\Rightarrow$
$\qquad\qquad$ predecessor(successor(i)) is defined and equals i
$\quad \wedge (\forall i \in T)$ predecessor(i) is defined $\Rightarrow$
$\qquad\qquad$ successor(predecessor(i)) is defined and equals i

As with successor, predecessor does not have to be total; the axioms of the concept relate its definition space to that of successor. We expect the cost of predecessor to be essentially identical to the cost of successor.

Lemma 6.14   If successor is defined on bidirectional iterators i and j,

$$successor(i) = successor(j) \Rightarrow i = j$$

In a weak range of bidirectional iterators, movement backward as far as the beginning of the range is possible:

```
template<typename I>
    requires(BidirectionalIterator(I))
I operator-(I l, DistanceType(I) n)
{
    // Precondition: n ≥ 0 ∧ (∃f ∈ I) weak_range(f, n) ∧ l = f + n
    while (!zero(n)) {
        n = predecessor(n);
        l = predecessor(l);
    }
    return l;
}
```

With bidirectional iterators, we can search backward. As we noted earlier, when searching a range of n iterators, there are n + 1 outcomes; this is true whether we search forward or backward. So we need a convention for representing half-open on left ranges of the form (f, l]. To indicate "not found," we return f, which forces us to return successor(i) if we find a satisfying element at iterator i:

```
template<typename I, typename P>
    requires(Readable(I) && BidirectionalIterator(I) &&
        UnaryPredicate(P) && ValueType(I) == Domain(P))
I find_backward_if(I f, I l, P p)
{
    // Precondition: (f, l] is a readable bounded half-open on left range
    while (l != f && !p(source(predecessor(l))))
        l = predecessor(l);
    return l;
}
```

Comparing this with find_if illustrates a program transformation: f and l interchange roles, source(i) becomes source(predecessor(i)), and successor(i) becomes predecessor(i). Under this transformation, in a nonempty range, l is dereferenceable, but f is not.

The program transformation just demonstrated can be applied to any algorithm that takes a range of forward iterators. Thus it is possible to implement an adapter type that, given a bidirectional iterator type, produces another bidirectional iterator type where successor becomes predecessor, predecessor becomes successor, and source becomes source of predecessor.[10] This adapter type allows any algorithm on iterators or forward iterators to work backward on bidirectional iterators, and it also allows any algorithm on bidirectional iterators to interchange the traversal directions.

Exercise 6.8 Rewrite find_backward_if with only one call of predecessor in the loop.

Exercise 6.9 As an example of an algorithm that uses both successor and predecessor, implement a predicate that determines whether a range is a palindrome: It reads the same way forward and backward.

---

10. In STL this is called a reverse iterator adapter.

6.9 Random-Access Iterators

Some iterator types satisfy the requirements of both indexed and bidirectional iterators. These types, called *random-access iterators,* provide the full power of computer
addresses:

$RandomAccessIterator(\mathsf{T}) \triangleq$
    $IndexedIterator(\mathsf{T}) \wedge BidirectionalIterator(\mathsf{T})$
  $\wedge \; TotallyOrdered(\mathsf{T})$
  $\wedge \; (\forall i, j \in \mathsf{T})\, i < j \Leftrightarrow i \prec j$
  $\wedge \; \mathsf{DifferenceType} : RandomAccessIterator \rightarrow Integer$
  $\wedge \; + : \mathsf{T} \times \mathsf{DifferenceType}(\mathsf{T}) \rightarrow \mathsf{T}$
  $\wedge \; - : \mathsf{T} \times \mathsf{DifferenceType}(\mathsf{T}) \rightarrow \mathsf{T}$
  $\wedge \; - : \mathsf{T} \times \mathsf{T} \rightarrow \mathsf{DifferenceType}(\mathsf{T})$
  $\wedge \; <$ takes constant time
  $\wedge \; -$ between an iterator and an integer takes constant time

DifferenceType(T) is large enough to contain distances and their additive inverses;
if i and j are iterators from a valid range, $i - j$ is always defined. It is possible to add
a negative integer to, or subtract it from, an iterator.

On weaker iterator types, the operations + and − are only defined within one
range. For random-access iterator types, this holds for < as well as for + and −. In
general, an operation on two iterators is defined only when they belong to the same
range.

> **Project 6.1**   Define axioms relating the operations of random-access iter-
> ators to each other.

We do not describe random-access iterators in great detail, because of the
following.

> **Theorem 6.1**   For any procedure defined on an explicitly given range of
> random-access iterators, there is another procedure defined on indexed it-
> erators with the same complexity.
>
> *Proof:* Since the operations on random-access iterators are only defined on iterators
> belonging to the same range, it is possible to implement an adapter type that, given
> an indexed iterator type, produces a random-access iterator type. The state of such
> an iterator contains an iterator f and an integer i and represents the iterator f + i.
> The iterator operations, such as +, −, and <, operate on i; source operates on f + i.

In other words, an iterator pointing to the beginning of the range, together with an index into the range, behave like a random-access iterator.

The theorem shows the theoretical equivalence of these concepts in any context in which the beginnings of ranges are known. In practice, we have found that there is no performance penalty for using the weaker concept. In some cases, however, a signature needs to be adjusted to include the beginning of the range.

Project 6.2   Implement a family of abstract procedures for finding a subsequence within a sequence. Describe the tradeoffs for selecting an appropriate algorithm.[11]

6.10 Conclusions

Algebra provides us with a hierarchy of concepts, such as semigroups, monoids, and groups, that allows us to state algorithms in the most general context. Similarly, the iterator concepts (Figure 6.1) allow us to state algorithms on sequential data structures in their most general context. The development of these concepts used three kinds of refinement: adding an operation, strengthening semantics, and tightening complexity requirement. In particular, the three concepts *iterator, forward iterator,* and *indexed iterator* differ not by their operations but only by their semantics and complexity. A variety of search algorithms for different iterator concepts, counted and bounded ranges, and range ordering serve as the foundation of sequential programming.

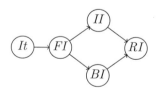

Figure 6.1 Iterator concepts.

---

11. Two of the best-known algorithms for this problem are Boyer and Moore [1977] and Knuth, et al. [1977]. Musser and Nishanov [1997] serves as a good foundation for the abstract setting for these algorithms.

Chapter 7
Coordinate Structures

*C*hapter 6 introduced a family of iterator concepts as the interface between algorithms and objects in data structures with immutable linear shape. This chapter
goes beyond iterators to coordinate structures with more complex shape. We introduce
bifurcate coordinates and implement algorithms on binary trees with the help of a
machine for iterative tree traversal. After discussing a concept schema for coordinate
structures, we conclude with algorithms for isomorphism, equivalence, and ordering.

7.1 Bifurcate Coordinates

Iterators allow us to traverse linear structures, which have a single successor at each
position. While there are data structures with an arbitrary number of successors, in
this chapter we study an important case of structures with exactly two successors
at every position, labeled left and right. In order to define algorithms on these
structures, we define the following concept:

$BifurcateCoordinate(\mathsf{T}) \triangleq$
  $Regular(\mathsf{T})$
  $\wedge$ WeightType : $BifurcateCoordinate \rightarrow Integer$
  $\wedge$ empty : $\mathsf{T} \rightarrow$ bool
  $\wedge$ has_left_successor : $\mathsf{T} \rightarrow$ bool
  $\wedge$ has_right_successor : $\mathsf{T} \rightarrow$ bool
  $\wedge$ left_successor : $\mathsf{T} \rightarrow \mathsf{T}$
  $\wedge$ right_successor : $\mathsf{T} \rightarrow \mathsf{T}$
  $\wedge$ $(\forall i, j \in \mathsf{T})$ (left_successor$(i) = j \vee$ right_successor$(i) = j) \Rightarrow \neg$empty$(j)$

The WeightType type function returns a type capable of counting all the objects in a traversal that uses a bifurcate coordinate. WeightType is analogous to
DistanceType for an iterator type.

115

The predicate empty is everywhere defined. If it returns true, none of the other procedures are defined. empty is the negation of the definition-space predicate for both has_left_successor and has_right_successor. has_left_successor is the definition-space predicate for left_successor, and has_right_successor is the definition-space predicate for right_successor. In other words, if a bifurcate coordinate is not empty, has_left_successor and has_right_successor are defined; if either one of them returns true, the corresponding successor function is defined. With iterators, algorithms use a limit or count to indicate the end of a range. With bifurcate coordinates, there are many positions at which branches end. Therefore it is more natural to introduce the predicates has_left_successor and has_right_successor for determining whether a coordinate has successors.

In this book we describe algorithms on *BifurcateCoordinate,* where all the operations are regular. This is different from the *Iterator* concept, where the most fundamental algorithms, such as find, do not require regularity of successor and where there are nonregular models, such as input streams. Structures where application of left_successor and right_successor change the shape of the underlying binary tree require a concept of *WeakBifurcateCoordinate,* where the operations are not regular.

The shape of a structure accessed via iterators is possibly cyclic for a weak range and is a linear segment for a counted or bounded range. In order to discuss the shape of a structure accessed via bifurcate coordinates, we need a notion of reachability.

A bifurcate coordinate y is a *proper descendant* of another coordinate x if y is the left or right successor of x or if it is a proper descendant of the left or right successor of x. A bifurcate coordinate y is a *descendant* of a coordinate x if $y = x$ or y is a proper descendant of x.

The descendants of x form a *directed acyclic graph* (DAG) if for all y in the descendants of x, y is not its own descendant. In other words, no sequence of successors of any coordinate leads back to itself. x is called the *root* of the DAG of its descendants. If the descendants of x form a DAG and are finite in number, they form a *finite DAG.* The *height* of a finite DAG is one more than the maximum sequence of successors starting from its root, or zero if it is empty.

A bifurcate coordinate y is *left reachable* from x if it is a descendant of the left successor of x, and similarly for *right reachable*.

The descendants of x form a *tree* if they form a finite DAG and for all y, z in the descendants of x, z is not both left reachable and right reachable from y. In other words, there is a unique sequence of successors from a coordinate to any of its descendants. The property of being a tree serves the same purpose for the algorithms in this chapter as the properties of being a bounded or counted range served in Chapter 6, with finiteness guaranteeing termination:

property(C : *BifurcateCoordinate*)
tree : C
   x ↦ the descendants of x form a tree

These are the recursive algorithms for computing the weight and height of a tree:

```
template<typename C>
    requires(BifurcateCoordinate(C))
WeightType(C) weight_recursive(C c)
{
    // Precondition: tree(c)
    typedef WeightType(C) N;
    if (empty(c)) return N(0);
    N l(0);
    N r(0);
    if (has_left_successor(c))
        l = weight_recursive(left_successor(c));
    if (has_right_successor(c))
        r = weight_recursive(right_successor(c));
    return successor(l + r);
}


template<typename C>
    requires(BifurcateCoordinate(C))
WeightType(C) height_recursive(C c)
{
    // Precondition: tree(c)
    typedef WeightType(C) N;
    if (empty(c)) return N(0);
    N l(0);
    N r(0);
    if (has_left_successor(c))
        l = height_recursive(left_successor(c));
    if (has_right_successor(c))
```

```
        r = height_recursive(right_successor(c));
    return successor(max(l, r));
}
```

Lemma 7.1   height_recursive(x) ≤ weight_recursive(x)

height_recursive correctly computes the height of a DAG but visits each coordinate as many times as there are paths to it; this fact means that weight_recursive does not correctly compute the weight of a DAG. Algorithms for traversing DAGs and cyclic structures require *marking:* a way of remembering which coordinates have been previously visited.

There are three primary depth-first tree-traversal orders. All three fully traverse the left descendants and then the right descendants. *Preorder* visits to a coordinate occur before the traversal of its descendants; *inorder* visits occur between the traversals of the left and right descendants; *postorder* visits occur after traversing all descendants. We name the three visits with the following type definition:

```
enum visit { pre, in, post };
```

We can perform any combination of the traversals with a single procedure that takes as a parameter another procedure taking the visit together with the coordinate:

```
template<typename C, typename Proc>
    requires(BifurcateCoordinate(C) &&
        Procedure(Proc) && Arity(Proc) == 2 &&
        visit == InputType(Proc, 0) &&
        C == InputType(Proc, 1))
Proc traverse_nonempty(C c, Proc proc)
{
    // Precondition: tree(c) ∧ ¬empty(c)
    proc(pre, c);
    if (has_left_successor(c))
        proc = traverse_nonempty(left_successor(c), proc);
    proc(in, c);
    if (has_right_successor(c))
        proc = traverse_nonempty(right_successor(c), proc);
    proc(post, c);
    return proc;
}
```

7.2 Bidirectional Bifurcate Coordinates

Recursive traversal requires stack space proportional to the height of the tree, which can be as large as the weight; this is often unacceptable for large, unbalanced trees. Also, the interface to traverse_nonempty does not allow concurrent traversal of multiple trees. In general, traversing more than one tree concurrently requires a stack per tree. If we combined a coordinate with a stack of previous coordinates, we would obtain a new coordinate type with an additional transformation for obtaining the predecessor. (It would be more efficient to use actions rather than transformations, to avoid copying the stack each time.) Such a coordinate would model the concept *bidirectional bifurcate coordinate*. There is a simpler and more flexible model of this concept: trees that include a predecessor link in each node. Such trees allow concurrent, constant-space traversals and make possible various rebalancing algorithms. The overhead for the extra link is usually justified.

$BidirectionalBifurcateCoordinate(\mathsf{T}) \triangleq$
  $\quad BifurcateCoordinate(\mathsf{T})$
  $\quad \wedge$ has_predecessor : $\mathsf{T} \to$ bool
  $\quad \wedge (\forall i \in \mathsf{T}) \, \neg$empty$(i) \Rightarrow$ has_predecessor(i) is defined
  $\quad \wedge$ predecessor : $\mathsf{T} \to \mathsf{T}$
  $\quad \wedge (\forall i \in \mathsf{T})$ has_left_successor$(i) \Rightarrow$
  $\qquad$ predecessor$($left_successor$(i))$ is defined and equals i
  $\quad \wedge (\forall i \in \mathsf{T})$ has_right_successor$(i) \Rightarrow$
  $\qquad$ predecessor$($right_successor$(i))$ is defined and equals i
  $\quad \wedge (\forall i \in \mathsf{T})$ has_predecessor$(i) \Rightarrow$
  $\qquad$ is_left_successor$(i) \vee$ is_right_successor(i)

where is_left_successor and is_right_successor are defined as follows:

```
template<typename T>
    requires(BidirectionalBifurcateCoordinate(T))
bool is_left_successor(T j)
{
    // Precondition: has_predecessor(j)
    T i = predecessor(j);
    return has_left_successor(i) && left_successor(i) == j;
}

template<typename T>
    requires(BidirectionalBifurcateCoordinate(T))
```

```
bool is_right_successor(T j)
{
    // Precondition: has_predecessor(j)
    T i = predecessor(j);
    return has_right_successor(i) && right_successor(i) == j;
}
```

Lemma 7.2   If x and y are bidirectional bifurcate coordinates,

$$\text{left\_successor}(x) = \text{left\_successor}(y) \Rightarrow x = y$$
$$\text{left\_successor}(x) = \text{right\_successor}(y) \Rightarrow x = y$$
$$\text{right\_successor}(x) = \text{right\_successor}(y) \Rightarrow x = y$$

Exercise 7.1   Would the existence of a coordinate x such that

$$\text{is\_left\_successor}(x) \wedge \text{is\_right\_successor}(x)$$

contradict the axioms of bidirectional bifurcate coordinates?

traverse_nonempty visits each coordinate three times, whether or not it has successors; maintaining this invariant makes the traversal uniform. The three visits to a coordinate always occur in the same order (pre, in, post), so given a current coordinate and the visit just performed on it, we can determine the next coordinate and the next state, using only the information from the coordinate and its predecessor. These considerations lead us to an iterative constant-space algorithm for traversing a tree with bidirectional bifurcate coordinates. The traversal depends on a *machine*—a sequence of statements used as a component of many algorithms:

```
template<typename C>
    requires(BidirectionalBifurcateCoordinate(C))
int traverse_step(visit& v, C& c)
{
    // Precondition: has_predecessor(c) ∨ v ≠ post
    switch (v) {
    case pre:
        if (has_left_successor(c))   {
                    c = left_successor(c);   return 1;
        }   v = in;                          return 0;
```

```
    case in:
        if (has_right_successor(c)) {
            v = pre; c = right_successor(c); return 1;
        }   v = post;                       return 0;
    case post:
        if (is_left_successor(c))
            v = in;
                    c = predecessor(c);       return -1;
    }
}
```

The value returned by the procedure is the change in height. An algorithm based on traverse_step uses a loop that terminates when the original coordinate is reached on the final (post) visit:

```
template<typename C>
    requires(BifurcateCoordinate(C))
bool reachable(C x, C y)
{
    // Precondition: tree(c)
    if (empty(x)) return false;
    C root = x;
    visit v = pre;
    do {
        if (x == y) return true;
        traverse_step(v, x);
    } while (x != root || v != post);
    return false;
}
```

Lemma 7.3   If reachable returns true, v = pre right before the return.

To compute the weight of a tree, we count the pre visits in a traversal:

```
template<typename C>
    requires(BidirectionalBifurcateCoordinate(C))
WeightType(C) weight(C c)
{
```

```
// Precondition: tree(c)
typedef WeightType(C) N;
if (empty(c)) return N(0);
C root = c;
visit v = pre;
N n(1); // Invariant: n is count of pre visits so far
do {
    traverse_step(v, c);
    if (v == pre) n = successor(n);
} while (c != root || v != post);
return n;
}
```

Exercise 7.2 Change weight to count in or post visits instead of pre.

To compute the height of a tree, we need to maintain the current height and the running maximum:

```
template<typename C>
    requires(BidirectionalBifurcateCoordinate(C))
WeightType(C) height(C c)
{
    // Precondition: tree(c)
    typedef WeightType(C) N;
    if (empty(c)) return N(0);
    C root = c;
    visit v = pre;
    N n(1); // Invariant: n is max of height of pre visits so far
    N m(1); // Invariant: m is height of current pre visit
    do {
        m = (m - N(1)) + N(traverse_step(v, c) + 1);
        n = max(n, m);
    } while (c != root || v != post);
    return n;
}
```

The extra −1 and +1 are in case WeightType is unsigned. The code would benefit from an accumulating version of max.

We can define an iterative procedure corresponding to traverse_nonempty. We include a test for the empty tree, since it is not executed on every recursive call:

```
template<typename C, typename Proc>
    requires(BidirectionalBifurcateCoordinate(C) &&
        Procedure(Proc) && Arity(Proc) == 2 &&
        visit == InputType(Proc, 0) &&
        C == InputType(Proc, 1))
Proc traverse(C c, Proc proc)
{
    // Precondition: tree(c)
    if (empty(c)) return proc;
    C root = c;
    visit v = pre;
    proc(pre, c);
    do {
        traverse_step(v, c);
        proc(v, c);
    } while (c != root || v != post);
    return proc;
}
```

Exercise 7.3   Use traverse_step and the procedures of Chapter 2 to determine whether the descendants of a bidirectional bifurcate coordinate form a DAG.

The property readable_bounded_range for iterators says that for every iterator in a range, source is defined. An analogous property for bifurcate coordinates is

property(C : *Readable*)
   requires(BifurcateCoordinate(C))
readable_tree : C
   $x \mapsto \text{tree}(x) \wedge (\forall y \in C)\,\text{reachable}(x, y) \Rightarrow \text{source}(y)$ is defined

There are two approaches to extending iterator algorithms, such as find and count, to bifurcate coordinates: implementing specialized versions or implementing an adapter type.

Project 7.1   Implement versions of algorithms in Chapter 6 for bidirectional bifurcate coordinates.

Project 7.2 Design an adapter type that, given a bidirectional bifurcate coordinate type, produces an iterator type that accesses coordinates in a traversal order (pre, in, or post) specified when an iterator is constructed.

7.3 Coordinate Structures

So far, we have defined individual concepts, each of which specifies a set of procedures and their semantics. Occasionally it is useful to define a *concept schema*, which is a way of describing some common properties of a family of concepts. While it is not possible to define an algorithm on a concept schema, it is possible to describe structures of related algorithms on different concepts belonging to the same concept schema. For example, we defined several iterator concepts describing linear traversals and bifurcate coordinate concepts describing traversal of binary trees. To allow traversal within arbitrary data structures, we introduce a concept schema called *coordinate structures*. A coordinate structure may have several interrelated coordinate types, each with diverse traversal functions. Coordinate structures abstract the navigational aspects of data structures, whereas composite objects, introduced in Chapter 12, abstract storage management and ownership. Multiple coordinate structures can describe the same set of objects.

A concept is a *coordinate structure* if it consists of one or more coordinate types, zero or more value types, one or more traversal functions, and zero or more access functions. Each traversal function maps one or more coordinate types and/or value types into a coordinate type, whereas each access function maps one or more coordinate types and/or value types into a value type. For example, when considered as a coordinate structure, a readable indexed iterator has one value type and two coordinate types: the iterator type and its distance type. The traversal functions are + (adding a distance to an iterator) and − (giving the distance between two iterators). There is one access function: source.

7.4 Isomorphism, Equivalence, and Ordering

Two collections of coordinates from the same coordinate structure concept are *isomorphic* if they have the same shape. More formally, they are isomorphic if there is a one-to-one correspondence between the two collections such that any valid application of a traversal function to coordinates from the first collection returns the coordinate corresponding to the same traversal function applied to the corresponding coordinates from the second collection.

Isomorphism does not depend on the values of the objects pointed to by the coordinates: Algorithms for testing isomorphism use only traversal functions. But isomorphism requires that the same access functions are defined, or not defined, for corresponding coordinates. For example, two bounded or counted ranges are isomorphic if they have the same size. Two weak ranges of forward iterators are isomorphic if they have the same orbit structure, as defined in Chapter 2. Two trees are isomorphic when both are empty; when both are nonempty, isomorphism is determined by the following code:

```
template<typename C0, typename C1>
    requires(BifurcateCoordinate(C0) &&
        BifurcateCoordinate(C1))
bool bifurcate_isomorphic_nonempty(C0 c0, C1 c1)
{
    // Precondition: tree(c0) ∧ tree(c1) ∧ ¬empty(c0) ∧ ¬empty(c1)
    if (has_left_successor(c0))
        if (has_left_successor(c1)) {
            if (!bifurcate_isomorphic_nonempty(
                    left_successor(c0), left_successor(c1)))
                return false;
        } else return false;
    else if (has_left_successor(c1)) return false;
    if (has_right_successor(c0))
        if (has_right_successor(c1)) {
            if (!bifurcate_isomorphic_nonempty(
                    right_successor(c0), right_successor(c1)))
                return false;
        } else return false;
    else if (has_right_successor(c1)) return false;
    return true;
}
```

Lemma 7.4   For bidirectional bifurcate coordinates, trees are isomorphic when simultaneous traversals take the same sequence of visits:

```
template<typename C0, typename C1>
    requires(BidirectionalBifurcateCoordinate(C0) &&
        BidirectionalBifurcateCoordinate(C1))
```

```
bool bifurcate_isomorphic(C0 c0, C1 c1)
{
    // Precondition: tree(c0) ∧ tree(c1)
    if (empty(c0)) return empty(c1);
    if (empty(c1)) return false;
    C0 root0 = c0;
    visit v0 = pre;
    visit v1 = pre;
    while (true) {
        traverse_step(v0, c0);
        traverse_step(v1, c1);
        if (v0 != v1) return false;
        if (c0 == root0 && v0 == post) return true;
    }
}
```

Chapter 6 contains algorithms for linear and bisection search, depending on, respectively, equality and total ordering, which are part of the notion of regularity. By inducing equality and ordering on collections of coordinates from a coordinate structure, we can search for collections of objects rather than for individual objects.

Two collections of coordinates from the same readable coordinate structure concept and with the same value types are *equivalent* under given equivalence relations (one per value type) if they are isomorphic and if applying the same access function to corresponding coordinates from the two collections returns equivalent objects. Replacing the equivalence relations with the equalities for the value types leads to a natural definition of equality on collections of coordinates.

Two readable bounded ranges are equivalent if they have the same size and if corresponding iterators have equivalent values:

```
template<typename I0, typename I1, typename R>
    requires(Readable(I0) && Iterator(I0) &&
        Readable(I1) && Iterator(I1) &&
        ValueType(I0) == ValueType(I1) &&
        Relation(R) && ValueType(I0) == Domain(R))
bool lexicographical_equivalent(I0 f0, I0 l0, I1 f1, I1 l1, R r)
{
    // Precondition: readable_bounded_range(f0, l0)
    // Precondition: readable_bounded_range(f1, l1)
    // Precondition: equivalence(r)
```

```
pair<I0, I1> p = find_mismatch(f0, l0, f1, l1, r);
return p.m0 == l0 && p.m1 == l1;
}
```

It is straightforward to implement lexicographical_equal by passing a function object implementing equality on the value type to lexicographical_equivalent:

```
template<typename T>
    requires(Regular(T))
struct equal
{
    bool operator()(const T& x, const T& y)
    {
        return x == y;
    }
};

template<typename I0, typename I1>
    requires(Readable(I0) && Iterator(I0) &&
        Readable(I1) && Iterator(I1) &&
        ValueType(I0) == ValueType(I1))
bool lexicographical_equal(I0 f0, I0 l0, I1 f1, I1 l1)
{
    return lexicographical_equivalent(f0, l0, f1, l1,
                                      equal<ValueType(I0)>());
}
```

Two readable trees are equivalent if they are isomorphic and if corresponding coordinates have equivalent values:

```
template<typename C0, typename C1, typename R>
    requires(Readable(C0) && BifurcateCoordinate(C0) &&
        Readable(C1) && BifurcateCoordinate(C1) &&
        ValueType(C0) == ValueType(C1) &&
        Relation(R) && ValueType(I0) == Domain(R))
bool bifurcate_equivalent_nonempty(C0 c0, C1 c1, R r)
{
    // Precondition: readable_tree(c0) ∧ readable_tree(c1)
    // Precondition: ¬empty(c0) ∧ ¬empty(c1)
```

```
    // Precondition: equivalence(r)
    if (!r(source(c0), source(c1))) return false;
    if (has_left_successor(c0))
        if (has_left_successor(c1)) {
            if (!bifurcate_equivalent_nonempty(
                    left_successor(c0), left_successor(c1), r))
                return false;
        } else return false;
    else if (has_left_successor(c1)) return false;
    if (has_right_successor(c0))
        if (has_right_successor(c1)) {
            if (!bifurcate_equivalent_nonempty(
                    right_successor(c0), right_successor(c1), r))
                return false;
        } else return false;
    else if (has_right_successor(c1)) return false;
    return true;
}
```

For bidirectional bifurcate coordinates, trees are equivalent if simultaneous traversals take the same sequence of visits and if corresponding coordinates have equivalent values:

```
template<typename C0, typename C1, typename R>
    requires(Readable(C0) &&
        BidirectionalBifurcateCoordinate(C0) &&
        Readable(C1) &&
        BidirectionalBifurcateCoordinate(C1) &&
        ValueType(C0) == ValueType(C1) &&
        Relation(R) && ValueType(C) == Domain(R))
bool bifurcate_equivalent(C0 c0, C1 c1, R r)
{
    // Precondition: readable_tree(c0) ∧ readable_tree(c1)
    // Precondition: equivalence(r)
    if (empty(c0)) return empty(c1);
    if (empty(c1)) return false;
    C0 root0 = c0;
    visit v0 = pre;
    visit v1 = pre;
```

```
    while (true) {
        if (v0 == pre && !r(source(c0), source(c1)))
            return false;
        traverse_step(v0, c0);
        traverse_step(v1, c1);
        if (v0 != v1) return false;
        if (c0 == root0 && v0 == post) return true;
    }
}
```

We can extend a weak (total) ordering to readable ranges of iterators by using lexicographical ordering, which ignores prefixes of equivalent (equal) values and considers a shorter range to precede a longer one:

```
template<typename I0, typename I1, typename R>
    requires(Readable(I0) && Iterator(I0) &&
        Readable(I1) && Iterator(I1) &&
        ValueType(I0) == ValueType(I1) &&
        Relation(R) && ValueType(I0) == Domain(R))
bool lexicographical_compare(I0 f0, I0 l0, I1 f1, I1 l1, R r)
{
    // Precondition: readable_bounded_range(f0, l0)
    // Precondition: readable_bounded_range(f1, l1)
    // Precondition: weak_ordering(r)
    while (true) {
        if (f1 == l1) return false;
        if (f0 == l0) return true;
        if (r(source(f0), source(f1))) return true;
        if (r(source(f1), source(f0))) return false;
        f0 = successor(f0);
        f1 = successor(f1);
    }
}
```

It is straightforward to specialize this to lexicographical_less by passing as r a function object capturing < on the value type:

```
template<typename T>
    requires(TotallyOrdered(T))
```

```
struct less
{
    bool operator()(const T& x, const T& y)
    {
        return x < y;
    }
};

template<typename I0, typename I1>
    requires(Readable(I0) && Iterator(I0) &&
        Readable(I1) && Iterator(I1) &&
        ValueType(I0) == ValueType(I1))
bool lexicographical_less(I0 f0, I0 l0, I1 f1, I1 l1)
{
    return lexicographical_compare(f0, l0, f1, l1,
                                   less<ValueType(I0)>());
}
```

Exercise 7.4   Explain why, in lexicographical_compare, the third and fourth
if statements could be interchanged, but the first and second cannot.

Exercise 7.5   Explain why we did not implement lexicographical_compare
by using find_mismatch.

We can also extend lexicographical ordering to bifurcate coordinates by ignor-
ing equivalent rooted subtrees and considering a coordinate without a left successor
to precede a coordinate having a left successor. If the current values and the left subtrees do not determine the outcome, consider a coordinate without a right successor
to precede a coordinate having a right successor.

Exercise 7.6   Implement bifurcate_compare_nonempty for readable bifurcate coordinates.

The readers who complete the preceding exercise will appreciate the simplicity
of comparing trees based on bidirectional coordinates and iterative traversal:

```
template<typename C0, typename C1, typename R>
    requires(Readable(C0) &&
        BidirectionalBifurcateCoordinate(C0) &&
        Readable(C1) &&
```

```
        BidirectionalBifurcateCoordinate(C1) &&
        Relation(R) && ValueType(C) == Domain(R))
bool bifurcate_compare(C0 c0, C1 c1, R r)
{
    // Precondition: readable_tree(c0) ∧ readable_tree(c1) ∧ weak_ordering(r)
    if (empty(c1)) return false;
    if (empty(c0)) return true;
    C0 root0 = c0;
    visit v0 = pre;
    visit v1 = pre;
    while (true) {
        if (v0 == pre) {
            if (r(source(c0), source(c1))) return true;
            if (r(source(c1), source(c0))) return false;
        }
        traverse_step(v0, c0);
        traverse_step(v1, c1);
        if (v0 != v1) return v0 > v1;
        if (c0 == root0 && v0 == post) return false;
    }
}
```

We can implement bifurcate_shape_compare by passing the relation that is always false to bifurcate_compare. This allows us to sort a range of trees and then use upper_bound to find an isomorphic tree in logarithmic time.

Project 7.3   Design a coordinate structure for a family of data structures, and extend isomorphism, equivalence, and ordering to this coordinate structure.

7.5   Conclusions

Linear structures play a fundamental role in computer science, and iterators provide a natural interface between such structures and the algorithms working on them. There are, however, nonlinear data structures with their own nonlinear coordinate structures. Bidirectional bifurcate coordinates provide an example of iterative algorithms quite different from algorithms on iterator ranges. We extend the notions of isomorphism, equality, and ordering to collections of coordinates of different topologies.

Chapter 8

Coordinates with Mutable Successors

T*his chapter introduces iterator and coordinate structure concepts that allow* relinking: *modifying* successor *or other traversal functions for a particular coordinate. Relinking allows us to implement rearrangements, such as sorting, that preserve the value of* source *at a coordinate. We introduce relinking machines that preserve certain structural properties of the coordinates. We conclude with a machine allowing certain traversals of a tree without the use of a stack or predecessor links, by temporarily relinking the coordinates during the traversal.*

8.1 Linked Iterators

In Chapter 6 we viewed the successor of a given interator as immutable: Applying successor to a particular iterator value always returns the same result. A *linked iterator* type is a forward iterator type for which a *linker object* exists; applying the linker object to an iterator allows the successor of that iterator to be changed. Such iterators are modeled by linked lists, where relationships between nodes can be changed. We use linker objects rather than a single set_successor function overloaded on the iterator type to allow different linkings of the same data structure. For example, doubly linked lists could be linked by setting both successor and predecessor links or by setting successor links only. This allows a multipass algorithm to minimize work by omitting maintenance of the predecessor links until the final pass. Thus we specify concepts for linked iterators indirectly, in terms of the corresponding linker objects. Informally, we still speak of linked iterator types. To define the requirements on linker objects, we define the following related concepts:

$ForwardLinker(S) \triangleq$
    IteratorType : $ForwardLinker \rightarrow ForwardIterator$
    $\wedge$ Let I = IteratorType(S) in:

$$(\forall s \in S)\,(s : I \times I \to \text{void})$$
$$\land\ (\forall s \in S)\,(\forall i, j \in I) \text{ if successor}(i) \text{ is defined,}$$
$$\text{then } s(i, j) \text{ establishes successor}(i) = j$$

$BackwardLinker(S) \triangleq$
     IteratorType : $BackwardLinker \to BidirectionalIterator$
     $\land$ Let I = IteratorType(S) in:
$$(\forall s \in S)\,(s : I \times I \to \text{void})$$
$$\land\ (\forall s \in S)\,(\forall i, j \in I) \text{ if predecessor}(j) \text{ is defined,}$$
$$\text{then } s(i, j) \text{ establishes } i = \text{predecessor}(j)$$

$BidirectionalLinker(S) \triangleq ForwardLinker(S) \land BackwardLinker(S)$

Two ranges are *disjoint* if they include no iterator in common. For half-open bounded ranges, this corresponds to the following:

property(I : *Iterator*)
disjoint : $I \times I \times I \times I$
     $(f0, l0, f1, l1) \mapsto (\forall i \in I)\,\neg(i \in [f0, l0) \land i \in [f1, l1))$

and similarly for other kinds of ranges. Since linked iterators are iterators, they benefit from all the notions we defined for ranges, but disjointness and all other properties of ranges can change over time on linked iterators. It is possible for disjoint ranges of forward iterators with only a forward linker—singly linked lists—to share the same limit—commonly referred to as *nil*.

8.2 Link Rearrangements

A *link rearrangement* is an algorithm taking one or more linked ranges, returning one or more linked ranges, and satisfying the following properties.

- Input ranges (either counted or bounded) are pairwise disjoint.
- Output ranges (either counted or bounded) are pairwise disjoint.
- Every iterator in an input range appears in one of the output ranges.
- Every iterator in an output range appeared in one of the input ranges.
- Every iterator in each output range designates the same object as before the rearrangement, and this object has the same value.

Note that successor and predecessor relationships that held in the input ranges may not hold in the output ranges.

A link rearrangement is *precedence preserving* if, whenever two iterators i ≺ j in an output range came from the same input range, i ≺ j originally held in the input range.

Implementing a link rearrangement requires care to satisfy the properties of disjointness, conservation, and ordering. We proceed by presenting three short procedures, or machines, each of which performs one step of traversal or linking, and then composing from these machines link rearrangements for splitting, combining, and reversing linked ranges. The first two machines establish or maintain the relationship f = successor(t) between two iterator objects passed by reference:

```
template<typename I>
    requires(ForwardIterator(I))
void advance_tail(I& t, I& f)
{
    // Precondition: successor(f) is defined
    t = f;
    f = successor(f);
}


template<typename S>
    requires(ForwardLinker(S))
struct linker_to_tail
{
    typedef IteratorType(S) I;
    S set_link;
    linker_to_tail(const S& set_link) : set_link(set_link) { }
    void operator()(I& t, I& f)
    {
        // Precondition: successor(f) is defined
        set_link(t, f);
        advance_tail(t, f);
    }
};
```

We can use advance_tail to find the last iterator in a nonempty bounded range:[1]

```
template<typename I>
    requires(ForwardIterator(I))
```

---

1. Observe that find_adjacent_mismatch_forward in Chapter 6 used advance_tail implicitly.

```
I find_last(I f, I l)
{
    // Precondition: bounded_range(f, l) ∧ f ≠ l
    I t;
    do
        advance_tail(t, f);
    while (f != l);
    return t;
}
```

We can use advance_tail and linker_to_tail together to split a range into two ranges based on the value of a *pseudopredicate* applied to each iterator. A *pseudopredicate* is not necessarily regular, and its result may depend on its own state as well as its inputs. For example, a pseudopredicate might ignore its arguments and return alternating false and true values. The algorithm takes a bounded range of linked iterators, a pseudopredicate on the linked iterator type, and a linker object. The algorithm returns a pair of ranges: iterators not satisfying the pseudopredicate and iterators satisfying it. It is useful to represent these returned ranges as closed bounded ranges [h, t], where h is the first, or *head*, iterator, and t is the last, or *tail*, iterator. Returning the tail of each range allows the caller to relink that iterator without having to traverse to it (using find_last, for example). However, either of the returned ranges could be empty, which we represent by returning h = t = l, where l is the limit of the input range. The successor links of the tails of the two returned ranges are not modified by the algorithm. Here is the algorithm:

```
template<typename I, typename S, typename Pred>
    requires(ForwardLinker(S) && I == IteratorType(S) &&
        UnaryPseudoPredicate(Pred) && I == Domain(Pred))
pair< pair<I, I>, pair<I, I> >
split_linked(I f, I l, Pred p, S set_link)
{
    // Precondition: bounded_range(f, l)
    typedef pair<I, I> P;
    linker_to_tail<S> link_to_tail(set_link);
    I h0 = l; I t0 = l;
    I h1 = l; I t1 = l;
    if (f == l)                                    goto s4;
    if (p(f)) { h1 = f; advance_tail(t1, f); goto s1; }
    else      { h0 = f; advance_tail(t0, f); goto s0; }
```

```
s0: if (f == 1)                                     goto s4;
    if (p(f)) { h1 = f; advance_tail(t1, f); goto s3; }
    else         {          advance_tail(t0, f); goto s0; }
s1: if (f == 1)                                     goto s4;
    if (p(f)) {          advance_tail(t1, f); goto s1; }
    else         { h0 = f; advance_tail(t0, f); goto s2; }
s2: if (f == 1)                                     goto s4;
    if (p(f)) {          link_to_tail(t1, f); goto s3; }
    else         {          advance_tail(t0, f); goto s2; }
s3: if (f == 1)                                     goto s4;
    if (p(f)) {          advance_tail(t1, f); goto s3; }
    else         {          link_to_tail(t0, f); goto s2; }
s4: return pair<P, P>(P(h0, t0), P(h1, t1));
}
```

The procedure is a state machine. The variables t0 and t1 point to the tails of the two output ranges, respectively. The states correspond to the following conditions:

s0: $\text{successor}(t0) = f \land \neg p(t0)$

s1: $\text{successor}(t1) = f \land p(t1)$

s2: $\text{successor}(t0) = f \land \neg p(t0) \land p(t1)$

s3: $\text{successor}(t1) = f \land \neg p(t0) \land p(t1)$

Relinking is necessary only when moving between states s2 and s3. goto statements from a state to the immediately following state are included for symmetry.

Lemma 8.1   For each of the ranges [h, t] returned by split_linked, $h = l \Leftrightarrow t = l$.

Exercise 8.1   Assuming that one of the ranges (h, t) returned by split_linked is not empty, explain what iterator t points to and what the value of $\text{successor}(t)$ is.

Lemma 8.2   split_linked is a precedence-preserving link rearrangement.

We can also use advance_tail and linker_to_tail to implement an algorithm to combine two ranges into a single range based on a pseudorelation applied to the heads of the remaining portions of the input ranges. A *pseudorelation* is a binary homogeneous pseudopredicate and thus not necessarily regular. The algorithm takes two bounded ranges of linked iterators, a pseudorelation on the linked iterator type, and a linker object. The algorithm returns a triple (f, t, l), where [f, l) is the half-open range of combined iterators, and t ∈ [f, l) is the last-visited iterator. A subsequent call to find_last(t, l) would return the last iterator in the range, allowing it to be linked to another range. Here is the algorithm:

```
template<typename I, typename S, typename R>
    requires(ForwardLinker(S) && I == IteratorType(S) &&
        PseudoRelation(R) && I == Domain(R))
triple<I, I, I>
combine_linked_nonempty(I f0, I l0, I f1, I l1, R r, S set_link)
{
    // Precondition: bounded_range(f0, l0) ∧ bounded_range(f1, l1)
    // Precondition: f0 ≠ l0 ∧ f1 ≠ l1 ∧ disjoint(f0, l0, f1, l1)
    typedef triple<I, I, I> T;
    linker_to_tail<S> link_to_tail(set_link);
    I h; I t;
    if (r(f1, f0)) { h = f1; advance_tail(t, f1); goto s1; }
    else           { h = f0; advance_tail(t, f0); goto s0; }
s0: if (f0 == l0)                                 goto s2;
    if (r(f1, f0)) {           link_to_tail(t, f1); goto s1; }
    else           {           advance_tail(t, f0); goto s0; }
s1: if (f1 == l1)                                 goto s3;
    if (r(f1, f0)) {           advance_tail(t, f1); goto s1; }
    else           {           link_to_tail(t, f0); goto s0; }
s2: set_link(t, f1); return T(h, t, l1);
s3: set_link(t, f0); return T(h, t, l0);
}
```

Exercise 8.2 Implement combine_linked, allowing for empty inputs. What value should be returned as the last-visited iterator?

The procedure is also a state machine. The variable t points to the tail of the output range. The states correspond to the following conditions:

s0: successor(t) = f0 ∧ ¬r(f1, t)

s1: successor(t) = f1 ∧ r(t, f0)

Relinking is necessary only when moving between states s0 and s1.

Lemma 8.3 If a call combine_linked_nonempty(f0, l0, f1, l1, r, s) returns (h, t, l), h equals f0 or f1 and, independently, l equals l0 or l1.

Lemma 8.4 When state s2 is reached, t is from the original range [f0, l0), successor(t) = l0, and f1 $\neq$ l1; when state s3 is reached, t is from the original range [f1, l1), successor(t) = l1, and f0 $\neq$ l0.

Lemma 8.5 combine_linked_nonempty is a precedence-preserving link rearrangement.

The third machine links to the head of a list rather than to its tail:

```
template<typename I, typename S>
    requires(ForwardLinker(S) && I == IteratorType(S))
struct linker_to_head
{
    S set_link;
    linker_to_head(const S& set_link) : set_link(set_link) { }
    void operator()(I& h, I& f)
    {
        // Precondition: successor(f) is defined
        IteratorType(S) tmp = successor(f);
        set_link(f, h);
        h = f;
        f = tmp;
    }
};
```

With this machine, we can reverse a range of iterators:

```
template<typename I, typename S>
    requires(ForwardLinker(S) && I == IteratorType(S))
I reverse_append(I f, I l, I h, S set_link)
{
    // Precondition: bounded_range(f, l) ∧ h ∉ [f, l)
    linker_to_head<I, S> link_to_head(set_link);
    while (f != l) link_to_head(h, f);
    return h;
}
```

To avoid sharing of proper tails, h should be the beginning of a disjoint linked list (for a singly linked list, nil is acceptable) or l. While we could have used l as the initial value for h (thus giving us reverse_linked), it is useful to pass a separate accumulation parameter.

8.3 Applications of Link Rearrangements

Given a predicate on the value type of a linked iterator type, we can use split_linked to partition a range. We need an adapter to convert from a predicate on values to a predicate on iterators:

```
template<typename I, typename P>
    requires(Readable(I) &&
        Predicate(P) && ValueType(I) == Domain(P))
struct predicate_source
{
    P p;
    predicate_source(const P& p) : p(p) { }
    bool operator()(I i)
    {
        return p(source(i));
    }
};
```

With this adapter, we can partition a range into values not satisfying the given predicate and those satisfying it:

```
template<typename I, typename S, typename P>
    requires(ForwardLinker(S) && I == IteratorType(S) &&
        UnaryPredicate(P) && ValueType(I) == Domain(P))
pair< pair<I, I>, pair<I, I> >
partition_linked(I f, I l, P p, S set_link)
{
    predicate_source<I, P> ps(p);
    return split_linked(f, l, ps, set_link);
}
```

Given a weak ordering on the value type of a linked iterator type, we can use combine_linked_nonempty to merge increasing ranges. Again, we need an adapter to convert from a relation on values to a relation on iterators:

```
template<typename I0, typename I1, typename R>
    requires(Readable(I0) && Readable(I1) &&
        ValueType(I0) == ValueType(I1) &&
        Relation(R) && ValueType(I0) == Domain(R))
struct relation_source
{
    R r;
    relation_source(const R& r) : r(r) { }
    bool operator()(I0 i0, I1 i1)
    {
        return r(source(i0), source(i1));
    }
};
```

After combining ranges with this relation, the only remaining work is to find the last iterator of the combined range and set it to $l1$:

```
template<typename I, typename S, typename R>
    requires(Readable(I) &&
        ForwardLinker(S) && I == IteratorType(S) &&
        Relation(R) && ValueType(I) == Domain(R))
pair<I, I> merge_linked_nonempty(I f0, I l0, I f1, I l1,
                                 R r, S set_link)
{
    // Precondition: f0 ≠ l0 ∧ f1 ≠ l1
    // Precondition: increasing_range(f0, l0, r)
    // Precondition: increasing_range(f1, l1, r)
    relation_source<I, I, R> rs(r);
    triple<I, I, I> t = combine_linked_nonempty(f0, l0, f1, l1,
                                                rs, set_link);
    set_link(find_last(t.m1, t.m2), l1);
    return pair<I, I>(t.m0, l1);
}
```

Lemma 8.6   If [f0, l0) and [f1, l1) are nonempty increasing bounded ranges, their merge with merge_linked_nonempty is an increasing bounded range.

Lemma 8.7   If i0 ∈ [f0, l0) and i1 ∈ [f1, l1) are iterators whose values are equivalent under r, in the merge of these ranges with merge_linked_nonempty, i0 ≺ i1.

Given merge_linked_nonempty, it is straightforward to implement a merge sort:

```
template<typename I, typename S, typename R>
    requires(Readable(I) &&
        ForwardLinker(S) && I == IteratorType(S) &&
        Relation(R) && ValueType(I) == Domain(R))
pair<I, I> sort_linked_nonempty_n(I f, DistanceType(I) n,
                                  R r, S set_link)
{
    // Precondition: counted_range(f, n) ∧ n > 0 ∧ weak_ordering(r)
    typedef DistanceType(I) N;
    typedef pair<I, I> P;
    if (n == N(1)) return P(f, successor(f));
    N h = half_nonnegative(n);
    P p0 = sort_linked_nonempty_n(f, h, r, set_link);
    P p1 = sort_linked_nonempty_n(p0.m1, n - h, r, set_link);
    return merge_linked_nonempty(p0.m0, p0.m1,
                                 p1.m0, p1.m1, r, set_link);
}
```

Lemma 8.8   sort_linked_nonempty_n is a link rearrangement.

Lemma 8.9   If ⟦f, n⟧ is a nonempty counted range, sort_linked_nonempty_n will rearrange it into an increasing bounded range.

A sort on a linked range is *stable* with respect to a weak ordering r if, whenever iterators i ≺ j in the input have equivalent values with respect to r, i ≺ j in the output.

Lemma 8.10   sort_linked_nonempty_n is stable with respect to the supplied weak ordering r.

Exercise 8.3 Determine formulas for the worst-case and average number of applications of the relation and of the linker object in sort_linked_ nonempty_n.

While the number of operations performed by sort_linked_nonempty_n is close to optimal, poor locality of reference limits its usefulness if the linked structure does not fit into cache memory. In such situations, if extra memory is available, one should copy the linked list to an array and sort the array.

Sorting a linked range does not depend on predecessor. Maintaining the invariant:

$$i = \text{predecessor}(\text{successor}(i))$$

requires a number of backward-linking operations proportional to the number of comparisons. We can avoid extra work by temporarily breaking the invariant. Suppose that I is a linked bidirectional iterator type, and that forward_linker and backward_linker are, respectively, forward and backward linker objects for I. We can supply forward_linker to the sort procedure—treating the list as singly linked—and then fix up the predecessor links by applying backward_linker to each iterator after the first:

```
pair<I, I> p = sort_linked_nonempty_n(f, n,
                                   r, forward_linker);
f = p.m0;
while (f != p.m1) {
    backward_linker(f, successor(f));
    f = successor(f);
};
```

Exercise 8.4 Implement a precedence-preserving linked rearrangement unique that takes a linked range and an equivalence relation on the value type of the iterators and that produces two ranges by moving all except the first iterator in any adjacent sequence of iterators with equivalent values to a second range.

8.4 Linked Bifurcate Coordinates

Allowing the modification of successor leads to link-rearrangement algorithms, such as combining and splitting. It is useful to have mutable traversal functions for other coordinate structures. We illustrate the idea with linked bifurcate coordinates.

For linked iterators, we passed the linking operation as a parameter because of the need to use different linking operations: for example, when restoring backward links after sort. For linked bifurcate coordinates, there does not appear to be a need for alternative versions of the linking operations, so we define them in the concept:

$LinkedBifurcateCoordinate(T) \triangleq$
    $BifurcateCoordinate(T)$
    $\wedge$ set_left_successor : $T \times T \rightarrow$ void
        $(i, j) \mapsto$ establishes left_successor(i) = j
    $\wedge$ set_right_successor : $T \times T \rightarrow$ void
        $(i, j) \mapsto$ establishes right_successor(i) = j

The definition space for set_left_successor and set_right_successor is the set of nonempty coordinates.

Trees constitute a rich set of possible data structures and algorithms. To conclude this chapter, we show a small set of algorithms to demonstrate an important programming technique. This technique, called *link reversal*, modifies links as the tree is traversed, restoring the original state after a complete traversal while requiring only constant additional space. Link reversal requires additional axioms that allow dealing with *empty* coordinates: ones on which the traversal functions are not defined:

$EmptyLinkedBifurcateCoordinate(T) \triangleq$
    $LinkedBifurcateCoordinate(T)$
    $\wedge$ empty(T())[2]
    $\wedge$ ¬empty(i) $\Rightarrow$
        left_successor(i) and right_successor(i) are defined
    $\wedge$ ¬empty(i) $\Rightarrow$
        (¬has_left_successor(i) $\Leftrightarrow$ empty(left_successor(i)))
    $\wedge$ ¬empty(i) $\Rightarrow$
        (¬has_right_successor(i) $\Leftrightarrow$ empty(right_successor(i)))

traverse_step from Chapter 7 is an efficient way to traverse via bidirectional bifurcating coordinates but requires the predecessor function. When the predecessor function is not available and recursive (stack-based) traversal is unacceptable because of unbalanced trees, link reversal can be used to temporarily store the link to the

---

2. In other words, empty is true on the default constructed value and possibly on other values as well.

predecessor in a link normally containing a successor, thus ensuring that there is a path back to the root.[3]

If we consider the left and right successors of a tree node together with the coordinate of a previous tree node as constituting a triple, we can perform a rotation of the three members of the triple with this machine:

```
template<typename C>
    requires(EmptyLinkedBifurcateCoordinate(C))
void tree_rotate(C& curr, C& prev)
{
    // Precondition: ¬empty(curr)
    C tmp = left_successor(curr);
    set_left_successor(curr, right_successor(curr));
    set_right_successor(curr, prev);
    if (empty(tmp)) { prev = tmp; return; }
    prev = curr;
    curr = tmp;
}
```

Repeated applications of tree_rotate allow traversal of an entire tree:

```
template<typename C, typename Proc>
    requires(EmptyLinkedBifurcateCoordinate(C) &&
        Procedure(Proc) && Arity(Proc) == 1 &&
        C == InputType(Proc, 0))
Proc traverse_rotating(C c, Proc proc)
{
    // Precondition: tree(c)
    if (empty(c)) return proc;
    C curr = c;
    C prev;
    do {
        proc(curr);
        tree_rotate(curr, prev);
```

---

3. Link reversal was introduced in Schorr and Waite [1967] and was independently discovered by L. P. Deutsch. A version without tag bits was published in Robson [1973] and Morris [1979]. We show the particular technique of rotating the links due to Lindstrom [1973] and independently by Dwyer [1974].

```
} while (curr != c);
do {
    proc(curr);
    tree_rotate(curr, prev);
} while (curr != c);
proc(curr);
tree_rotate(curr, prev);
return proc;
}
```

Theorem 8.1 Consider a call of traverse_rotating(c, proc) and any non-empty descendant i of c, where i has initial left and right successors l and r and predecessor p. Then

1. The left and right successors of i go through three transitions:

$$(l, r) \overset{pre}{\to} (r, p) \overset{in}{\to} (p, l) \overset{post}{\to} (l, r)$$

2. If n_l and n_r are the weights of l and r, the transitions $(r, p) \overset{in}{\to} (p, l)$ and $(p, l) \overset{post}{\to} (l, r)$ take $3n_l + 1$ and $3n_r + 1$ calls of tree_rotate, respectively.

3. If k is a running count of the calls of tree_rotate, the value of k mod 3 is distinct for each of the three transitions of the successors of i.

4. During the call of traverse_rotating(c, proc), the total number of calls of tree_rotate is 3n, where n is the weight of c.

   Proof: By induction on n, the weight of c.

Exercise 8.5 Draw diagrams of each state of the traversal by traverse_rotating of a complete binary tree with seven nodes.

traverse_rotating performs the same sequence of preorder, inorder, and postorder visits as traverse_nonempty from Chapter 7. Unfortunately, we do not know how to determine whether a particular visit to a coordinate is the pre, in, or post visit. There are still useful things we can compute with traverse_rotating, such as the weight of a tree:

```
template<typename T, typename N>
    requires(Integer(N))
```

```
struct counter
{
    N n;
    counter() : n(0) { }
    counter(N n) : n(n) { }
    void operator()(const T&) { n = successor(n); }
};
```

```
template<typename C>
    requires(EmptyLinkedBifurcateCoordinate(C))
WeightType(C) weight_rotating(C c)
{
    // Precondition: tree(c)
    typedef WeightType(C) N;
    return traverse_rotating(c, counter<C, N>()).n / N(3);
}
```

We can also arrange to visit each coordinate exactly once by counting visits modulo 3:

```
template<typename N, typename Proc>
    requires(Integer(N) &&
        Procedure(Proc) && Arity(Proc) == 1)
struct phased_applicator
{
    N period;
    N phase;
    N n;
    // Invariant: n, phase ∈ [0, period)
    Proc proc;
    phased_applicator(N period, N phase, N n, Proc proc) :
        period(period), phase(phase), n(n), proc(proc) { }
    void operator()(InputType(Proc, 0) x)
    {
        if (n == phase) proc(x);
        n = successor(n);
        if (n == period) n = 0;
    }
};
```

```
template<typename C, typename Proc>
    requires(EmptyLinkedBifurcateCoordinate(C) &&
        Procedure(Proc) && Arity(Proc) == 1 &&
        C == InputType(Proc, 0))
Proc traverse_phased_rotating(C c, int phase, Proc proc)
{
    // Precondition: tree(c) ∧ 0 ≤ phase < 3
    phased_applicator<int, Proc> applicator(3, phase, 0, proc);
    return traverse_rotating(c, applicator).proc;
}
```

Project 8.1   Consider using tree_rotate to implement isomorphism, equivalence, and ordering on binary trees.

8.5 Conclusions

Linked coordinate structures with mutable traversal functions allow useful rearrangement algorithms, such as sorting linked ranges. Systematic composition of such algorithms from simple machinelike components leads to efficient code with precise mathematical properties. Disciplined use of goto is a legitimate way of implementing state machines. Invariants involving more than one object may be temporarily violated during an update of one of the objects. An algorithm defines a scope inside which invariants may be broken as long as they are restored before the scope is exited.

Chapter 9

Copying

T*his chapter introduces writable iterators, whose access functions allow the value of iterators to be modified. We illustrate the use of writable iterators with a family of copy algorithms constructed from simple machines that copy one object and update the input and output iterators. Careful specification of preconditions allows input and output ranges to overlap during copying. When two nonoverlapping ranges of the same size are mutable, a family of swapping algorithms can be used to exchange their contents.*

9.1 Writability

This chapter discusses the second kind of access to iterators and other coordinate structures: writability. A type is *writable* if a unary procedure sink is defined on it; sink can only be used on the left side of an assignment whose right side evaluates to an object of ValueType(T):

Writable(T) $\triangleq$
    ValueType : *Writable* → *Regular*
    $\land$ ($\forall x \in$ T) ($\forall v \in$ ValueType(T)) sink(x) ← v is a well-formed statement

The only use of sink(x) justified by the concept *Writable* is on the left side of an assignment. Of course, other uses may be supported by a particular type modeling *Writable*.

sink does not have to be total; there may be objects of a writable type on which sink is not defined. As with readability, the concept does not provide a definition-space predicate to determine whether sink is defined for a particular object. Validity of its use in an algorithm must be derivable from preconditions.

For a particular state of an object x, only a single assignment to sink(x) can be justified by the concept *Writable;* a specific type might provide a protocol allowing subsequent assignments to sink(x).[1]

A writable object x and a readable object y are *aliased* if sink(x) and source(y) are both defined and if assigning any value v to sink(x) causes it to appear as the value of source(y):

> **property**(T : *Writable*, U : *Readable*)
>> **requires**(ValueType(T) = ValueType(U))
>
> aliased : T × U
>> (x, y) ↦ sink(x) is defined ∧
>>> source(y) is defined ∧
>>> ($\forall v \in$ ValueType(T)) sink(x) $\leftarrow v$ establishes source(y) = v

The final kind of access is *mutability*, which combines readability and writability in a consistent way:

Mutable(T) ≜
> *Readable*(T) ∧ *Writable*(T)
> ∧ ($\forall x \in$ T) sink(x) is defined ⇔ source(x) is defined
> ∧ ($\forall x \in$ T) sink(x) is defined ⇒ aliased(x, x)
> ∧ deref : T → ValueType(T) &
> ∧ ($\forall x \in$ T) sink(x) is defined ⇔ deref(x) is defined

For a mutable iterator, replacing source(x) or sink(x) with deref(x) does not affect a program's meaning or performance.

A range of iterators from a type modeling *Writable* and *Iterator* is *writable* if sink is defined on all the iterators in the range:

> **property**(I : *Writable*)
>> **requires**(*Iterator*(I))
>
> writable_bounded_range : I × I
>> (f, l) ↦ bounded_range(f, l) ∧ ($\forall i \in$ [f, l)) sink(i) is defined

writable_weak_range and writable_counted_range are defined similarly.

With a readable iterator i, source(i) may be called more than once and always returns the same value: It is regular. This allows us to write simple, useful algorithms, such as find_if. With a writable iterator j, however, assignment to sink(j) is

---

1. Jerry Schwarz suggests a potentially more elegant interface: replacing sink with a procedure store such that store(v, x) is equivalent to sink(x) $\leftarrow v$.

not repeatable: A call to successor must separate two assignments through an iterator. The asymmetry between readable and writable iterators is intentional: It does not seem to eliminate useful algorithms, and it allows models, such as output streams, that are not buffered. Nonregular successor in the *Iterator* concept and nonregular sink enable algorithms to be used with input and output streams and not just in-memory data structures.

A range of iterators from a type modeling *Mutable* and *ForwardIterator* is *mutable* if sink, and thus source and deref, are defined on all the iterators in the range. Only multipass algorithms both read from and write to the same range. Thus for mutable ranges we require at least forward iterators and we drop the requirement that two assignments to an iterator must be separated by a call to successor:

> **property**(I : *Mutable*)
>   **requires**(*ForwardIterator*(I))
> mutable_bounded_range : I × I
>   (f, l) ↦ bounded_range(f, l) ∧ (∀i ∈ [f, l)) sink(i) is defined

mutable_weak_range and mutable_counted_range are defined similarly.

9.2 Position-Based Copying

We present a family of algorithms for copying objects from one or more input ranges to one or more output ranges. In general, the postconditions of these algorithms specify equality between objects in output ranges and the original values of objects in input ranges. When input and output ranges do not *overlap*, it is straightforward to establish the desired postcondition. It is, however, often useful to copy objects between overlapping ranges, so the precondition of each algorithm specifies what kind of overlap is allowed.

The basic rule for overlap is that if an iterator within an input range is aliased with an iterator within an output range, the algorithm may not apply source to the input iterator after applying sink to the output iterator. We develop precise conditions, and general properties to express them, as we present the algorithms.

The machines from which we compose the copying algorithms all take two iterators by reference and are responsible for both copying and updating the iterators. The most frequently used machine copies one object and then increments both iterators:

```
template<typename I, typename O>
    requires(Readable(I) && Iterator(I) &&
        Writable(O) && Iterator(O) &&
```

```
          ValueType(I) == ValueType(O))
void copy_step(I& f_i, O& f_o)
{
```
    // *Precondition:* source(f_i) *and* sink(f_o) *are defined*
```
    sink(f_o) = source(f_i);
    f_i = successor(f_i);
    f_o = successor(f_o);
}
```

The general form of the copy algorithms is to perform a copying step until the termination condition is satisfied. For example, copy copies a half-open bounded range to an output range specified by its first iterator:

```
template<typename I, typename O>
    requires(Readable(I) && Iterator(I) &&
        Writable(O) && Iterator(O) &&
        ValueType(I) == ValueType(O))
O copy(I f_i, I l_i, O f_o)
{
```
    // *Precondition:* not_overlapped_forward($f_i, l_i, f_o, f_o + (l_i - f_i)$)
```
    while (f_i != l_i) copy_step(f_i, f_o);
    return f_o;
}
```

copy returns the limit of the output range because it might not be known to the caller. The output iterator type might not allow multiple traversals, in which case if the limit were not returned, it would not be recoverable.

The postcondition for copy is that the sequence of values in the output range is equal to the original sequence of values in the input range. In order to satisfy this postcondition, the precondition must ensure readability and writability, respectively, of the input and output ranges; sufficient size of the output range; and, if the input and output ranges overlap, that no input iterator is read after an aliased output iterator is written. These conditions are formalized with the help of the property not_overlapped_forward. A readable range and a writable range are not *overlapped forward* if any aliased iterators occur at an index within the input range that does not exceed the index in the output range:

property(I : *Readable*, O : *Writable*)
    requires(*Iterator*(I) $\land$ *Iterator*(O))

not_overlapped_forward : $I \times I \times O \times O$
$\qquad$ $(f_i, l_i, f_o, l_o) \mapsto$
$\qquad\qquad$ readable_bounded_range$(f_i, l_i) \wedge$
$\qquad\qquad$ writable_bounded_range$(f_o, l_o) \wedge$
$\qquad\qquad$ $(\forall k_i \in [f_i, l_i))(\forall k_o \in [f_o, l_o))$
$\qquad\qquad\qquad$ aliased$(k_o, k_i) \Rightarrow k_i - f_i \le k_o - f_o$

Sometimes, the sizes of the input and output ranges may be different:

```
template<typename I, typename O>
    requires(Readable(I) && Iterator(I) &&
        Writable(O) && Iterator(O) &&
        ValueType(I) == ValueType(O))
pair<I, O> copy_bounded(I f_i, I l_i, O f_o, O l_o)
{
    // Precondition: not_overlapped_forward(f_i, l_i, f_o, l_o)
    while (f_i != l_i && f_o != l_o) copy_step(f_i, f_o);
    return pair<I, O>(f_i, f_o);
}
```

While the ends of both ranges are known to the caller, returning the pair allows the caller to determine which range is smaller and where in the larger range copying stopped. Compared to copy, the output precondition is weakened: The output range could be shorter than the input range. One could even argue that the weakest precondition should be

$$\text{not\_overlapped\_forward}(f_i, f_i + n, f_o, f_o + n)$$

where $n = \min(l_i - f_i, l_o - f_o)$.

This auxiliary machine handles the termination condition for counted ranges:

```
template<typename N>
    requires(Integer(N))
bool count_down(N& n)
{
    // Precondition: n ≥ 0
    if (zero(n)) return false;
    n = predecessor(n);
    return true;
}
```

copy_n copies a half-open counted range to an output range specified by its first iterator:

```
template<typename I, typename O, typename N>
    requires(Readable(I) && Iterator(I) &&
        Writable(O) && Iterator(O) &&
        ValueType(I) == ValueType(O) &&
        Integer(N))
pair<I, O> copy_n(I f_i, N n, O f_o)
{
    // Precondition: not_overlapped_forward(f_i, f_{i+n}, f_o, f_{o+n})
    while (count_down(n)) copy_step(f_i, f_o);
    return pair<I, O>(f_i, f_o);
}
```

The effect of copy_bounded for two counted ranges is obtained by calling copy_n with the minimum of the two sizes.

When ranges overlap forward, it still is possible to copy if the iterator types model *BidirectionalIterator* and thus allow backward movement. That leads to the next machine:

```
template<typename I, typename O>
    requires(Readable(I) && BidirectionalIterator(I) &&
        Writable(O) && BidirectionalIterator(O) &&
        ValueType(I) == ValueType(O))
void copy_backward_step(I& l_i, O& l_o)
{
    // Precondition: source(predecessor(l_i)) and sink(predecessor(l_o))
    //                        are defined
    l_i = predecessor(l_i);
    l_o = predecessor(l_o);
    sink(l_o) = source(l_i);
}
```

Since we deal with half-open ranges and start at the limit, we need to decrement before copying, which leads to copy_backward:

```
template<typename I, typename O>
    requires(Readable(I) && BidirectionalIterator(I) &&
        Writable(O) && BidirectionalIterator(O) &&
```

```
                ValueType(I) == ValueType(O))
O copy_backward(I f_i, I l_i, O l_o)
{
        // Precondition: not_overlapped_backward(f_i, l_i, l_o - (l_i - f_i), l_o)
        while (f_i != l_i) copy_backward_step(l_i, l_o);
        return l_o;
}
```

copy_backward_n is similar.

The postcondition for copy_backward is analogous to copy and is formalized with the help of the property not_overlapped_backward. A readable range and a writable range are not *overlapped backward* if any aliased iterators occur at an index from the limit of the input range that does not exceed the index from the limit of the output range:

property(I : *Readable*, O : *Writable*)
   requires(*Iterator*(I) $\land$ *Iterator*(O))
not_overlapped_backward : I $\times$ I $\times$ O $\times$ O
   $(f_i, l_i, f_o, l_o) \mapsto$
      readable_bounded_range$(f_i, l_i) \land$
      writable_bounded_range$(f_o, l_o) \land$
      $(\forall k_i \in [f_i, l_i))(\forall k_o \in [f_o, l_o))$
         aliased$(k_o, k_i) \Rightarrow l_i - k_i \leq l_o - k_o$

If either of the ranges is of an iterator type modeling *BidirectionalIterator*, we can reverse the direction of the output range with respect to the input range by using a machine that moves backward in the output or one that moves backward in the input:

```
template<typename I, typename O>
    requires(Readable(I) && BidirectionalIterator(I) &&
            Writable(O) && Iterator(O) &&
            ValueType(I) == ValueType(O))
void reverse_copy_step(I& l_i, O& f_o)
{
        // Precondition: source(predecessor(l_i)) and sink(f_o) are defined
        l_i = predecessor(l_i);
        sink(f_o) = source(l_i);
        f_o = successor(f_o);
}
```

```
template<typename I, typename O>
    requires(Readable(I) && Iterator(I) &&
        Writable(O) && BidirectionalIterator(O) &&
        ValueType(I) == ValueType(O))
void reverse_copy_backward_step(I& f_i, O& l_o)
{
```
    // *Precondition:* source(f_i) *and* sink(predecessor(l_o)) *are defined*
```
    l_o = predecessor(l_o);
    sink(l_o) = source(f_i);
    f_i = successor(f_i);
}
```

leading to the following algorithms:

```
template<typename I, typename O>
    requires(Readable(I) && BidirectionalIterator(I) &&
        Writable(O) && Iterator(O) &&
        ValueType(I) == ValueType(O))
O reverse_copy(I f_i, I l_i, O f_o)
{
```
    // *Precondition:* not_overlapped($f_i, l_i, f_o, f_o + (l_i - f_i)$)
```
    while (f_i != l_i) reverse_copy_step(l_i, f_o);
    return f_o;
}
```

```
template<typename I, typename O>
    requires(Readable(I) && Iterator(I) &&
        Writable(O) && BidirectionalIterator(O) &&
        ValueType(I) == ValueType(O))
O reverse_copy_backward(I f_i, I l_i, O l_o)
{
```
    // *Precondition:* not_overlapped($f_i, l_i, l_o - (l_i - f_i), l_o$)
```
    while (f_i != l_i) reverse_copy_backward_step(f_i, l_o);
    return l_o;
}
```

reverse_copy_n and reverse_copy_backward_n are similar.

The postcondition for both reverse_copy and reverse_copy_backward is that the output range is a reversed copy of the original sequence of values of the input range. The practical, but not the weakest, precondition is that the input and output ranges do not overlap, which we formalize with the help of the property not_overlapped. A readable range and a writable range are not *overlapped* if they have no aliased iterators in common:

property(I : *Readable*, O : *Writable*)
  requires(Iterator(I) ∧ Iterator(O))
not_overlapped : $I \times I \times O \times O$
  $(f_i, l_i, f_o, l_o) \mapsto$
    readable_bounded_range(f_i, l_i) ∧
    writable_bounded_range(f_o, l_o) ∧
    $(\forall k_i \in [f_i, l_i)) (\forall k_o \in [f_o, l_o)) \neg$aliased$(k_o, k_i)$

Exercise 9.1   Find the weakest preconditions for reverse_copy and its companion reverse_copy_backward.

While the main reason to introduce copy_backward as well as copy is to handle ranges that are overlapped in either direction, the reason for introducing reverse_copy_backward as well as reverse_copy is to allow greater flexibility in terms of iterator requirements.

9.3 Predicate-Based Copying

The algorithms presented so far copy every object in the input range to the output range, and their postconditions do not depend on the value of any iterator. The algorithms in this section take a predicate argument and use it to control each copying step.

For example, making the copying step conditional on a unary predicate leads to copy_select:

```
template<typename I, typename O, typename P>
    requires(Readable(I) && Iterator(I) &&
        Writable(O) && Iterator(O) &&
        ValueType(I) == ValueType(O) &&
        UnaryPredicate(P) && I == Domain(P))
O copy_select(I f_i, I l_i, O f_t, P p)
{
    // Precondition: not_overlapped_forward(f_i, l_i, f_t, f_t + n_t)
    // where n_t is an upper bound for the number of iterators satisfying p
    while (f_i != l_i)
        if (p(f_i)) copy_step(f_i, f_t);
```

```
        else f_i = successor(f_i);
    return f_t;
}
```

The worst case for n_t is $l_i - f_i$; the context might ensure a smaller value.

In the most common case, the predicate is applied not to the iterator but to its value:

```
template<typename I, typename O, typename P>
    requires(Readable(I) && Iterator(I) &&
        Writable(O) && Iterator(O) &&
        ValueType(I) == ValueType(O) &&
        UnaryPredicate(P) && ValueType(I) == Domain(P))
O copy_if(I f_i, I l_i, O f_t, P p)
{
    // Precondition: same as for copy_select
    predicate_source<I, P> ps(p);
    return copy_select(f_i, l_i, f_t, ps);
}
```

In Chapter 8 we presented split_linked and combine_linked_nonempty operating on linked ranges of iterators. There are analogous copying algorithms:

```
template<typename I, typename O_f, typename O_t, typename P>
    requires(Readable(I) && Iterator(I) &&
        Writable(O_f) && Iterator(O_f) &&
        Writable(O_t) && Iterator(O_t) &&
        ValueType(I) == ValueType(O_f) &&
        ValueType(I) == ValueType(O_t) &&
        UnaryPredicate(P) && I == Domain(P))
pair<O_f, O_t> split_copy(I f_i, I l_i, O_f f_f, O_t f_t,
                          P p)
{
    // Precondition: see below
    while (f_i != l_i)
        if (p(f_i)) copy_step(f_i, f_t);
        else        copy_step(f_i, f_f);
    return pair<O_f, O_t>(f_f, f_t);
}
```

Exercise 9.2 Write the postcondition for split_copy.

To satisfy its postcondition, a call of split_copy must ensure that the two output ranges do not overlap at all. It is permissible for either of the output ranges to overlap the input range as long as they do not overlap forward. This results in the following precondition:

not_write_overlapped(f_f, n_f, f_t, n_t) $\wedge$
   ((not_overlapped_forward(f_i, l_i, f_f, $f_f + n_f$) $\wedge$ not_overlapped(f_i, l_i, f_t, l_t)) $\vee$
   (not_overlapped_forward(f_i, l_i, f_t, $f_t + n_t$) $\wedge$ not_overlapped(f_i, l_i, f_f, l_f)))

where n_f and n_t are upper bounds for the number of iterators not satisfying and satisfying p, respectively.

The definition of the property not_write_overlapped depends on the notion of *write aliasing:* two writable objects x and y such that sink(x) and sink(y) are both defined, and any observer of the effect of writes to x also observes the effect of writes to y:

property(T : *Writable*, U : *Writable*)
   requires(ValueType(T) = ValueType(U))
write_aliased : T $\times$ U
   (x, y) $\mapsto$ sink(x) is defined $\wedge$ sink(y) is defined $\wedge$
      ($\forall$V $\in$ *Readable*) ($\forall v \in$ V) aliased(x, v) $\Leftrightarrow$ aliased(y, v)

That leads to the definition of *not write overlapped*, or writable ranges that have no aliased sinks in common:

property(O_0 : *Writable*, O_1 : *Writable*)
   requires(Iterator(O_0) $\wedge$ Iterator(O_1))
not_write_overlapped : $O_0 \times O_0 \times O_1 \times O_1$
   (f_0, l_0, f_1, l_1) $\mapsto$
      writable_bounded_range(f_0, l_0) $\wedge$
      writable_bounded_range(f_1, l_1) $\wedge$
      ($\forall k_0 \in [f_0, l_0)$)($\forall k_1 \in [f_1, l_1)$) $\neg$write_aliased(k_0, k_1)

As with select_copy, the predicate in the most common case of split_copy is applied not to the iterator but to its value:[2]

```
template<typename I, typename O_f, typename O_t, typename P>
    requires(Readable(I) && Iterator(I) &&
        Writable(O_f) && Iterator(O_f) &&
        Writable(O_t) && Iterator(O_t) &&
        ValueType(I)  == ValueType(O_f) &&
```

---

2. The interface was suggested to us by T. K. Lakshman.

```
              ValueType(I) == ValueType(O_t) &&
              UnaryPredicate(P) && ValueType(I) == Domain(P))
pair<O_f, O_t> partition_copy(I f_i, I l_i, O_f f_f, O_t f_t,
                              P p)
{
    // Precondition: same as split_copy
    predicate_source<I, P> ps(p);
    return split_copy(f_i, l_i, f_f, f_t, ps);
}
```

The values of each of the two output ranges are in the same relative order as in the input range; partition_copy_n is similar.

The code for combine_copy is equally simple:

```
template<typename I0, typename I1, typename O, typename R>
    requires(Readable(I0) && Iterator(I0) &&
        Readable(I1) && Iterator(I1) &&
        Writable(O) && Iterator(O) &&
        BinaryPredicate(R) &&
        ValueType(I0) == ValueType(O) &&
        ValueType(I1) == ValueType(O) &&
        I0 == InputType(R, 1) && I1 == InputType(R, 0))
O combine_copy(I0 f_i0, I0 l_i0, I1 f_i1, I1 l_i1, O f_o, R r)
{
    // Precondition: see below
    while (f_i0 != l_i0 && f_i1 != l_i1)
        if (r(f_i1, f_i0)) copy_step(f_i1, f_o);
        else               copy_step(f_i0, f_o);
    return copy(f_i1, l_i1, copy(f_i0, l_i0, f_o));
}
```

For combine_copy, read overlap between the input ranges is acceptable. Furthermore, it is permissible for one of the input ranges to overlap with the output range, but such overlap cannot be in the forward direction and must be offset in the backward direction by at least the size of the other input range, as described by the property backward_offset used in the precondition of combine_copy:

$$(\text{backward\_offset}(f_{i_0}, l_{i_0}, f_o, l_o, l_{i_1} - f_{i_1}) \land \text{not\_overlapped}(f_{i_1}, l_{i_1}, f_o, l_o)) \lor$$
$$(\text{backward\_offset}(f_{i_1}, l_{i_1}, f_o, l_o, l_{i_0} - f_{i_0}) \land \text{not\_overlapped}(f_{i_0}, l_{i_0}, f_o, l_o))$$

where $l_o = f_o + (l_{i_0} - f_{i_0}) + (l_{i_1} - f_{i_1})$ is the limit of the output range.

The property backward_offset is satisfied by a readable range, a writable range, and an offset $n \geq 0$ if any aliased iterators occur at an index within the input range that, when increased by n, does not exceed the index in the output range:

property$(I : Readable, O : Writable, N : Integer)$
   requires$(Iterator(I) \wedge Iterator(O))$
backward_offset $: I \times I \times O \times O \times N$
   $(f_i, l_i, f_o, l_o, n) \mapsto$
      readable_bounded_range$(f_i, l_i) \wedge$
      $n \geq 0 \wedge$
      writable_bounded_range$(f_o, l_o) \wedge$
      $(\forall k_i \in [f_i, l_i))(\forall k_o \in [f_o, l_o))$
         aliased$(k_o, k_i) \Rightarrow k_i - f_i + n \leq k_o - f_o$

Note that not_overlapped_forward$(f_i, l_i, f_o, l_o) =$ backward_offset$(f_i, l_i, f_o, l_o, 0)$.

Exercise 9.3   Write the postcondition for combine_copy, and prove that it is satisfied whenever the precondition holds.

combine_copy_backward is similar. To ensure that the same postcondition holds, the order of the if clauses must be reversed from the order in combine_copy:

```
template<typename I0, typename I1, typename O, typename R>
    requires(Readable(I0) && BidirectionalIterator(I0) &&
        Readable(I1) && BidirectionalIterator(I1) &&
        Writable(O) && BidirectionalIterator(O) &&
        BinaryPredicate(R) &&
        ValueType(I0) == ValueType(O) &&
        ValueType(I1) == ValueType(O) &&
        I0 == InputType(R, 1) && I1 == InputType(R, 0))
O combine_copy_backward(I0 f_i0, I0 l_i0, I1 f_i1, I1 l_i1,
                        O l_o, R r)
{
    // Precondition: see below
    while (f_i0 != l_i0 && f_i1 != l_i1) {
        if (r(predecessor(l_i1), predecessor(l_i0)))
            copy_backward_step(l_i0, l_o);
        else
            copy_backward_step(l_i1, l_o);
    }
}
```

```
   return copy_backward(f_i0, l_i0,
                        copy_backward(f_i1, l_i1, l_o));
}
```

The precondition for combine_copy_backward is

$$(\text{forward\_offset}(f_{i_0}, l_{i_0}, f_o, l_o, l_{i_1} - f_{i_1}) \wedge \text{not\_overlapped}(f_{i_1}, l_{i_1}, f_o, l_o)) \vee$$
$$(\text{forward\_offset}(f_{i_1}, l_{i_1}, f_o, l_o, l_{i_0} - f_{i_0}) \wedge \text{not\_overlapped}(f_{i_0}, l_{i_0}, f_o, l_o))$$

where $f_o = l_o - (l_{i_0} - f_{i_0}) + (l_{i_1} - f_{i_1})$ is the first iterator of the output range.

The property forward_offset is satisfied by a readable range, a writable range, and an offset $n \geq 0$ if any aliased iterators occur at an index from the limit of the input range that, increased by n, does not exceed the index from the limit of the output range:

property(I : *Readable*, O : *Writable*, N : *Integer*)
   requires(*Iterator*(I) $\wedge$ *Iterator*(O))
forward_offset : I $\times$ I $\times$ O $\times$ O $\times$ N
   $(f_i, l_i, f_o, l_o, n) \mapsto$
      readable_bounded_range$(f_i, l_i) \wedge$
      $n \geq 0 \wedge$
      writable_bounded_range$(f_o, l_o) \wedge$
      $(\forall k_i \in [f_i, l_i))(\forall k_o \in [f_o, l_o))$
         aliased$(k_o, k_i) \Rightarrow l_i - k_i + n \leq l_o - k_o$

Note that not_overlapped_backward(f_i, l_i, f_o, l_o) = forward_offset$(f_i, l_i, f_o, l_o, 0)$.

Exercise 9.4 Write the postcondition for combine_copy_backward, and prove that it is satisfied whenever the precondition holds.

When the forward and backward combining copy algorithms are passed a weak ordering on the the value type, they merge increasing ranges:

```
template<typename I0, typename I1, typename O, typename R>
    requires(Readable(I0) && Iterator(I0) &&
        Readable(I1) && Iterator(I1) &&
        Writable(O) && Iterator(O) &&
        Relation(R) &&
        ValueType(I0) == ValueType(O) &&
```

```
            ValueType(I1) == ValueType(O) &&
            ValueType(I0) == Domain(R))
O merge_copy(I0 f_i0, I0 l_i0, I1 f_i1, I1 l_i1, O f_o, R r)
{
```
    // *Precondition: in addition to that for* combine_copy
    //   weak_ordering(r) $\wedge$
    //   increasing_range(f_{i_0}, l_{i_0}, r) $\wedge$ increasing_range(f_{i_1}, l_{i_1}, r)
```
    relation_source<I1, I0, R> rs(r);
    return combine_copy(f_i0, l_i0, f_i1, l_i1, f_o, rs);
}
template<typename I0, typename I1, typename O, typename R>
    requires(Readable(I0) && BidirectionalIterator(I0) &&
        Readable(I1) && BidirectionalIterator(I1) &&
        Writable(O) && BidirectionalIterator(O) &&
        Relation(R) &&
        ValueType(I0) == ValueType(O) &&
        ValueType(I1) == ValueType(O) &&
        ValueType(I0) == Domain(R))
O merge_copy_backward(I0 f_i0, I0 l_i0, I1 f_i1, I1 l_i1, O l_o,
                      R r)

{
```
    // *Precondition: in addition to that for* combine_copy_backward
    //   weak_ordering(r) $\wedge$
    //   increasing_range(f_{i_0}, l_{i_0}, r) $\wedge$ increasing_range(f_{i_1}, l_{i_1}, r)
```
    relation_source<I1, I0, R> rs(r);
    return combine_copy_backward(f_i0, l_i0, f_i1, l_i1, l_o,
                                 rs);

}
```

Exercise 9.5 Implement combine_copy_n and combine_copy_backward_n with the appropriate return values.

Lemma 9.1 If the sizes of the input ranges are n_0 and n_1, merge_copy and merge_copy_backward perform $n_0 + n_1$ assignments and, in the worst case, $n_0 + n_1 - 1$ comparisons.

Exercise 9.6 Determine the best case and average number of comparisons.

Project 9.1 Modern computing systems include highly optimized library procedures for copying memory; for example, `memmove` and `memcpy`, which use optimization techniques not discussed in this book. Study the procedures provided on your platform, determine the techniques they use (for example, loop unrolling and software pipelining), and design abstract procedures expressing as many of these techniques as possible. What type requirements and preconditions are necessary for each technique? What language extensions would allow a compiler full flexibility to carry out these optimizations?

9.4 Swapping Ranges

Instead of copying one range into another, it is sometimes useful to *swap* two ranges of the same size: to exchange the values of objects in corresponding positions. Swapping algorithms are very similar to copying algorithms, except that assignment is replaced by a procedure that exchanges the values of objects pointed to by two mutable iterators:

```
template<typename I0, typename I1>
    requires(Mutable(I0) && Mutable(I1) &&
        ValueType(I0) == ValueType(I1))
void exchange_values(I0 x, I1 y)
{
    // Precondition: deref(x) and deref(y) are defined
    ValueType(I0) t = source(x);
            sink(x) = source(y);
            sink(y) = t;
}
```

Exercise 9.7 What is the postcondition of `exchange_values`?

Lemma 9.2 The effects of `exchange_values(i, j)` and `exchange_values(j, i)` are equivalent.

We would like the implementation of `exchange_values` to avoid actually constructing or destroying any objects but simply to exchange the values of two objects, so that its cost does not increase with the amount of resources owned by the objects. We accomplish this goal in Chapter 12 with a notion of *underlying type*.

As with copying, we construct the swapping algorithms from machines that take two iterators by reference and are responsible for both exchanging and updating the iterators. One machine exchanges two objects and then increments both iterators:

```
template<typename I0, typename I1>
    requires(Mutable(I0) && ForwardIterator(I0) &&
        Mutable(I1) && ForwardIterator(I1) &&
        ValueType(I0) == ValueType(I1))
void swap_step(I0& f0, I1& f1)
{
```
      // *Precondition:* deref(f_0) *and* deref(f_1) *are defined*
```
    exchange_values(f0, f1);
    f0 = successor(f0);
    f1 = successor(f1);
}
```

This leads to the first algorithm, which is analogous to copy:

```
template<typename I0, typename I1>
    requires(Mutable(I0) && ForwardIterator(I0) &&
        Mutable(I1) && ForwardIterator(I1) &&
        ValueType(I0) == ValueType(I1))
I1 swap_ranges(I0 f0, I0 l0, I1 f1)
{
```
      // *Precondition:* mutable_bounded_range(f_0, l_0)
      // *Precondition:* mutable_counted_range(f_1, $l_0 - f_0$)
```
    while (f0 != l0) swap_step(f0, f1);
    return f1;
}
```

The second algorithm is analogous to copy_bounded:

```
template<typename I0, typename I1>
    requires(Mutable(I0) && ForwardIterator(I0) &&
        Mutable(I1) && ForwardIterator(I1) &&
        ValueType(I0) == ValueType(I1))
pair<I0, I1> swap_ranges_bounded(I0 f0, I0 l0, I1 f1, I1 l1)
{
```
      // *Precondition:* mutable_bounded_range(f_0, l_0)

```
    // Precondition: mutable_bounded_range(f1, l1)
    while (f0 != l0 && f1 != l1) swap_step(f0, f1);
    return pair<I0, I1>(f0, f1);
}
```

The third algorithm is analogous to copy_n:

```
template<typename I0, typename I1, typename N>
    requires(Mutable(I0) && ForwardIterator(I0) &&
        Mutable(I1) && ForwardIterator(I1) &&
        ValueType(I0) == ValueType(I1) &&
        Integer(N))
pair<I0, I1> swap_ranges_n(I0 f0, I1 f1, N n)
{
    // Precondition: mutable_counted_range(f0, n)
    // Precondition: mutable_counted_range(f1, n)
    while (count_down(n)) swap_step(f0, f1);
    return pair<I0, I1>(f0, f1);
}
```

When the ranges passed to the range-swapping algorithms do not overlap, it is apparent that their effect is to exchange the values of objects in corresponding positions. In the next chapter, we derive the postcondition for the overlapping case.

Reverse copying results in a copy in which positions are reversed from the original; reverse swapping is analogous. It requires a second machine, which moves backward in the first range and forward in the second range:

```
template<typename I0, typename I1>
    requires(Mutable(I0) && BidirectionalIterator(I0) &&
        Mutable(I1) && ForwardIterator(I1) &&
        ValueType(I0) == ValueType(I1))
void reverse_swap_step(I0& l0, I1& f1)
{
    // Precondition: deref(predecessor(l0)) and deref(f1) are defined
    l0 = predecessor(l0);
    exchange_values(l0, f1);
    f1 = successor(f1);
}
```

Because of the symmetry of exchange_values, reverse_swap_ranges can be used whenever at least one iterator type is bidirectional; no backward versions are needed:

```
template<typename I0, typename I1>
    requires(Mutable(I0) && BidirectionalIterator(I0) &&
        Mutable(I1) && ForwardIterator(I1) &&
        ValueType(I0) == ValueType(I1))
I1 reverse_swap_ranges(I0 f0, I0 l0, I1 f1)
{
    // Precondition: mutable_bounded_range(f0, l0)
    // Precondition: mutable_counted_range(f1, l0 − f0)
    while (f0 != l0) reverse_swap_step(l0, f1);
    return f1;
}
```

```
template<typename I0, typename I1>
    requires(Mutable(I0) && BidirectionalIterator(I0) &&
        Mutable(I1) && ForwardIterator(I1) &&
        ValueType(I0) == ValueType(I1))
pair<I0, I1>reverse_swap_ranges_bounded(I0 f0, I0 l0,
                                        I1 f1, I1 l1)
{
    // Precondition: mutable_bounded_range(f0, l0)
    // Precondition: mutable_bounded_range(f1, l1)
    while (f0 != l0 && f1 != l1)
        reverse_swap_step(l0, f1);
    return pair<I0, I1>(l0, f1);
}
```

```
template<typename I0, typename I1, typename N>
    requires(Mutable(I0) && BidirectionalIterator(I0) &&
        Mutable(I1) && ForwardIterator(I1) &&
        ValueType(I0) == ValueType(I1) &&
        Integer(N))
pair<I0, I1> reverse_swap_ranges_n(I0 l0, I1 f1, N n)
{
    // Precondition: mutable_counted_range(l0 − n, n)
```

```
// Precondition: mutable_counted_range(f₁, n)
while (count_down(n)) reverse_swap_step(l0, f1);
return pair<I0, I1>(l0, f1);
}
```

9.5 Conclusions

Extending an iterator type with sink leads to writability and mutability. Although the axiom for sink is simple, the issues of aliasing and of concurrent updates—which this book does not treat—make imperative programming complicated. In particular, defining preconditions that deal with aliasing through different iterator types requires great care. Copying algorithms are simple, powerful, and widely used. Composing these algorithms from simple machines helps to organize them into a family by identifying commonalities and suggesting additional variations. Using value exchange instead of value assignment leads to an analogous but slightly smaller family of useful range-swapping algorithms.

Chapter 10

Rearrangements

T *his chapter introduces the concept of permutation and a taxonomy for a class of algorithms, called rearrangements, that permute the elements of a range to satisfy a given postcondition. We provide iterative algorithms of reverse for bidirectional and random-access iterators, and a divide-and-conquer algorithm for reverse on forward iterators. We show how to transform divide-and-conquer algorithms to make them run faster when extra memory is available. We describe three rotation algorithms corresponding to different iterator concepts, where rotation is the interchange of two adjacent ranges of not necessarily equal size. We conclude with a discussion of how to package algorithms for compile-time selection based on their requirements.*

10.1 Permutations

A transformation f is an *into* transformation if, for all x in its definition space, there exists a y in its definition space such that $y = f(x)$. A transformation f is an *onto* transformation if, for all y in its definition space, there exists an x in its definition space such that $y = f(x)$. A transformation f is a *one-to-one* transformation if, for all x, x′ in its definition space, $f(x) = f(x') \Rightarrow x = x'$.

Lemma 10.1 A transformation on a finite definition space is an onto transformation if and only if it is both an into and one-to-one transformation.

Exercise 10.1 Find a transformation of the natural numbers that is both an into and onto transformation but not a one-to-one transformation, and one that is both an into and one-to-one transformation but not an onto transformation.

A *fixed point* of a transformation is an element x such that $f(x) = x$. An *identity transformation* is one that has every element of its definition space as a fixed point. We denote the identity transformation on a set S as $identity_S$.

A *permutation* is an onto transformation on a finite definition space. An example of a permutation on $[0, 6)$:

$$p(0) = 5$$
$$p(1) = 2$$
$$p(2) = 4$$
$$p(3) = 3$$
$$p(4) = 1$$
$$p(5) = 0$$

If p and q are two permutations on a set S, the *composition* $q \circ p$ takes $x \in S$ to $q(p(x))$.

Lemma 10.2   The composition of permutations is a permutation.

Lemma 10.3   Composition of permutations is associative.

Lemma 10.4   For every permutation p on a set S, there is an *inverse permutation* p^{-1} such that $p^{-1} \circ p = p \circ p^{-1} = identity_S$.

The permutations on a set form a group under composition.

Lemma 10.5   Every finite group is a subgroup of a permutation group of its elements, where every permutation in the subgroup is generated by multiplying all the elements by an individual element.

For example, the multiplication group modulo 5 has the following multiplication table:

×	1	2	3	4
1	1	2	3	4
2	2	4	1	3
3	3	1	4	2
4	4	3	2	1

Every row and column of the multiplication table is a permutation. Since not every one of the $4! = 24$ permutations of four elements appears in it, the multiplication group modulo 5 is therefore a proper subgroup of the permutation group of four elements.

A *cycle* is a circular orbit within a permutation. A *trivial cycle* is one with a cycle size of 1; the element in a trivial cycle is a fixed point. A permutation containing a single nontrivial cycle is called a *cyclic permutation*. A *transposition* is a cyclic permutation with a cycle size of 2.

Lemma 10.6   Every element in a permutation belongs to a unique cycle.

Lemma 10.7   Any permutation of a set with n elements contains $k \leq n$ cycles.

Lemma 10.8   Disjoint cyclic permutations commute.

Exercise 10.2   Show an example of two nondisjoint cyclic permutations that do not commute.

Lemma 10.9   Every permutation can be represented as a product of the cyclic permutations corresponding to its cycles.

Lemma 10.10   The inverse of a permutation is the product of the inverses of its cycles.

Lemma 10.11   Every cyclic permutation is a product of transpositions.

Lemma 10.12   Every permutation is a product of transpositions.

A *finite set* S of size n is a set for which there exists a pair of functions

$$\text{choose}_S : [0, n) \rightarrow S$$
$$\text{index}_S : S \rightarrow [0, n)$$

satisfying

$$\text{choose}_S(\text{index}_S(x)) = x$$
$$\text{index}_S(\text{choose}_S(i)) = i$$

In other words, S can be put into one-to-one correspondence with a range of natural numbers.

If p is a permutation on a finite set S of size n, there is a corresponding *index permutation* p' on $[0, n)$ defined as

$$p'(i) = index_S(p(choose_S(i)))$$

Lemma 10.13 $p(x) = choose_S(p'(index_S(x)))$

We will frequently define permutations by the corresponding index permutations.

10.2 Rearrangements

A *rearrangement* is an algorithm that copies the objects from an input range to an output range such that the mapping between the indices of the input and output ranges is a permutation. This chapter deals with *position-based* rearrangements, where the destination of a value depends only on its original position and not on the value itself. The next chapter deals with *predicate-based* rearrangements, where the destination of a value depends only on the result of applying a predicate to a value, and *ordering-based* rearrangements, where the destination of a value depends only on the ordering of values.

In Chapter 8 we studied link rearrangements, such as reverse_linked, where links are modified to establish a rearrangement. In Chapter 9 we studied copying rearrangements, such as copy and reverse_copy. In this and the next chapter we study *mutative* rearrangements, where the input and output ranges are identical.

Every mutative rearrangement corresponds to two permutations: a *to-permutation* mapping an iterator i to the iterator pointing to the destination of the element at i and a *from-permutation* mapping an iterator i to the iterator pointing to the origin of the element moved to i.

Lemma 10.14   The to-permutation and from-permutation for a rearrangement are inverses of each other.

If the to-permutation is known, we can rearrange a cycle with this algorithm:

```
template<typename I, typename F>
    requires(Mutable(I) && Transformation(F) && I == Domain(F))
void cycle_to(I i, F f)
{
    // Precondition: The orbit of i under f is circular
    // Precondition: (∀n ∈ ℕ) deref(fⁿ(i)) is defined
```

```
    I k = f(i);
    while (k != i) {
        exchange_values(i, k);
        k = f(k);
    }
}
```

After cycle_to(i, f), the value of source(f(j)) and the original value of source(j) are equal for all j in the orbit of i under f. The call performs $3(n - 1)$ assignments for a cycle of size n.

Exercise 10.3 Implement a version of cycle_to that performs $2n - 1$ assignments.

If the from-permutation is known, we can rearrange a cycle with this algorithm:

```
template<typename I, typename F>
    requires(Mutable(I) && Transformation(F) && I == Domain(F))
void cycle_from(I i, F f)
{
    // Precondition: The orbit of i under f is circular
    // Precondition: (∀n ∈ ℕ) deref(fⁿ(i)) is defined
    ValueType(I) tmp = source(i);
    I j = i;
    I k = f(i);
    while (k != i) {
        sink(j) = source(k);
        j = k;
        k = f(k);
    }
    sink(j) = tmp;
}
```

After cycle_from(i, f), the value of source(j) and the original value of source(f(j)) are equal for all j in the orbit of i under f. The call performs $n + 1$ assignments, whereas implementing it with exchange_values would perform $3(n - 1)$ assignments. Observe that we require only mutability on the type I; we do not need any traversal functions, because the transformation f performs the traversal. In addition to the from-permutation, implementing a mutative rearrangement using cycle_from requires a way to obtain a representative element from each cycle. In some cases the cycle structure and representatives of the cycles are known.

Exercise 10.4 Implement an algorithm that performs an arbitrary rearrangement of a range of indexed iterators. Use an array of n Boolean values to mark elements as they are placed, and scan this array for an unmarked value to determine a representive of the next cycle.

Exercise 10.5 Assuming iterators with total ordering, design an algorithm that uses constant storage to determine whether an iterator is a representative for a cycle; use this algorithm to implement an arbitrary rearrangement.

Lemma 10.15 Given a from-permutation, it is possible to perform a mutative rearrangement using $n + c_N - c_T$ assignments, where n is the number of elements, c_N the number of nontrivial cycles, and c_T the number of trivial cycles.

10.3 Reverse Algorithms

A simple but useful position-based mutative rearrangement is reversing a range. This rearrangement is induced by the *reverse permutation* on a finite set with n elements, which is defined by the index permutation

$$p(i) = (n - 1) - i$$

Lemma 10.16 The number of nontrivial cycles in a reverse permutation is $\lfloor n/2 \rfloor$; the number of trivial cycles is $n \bmod 2$.

Lemma 10.17 $\lfloor n/2 \rfloor$ is the largest possible number of nontrivial cycles in a permutation.

The definition of reverse directly gives the following algorithm for indexed iterators:[1]

```
template<typename I>
    requires(Mutable(I) && IndexedIterator(I))
```

---

1. A reverse algorithm could return the range of elements that were not moved: the middle element when the size of the range is odd or the empty range between the two "middle" elements when the size of the range is even. We do not know of an example when this return value is useful and, therefore, return void. Of course, for versions taking a counted range of forward iterators, it is useful to return the limit.

```
void reverse_n_indexed(I f, DistanceType(I) n)
{
    // Precondition: mutable_counted_range(f, n)
    DistanceType(I) i(0);
    n = predecessor(n);
    while (i < n) {
        // n = (n_original − 1) − i
        exchange_values(f + i, f + n);
        i = successor(i);
        n = predecessor(n);
    }
}
```

If the algorithm is used with forward or bidirectional iterators, it performs a quadratic number of iterator increments. For bidirectional iterators, two tests per iteration are required:

```
template<typename I>
    requires(Mutable(I) && BidirectionalIterator(I))
void reverse_bidirectional(I f, I l)
{
    // Precondition: mutable_bounded_range(f, l)
    while (true) {
        if (f == l) return;
        l = predecessor(l);
        if (f == l) return;
        exchange_values(f, l);
        f = successor(f);
    }
}
```

When the size of the range is known, reverse_swap_ranges_n can be used:

```
template<typename I>
    requires(Mutable(I) && BidirectionalIterator(I))
void reverse_n_bidirectional(I f, I l, DistanceType(I) n)
{
    // Precondition: mutable_bounded_range(f, l) ∧ 0 ≤ n ≤ l − f
    reverse_swap_ranges_n(l, f, half_nonnegative(n));
}
```

The order of the first two arguments to reverse_swap_ranges_n is determined by the fact that it moves backward in the first range. Passing $n < l - f$ to reverse_n_bidirectional leaves values in the middle in their original positions.

When a data structure provides forward iterators, they are sometimes linked iterators, in which case reverse_linked can be used. In other cases extra buffer memory may be available, allowing the following algorithm to be used:

```
template<typename I, typename B>
    requires(Mutable(I) && ForwardIterator(I) &&
        Mutable(B) && BidirectionalIterator(B) &&
        ValueType(I) == ValueType(B))
I reverse_n_with_buffer(I f_i, DistanceType(I) n, B f_b)
{
    // Precondition: mutable_counted_range(f_i, n)
    // Precondition: mutable_counted_range(f_b, n)
    return reverse_copy(f_b, copy_n(f_i, n, f_b).m1, f_i);
}
```

reverse_n_with_buffer performs $2n$ assignments.

We will use this approach of copying to a buffer and back for other rearrangements.

If no buffer memory is available but logarithmic storage is available as stack space, a divide-and-conquer algorithm is possible: Split the range into two parts, reverse each part, and, finally, interchange the parts with swap_ranges_n.

Lemma 10.18 Splitting as evenly as possible minimizes the work.

Returning the limit allows us to optimize traversal to the midpoint by using the technique we call *auxiliary computation during recursion:*

```
template<typename I>
    requires(Mutable(I) && ForwardIterator(I))
I reverse_n_forward(I f, DistanceType(I) n)
{
    // Precondition: mutable_counted_range(f, n)
    typedef DistanceType(I) N;
    if (n < N(2)) return f + n;
    N h = half_nonnegative(n);
    N n_mod_2 = n - twice(h);
```

```
    I m = reverse_n_forward(f, h) + n_mod_2;
    I l = reverse_n_forward(m, h);
    swap_ranges_n(f, m, h);
    return l;
}
```

The correctness of reverse_n_forward depends on the following.

Lemma 10.19 The reverse permutation on $[0, n)$ is the only permutation satisfying $i < j \Rightarrow p(j) < p(i)$.

This condition obviously holds for ranges of size 1. The recursive calls inductively establish that the condition holds within each half. The condition between the halves and the skipped middle element, if any, is reestablished with swap_ranges_n.

Lemma 10.20 For a range of length $n = \sum_{i=0}^{\lfloor \log n \rfloor} a_i 2^i$, where a_i is the ith digit in the binary representation of n, the number of assignments is $\frac{3}{2} \sum_{i=0}^{\lfloor \log n \rfloor} a_i i 2^i$.

reverse_n_forward requires a logarithmic amount of space for the call stack. A *memory-adaptive* algorithm uses as much additional space as it can acquire to maximize performance. A few percent of additional space gives a large performance improvement. That leads to the following algorithm, which uses divide and conquer and switches to the linear-time reverse_n_with_buffer whenever the subproblem fits into the buffer:

```
template<typename I, typename B>
    requires(Mutable(I) && ForwardIterator(I) &&
        Mutable(B) && BidirectionalIterator(B) &&
        ValueType(I) == ValueType(B))
I reverse_n_adaptive(I f_i, DistanceType(I) n_i,
                     B f_b, DistanceType(I) n_b)
{
    // Precondition: mutable_counted_range(f_i, n_i)
    // Precondition: mutable_counted_range(f_b, n_b)
    typedef DistanceType(I) N;
    if (n_i < N(2))
        return f_i + n_i;
    if (n_i <= n_b)
```

```
      return reverse_n_with_buffer(f_i, n_i, f_b);
  N h_i = half_nonnegative(n_i);
  N n_mod_2 = n_i - twice(h_i);
  I m_i = reverse_n_adaptive(f_i, h_i, f_b, n_b) + n_mod_2;
  I l_i = reverse_n_adaptive(m_i, h_i, f_b, n_b);
  swap_ranges_n(f_i, m_i, h_i);
  return l_i;
}
```

Exercise 10.6   Derive a formula for the number of assignments performed by reverse_n_adaptive for given range and buffer sizes.

10.4 Rotate Algorithms

The permutation p of n elements defined by an index permutation $p(i) = (i + k)$ mod n is called the k-*rotation*.

Lemma 10.21   The inverse of a k-rotation of n elements is an $(n - k)$-rotation.

An element with index i is in the cycle

$$\{i, (i + k) \bmod n, (i + 2k) \bmod n, \ldots\} = \{(i + uk) \bmod n\}$$

The length of the cycle is the smallest positive integer m such that

$$i = (i + mk) \bmod n$$

This is equivalent to $mk \bmod n = 0$, which shows the length of the cycle to be independent of i. Since m is the smallest positive number such that $mk \bmod n = 0$, $\mathrm{lcm}(k, n) = mk$. Using the standard identity

$$\mathrm{lcm}(a, b)\,\gcd(a, b) = ab$$

we obtain that the size of the cycle is

$$m = \frac{\mathrm{lcm}(k, n)}{k} = \frac{kn}{\gcd(k, n)k} = \frac{n}{\gcd(k, n)}$$

The number of cycles, therefore, is $\gcd(k, n)$.

Consider two elements in a cycle: $(i + uk) \bmod n$ and $(i + vk) \bmod n$. The distance between them is

$$|(i + uk) \bmod n - (i + vk) \bmod n| = (u - v)k \bmod n$$
$$= (u - v)k - pn$$

where $p = \text{quotient}((u - v)k, n)$. Since both k and n are divisible by $d = \gcd(k, n)$, so is the distance. Therefore the distance between different elements in the same cycle is at least d, and elements with indices in $[0, d)$ belong to disjoint cycles.

k-rotation rearrangement of a range $[f, l)$ is equivalent to interchanging the relative positions of the values in the subranges $[f, m)$ and $[m, l)$, where $m = f + ((l - f) - k) = l - k$. m is a more useful input than k. When forward or bidirectional iterators are involved, it avoids performing linear-time operations to compute m from k. Returning the iterator $m' = f + k$ pointing to the new position of the element at f is useful for many other algorithms.[2]

Lemma 10.22 Rotating a range $[f, l)$ around the iterator m and then rotating it around the returned value m' returns m and restores the range to its original state.

We can use cycle_from to implement a k-rotation rearrangement of a range of indexed or random-access iterators. The to-permutation is $p(i) = (i+k) \bmod n$, and the from-permutation is its inverse: $p^{-1}(i) = (i+(n-k)) \bmod n$, where $n-k = m-f$. We want to avoid evaluating mod, and we observe that

$$p^{-1}(i) = \begin{cases} i + (n - k) & \text{if } i < k \\ i - k & \text{if } i \geq k \end{cases}$$

That leads to the following function object for random-access iterators:

```
template<typename I>
    requires(RandomAccessIterator(I))
struct k_rotate_from_permutation_random_access
{
    DistanceType(I) k;
    DistanceType(I) n_minus_k;
```

---

2. Joseph Tighe suggests returning a pair, m and m', in the order constituting a valid range; although it is an interesting suggestion and preserves all the information, we do not yet know of a compelling use of such an interface.

```
    I m_prime;
    k_rotate_from_permutation_random_access(I f, I m, I l) :
        k(l - m), n_minus_k(m - f), m_prime(f + (l - m))
    {
        // Precondition: bounded_range(f, l) ∧ m ∈ [f, l)
    }
    I operator()(I x)
    {
        // Precondition: x ∈ [f, l)
        if (x < m_prime) return x + n_minus_k;
        else             return x - k;
    }
};
```

For indexed iterators, the absence of natural ordering and subtraction of a distance from an iterator costs an extra addition or two:

```
template<typename I>
    requires(IndexedIterator(I))
struct k_rotate_from_permutation_indexed
{
    DistanceType(I) k;
    DistanceType(I) n_minus_k;
    I f;
    k_rotate_from_permutation_indexed(I f, I m, I l) :
        k(l - m), n_minus_k(m - f), f(f)
    {
        // Precondition: bounded_range(f, l) ∧ m ∈ [f, l)
    }
    I operator()(I x)
    {
        // Precondition: x ∈ [f, l)
        DistanceType(I) i = x - f;
        if (i < k) return x + n_minus_k;
        else       return f + (i - k);
    }
};
```

This procedure rotates every cycle:

```
template<typename I, typename F>
    requires(Mutable(I) && IndexedIterator(I) &&
        Transformation(F) && I == Domain(F))
I rotate_cycles(I f, I m, I l, F from)
{
    // Precondition: mutable_bounded_range(f, l) ∧ m ∈ [f, l]
    // Precondition: from is a from-permutation on [f, l)
    typedef DistanceType(I) N;
    N d = gcd<N, N>(m - f, l - m);
    while (count_down(d)) cycle_from(f + d, from);
    return f + (l - m);
}
```

This algorithm was first published in Fletcher and Silver [1966] except that they used cycle_to where we use cycle_from. These procedures select the appropriate function object:

```
template<typename I>
    requires(Mutable(I) && IndexedIterator(I))
I rotate_indexed_nontrivial(I f, I m, I l)
{
    // Precondition: mutable_bounded_range(f, l) ∧ f ≺ m ≺ l
    k_rotate_from_permutation_indexed<I> p(f, m, l);
    return rotate_cycles(f, m, l, p);
}
```

```
template<typename I>
    requires(Mutable(I) && RandomAccessIterator(I))
I rotate_random_access_nontrivial(I f, I m, I l)
{
    // Precondition: mutable_bounded_range(f, l) ∧ f ≺ m ≺ l
    k_rotate_from_permutation_random_access<I> p(f, m, l);
    return rotate_cycles(f, m, l, p);
}
```

The number of assignments is $n + c_N - c_T = n + \gcd(n, k)$. Recall that n is the number of elements, c_N the number of nontrivial cycles, and c_T the number of trivial cycles. The expected value of gcd(n, k) for $1 \leq n, k \leq m$ is $\frac{6}{\pi^2} \ln m + C + O(\frac{\ln m}{\sqrt{m}})$ (see Diaconis and Erdös [2004]).

The following property leads to a rotation algorithm for bidirectional iterators.

Lemma 10.23   The k-rotation on $[0, n)$ is the only permutation p that inverts the relative ordering between the subranges $[0, n-k)$ and $[n-k, n)$ but preserves the relative ordering within each subrange:

1. $i < n - k \land n - k \leq j < n \Rightarrow p(j) < p(i)$
2. $i < j < n - k \lor n - k \leq i < j \Rightarrow p(i) < p(j)$

The reverse rearrangement satisfies condition 1 but not 2. Applying reverse to subranges $[0, n - k)$ and $[n - k, n)$ and then applying reverse to the entire range will satisfy both conditions:

```
reverse_bidirectional(f, m);
reverse_bidirectional(m, l);
reverse_bidirectional(f, l);
```

Finding the return value m' is handled by using reverse_swap_ranges_bounded:[3]

```
template<typename I>
    requires(Mutable(I) && BidirectionalIterator(I))
I rotate_bidirectional_nontrivial(I f, I m, I l)
{
    // Precondition: mutable_bounded_range(f, l) ∧ f ≺ m ≺ l
    reverse_bidirectional(f, m);
    reverse_bidirectional(m, l);
    pair<I, I> p = reverse_swap_ranges_bounded(m, l, f, m);
    reverse_bidirectional(p.m1, p.m0);
    if (m == p.m0) return p.m1;
    else           return p.m0;
}
```

Lemma 10.24   The number of assignments is $3(\lfloor n/2 \rfloor + \lfloor k/2 \rfloor + \lfloor (n-k)/2 \rfloor)$, which is $3n$ when both n and k are even and $3(n-2)$ otherwise.

---

3. The use of reverse_swap_ranges_bounded to determine m' was suggested to us by Wilson Ho and Raymond Lo.

Given a range [f, l) and an iterator m in that range, a call

$$p \leftarrow \text{swap\_ranges\_bounded}(f, m, m, l)$$

sets p to a pair of iterators such that

$$p.m0 = m \lor p.m1 = l$$

If $p.m0 = m \land p.m0 = l$, we are done. Otherwise [f, p.m0) are in the final position and, depending on whether $p.m0 = m$ or $p.m1 = l$, we need to rotate [p.m0, l) around p.m1 or m, respectively. This immediately leads to the following algorithm, first published in Gries and Mills [1981]:

```
template<typename I>
    requires(Mutable(I) && ForwardIterator(I))
void rotate_forward_annotated(I f, I m, I l)
{
    // Precondition: mutable_bounded_range(f, l) ∧ f ≺ m ≺ l
                                            DistanceType(I) a = m - f;
                                            DistanceType(I) b = l - m;
    while (true) {
        pair<I, I> p = swap_ranges_bounded(f, m, m, l);
        if (p.m0 == m && p.m1 == l) { assert(a == b);
            return;
        }
        f = p.m0;
        if (f == m) {                       assert(b > a);
            m = p.m1;                       b = b - a;
        } else {                            assert(a > b);
                                            a = a - b;
        }
    }
}
```

Lemma 10.25 The first time the else clause is taken, f = m′, the standard return value for rotate.

The *annotation variables* a and b remain equal to the sizes of the two subranges to be swapped. At the same time, they perform subtractive gcd of the initial sizes.

Each call of exchange_values performed by swap_ranges_bounded puts one value into its final position, except during the final call of swap_ranges_bounded, when each call of exchange_values puts two values into their final positions. Since the final call of swap_ranges_bounded performs gcd(n, k) calls of exchange_values, the total number of calls to exchange_values is n − gcd(n, k).

The previous lemma suggests one way to implement a complete rotate_forward: Create a second copy of the code that saves a copy of f in the `else` clause and then invokes rotate_forward_annotated to complete the rotation. This can be transformed into the following two procedures:

```
template<typename I>
    requires(Mutable(I) && ForwardIterator(I))
void rotate_forward_step(I& f, I& m, I l)
{
    // Precondition: mutable_bounded_range(f, l) ∧ f ≺ m ≺ l
    I c = m;
    do {
        swap_step(f, c);
        if (f == m) m = c;
    } while (c != l);
}


template<typename I>
    requires(Mutable(I) && ForwardIterator(I))
I rotate_forward_nontrivial(I f, I m, I l)
{
    // Precondition: mutable_bounded_range(f, l) ∧ f ≺ m ≺ l
    rotate_forward_step(f, m, l);
    I m_prime = f;
    while (m != l) rotate_forward_step(f, m, l);
    return m_prime;
}
```

Exercise 10.7 Verify that rotate_forward_nontrivial rotates [f, l) around m and returns m′.

Sometimes, it is useful to *partially rotate* a range, moving the correct objects to [f, m′) but leaving the objects in [m′, l) in some rearrangement of the objects originally in [f, m). For example, this can be used to move undesired objects to the end of a sequence in preparation for erasing them. We can accomplish this with the following algorithm:

```
template<typename I>
    requires(Mutable(I) && ForwardIterator(I))
I rotate_partial_nontrivial(I f, I m, I l)
{
    // Precondition: mutable_bounded_range(f, l) ∧ f ≺ m ≺ l
    return swap_ranges(m, l, f);
}
```

Lemma 10.26 The postcondition for rotate_partial_nontrivial is that it performs a partial rotation such that the objects in positions $[m', l)$ are k-rotated where $k = -(l - f) \bmod (m - f)$.

A backward version of rotate_partial_nontrivial that uses a backward version of swap_ranges could be useful sometimes.

When extra buffer memory is available, the following algorithm may be used:

```
template<typename I, typename B>
    requires(Mutable(I) && ForwardIterator(I) &&
        Mutable(B) && ForwardIterator(B))
I rotate_with_buffer_nontrivial(I f, I m, I l, B f_b)
{
    // Precondition: mutable_bounded_range(f, l) ∧ f ≺ m ≺ l
    // Precondition: mutable_counted_range(f_b, l - f)
    B l_b = copy(f, m, f_b);
    I m_prime = copy(m, l, f);
    copy(f_b, l_b, m_prime);
    return m_prime;
}
```

rotate_with_buffer_nontrivial performs $(l - f) + (m - f)$ assignments, whereas the following algorithm performs $(l - f) + (l - m)$ assignments. When rotating a range of bidirectional iterators, the algorithm minimizing the number of assignments could be chosen, although computing the differences at runtime requires a linear number of successor operations:

```
template<typename I, typename B>
    requires(Mutable(I) && BidirectionalIterator(I) &&
        Mutable(B) && ForwardIterator(B))
```

```
I rotate_with_buffer_backward_nontrivial(I f, I m, I l, B f_b)
{
```
    // *Precondition:* mutable_bounded_range(f, l) $\land$ f $\prec$ m $\prec$ l
    // *Precondition:* mutable_counted_range(f_b, l $-$ f)
```
    B l_b = copy(m, l, f_b);
    copy_backward(f, m, l);
    return copy(f_b, l_b, f);
}
```

10.5 Algorithm Selection

In Section 10.3 we presented reverse algorithms with a variety of iterator requirements and procedure signatures, including versions taking counted and bounded
ranges. It is worth defining variations that make the most convenient signatures
available for additional iterator types. For example, an additional constant-time
iterator difference leads to the algorithm for reversing a bounded range of indexed
iterators:

```
template<typename I>
    requires(Mutable(I) && IndexedIterator(I))
void reverse_indexed(I f, I l)
{
```
    // *Precondition:* mutable_bounded_range(f, l)
```
    reverse_n_indexed(f, l - f);
}
```

When a range of forward iterators must be reversed, there is usually enough
extra memory available to allow reverse_n_adaptive to run efficiently. When the size
of the range to be reversed is moderate, it can be obtained in the usual way (for
example, malloc). However, when the size is very large, there might not be enough
available physical memory to allocate a buffer of this size. Because algorithms such
as reverse_n_adaptive run efficiently even when the size of the buffer is small in
proportion to the range being mutated, it is useful for the system to provide a
way to allocate a *temporary buffer.* The allocation may reserve less memory than
requested; in a system with virtual memory, the allocated memory has physical
memory assigned to it. A temporary buffer is intended for short-term use and is
guaranteed to be returned when the algorithm terminates.

For example, the following algorithm uses a type temporary_buffer:

```
template<typename I>
    requires(Mutable(I) && ForwardIterator(I))
void reverse_n_with_temporary_buffer(I f, DistanceType(I) n)
{
    // Precondition: mutable_counted_range(f, n)
    temporary_buffer<ValueType(I)> b(n);
    reverse_n_adaptive(f, n, begin(b), size(b));
}
```

The constructor b(n) allocates memory to hold some number $m \leq n$ adjacent objects of type ValueType(I); size(b) returns the number m, and begin(b) returns an iterator pointing to the beginning of this range. The destructor for b deallocates the memory.

For the same problem, there are often different algorithms for different type requirements. For example, for rotate there are three useful algorithms for indexed (and random access), bidirectional, and forward iterators. It is possible to automatically select from a family of algorithms, based on the requirements the types satisfy. We accomplish this by using a mechanism known as *concept dispatch*. We start by defining a top-level dispatch procedure, which in this case also handles trivial rotates:

```
template<typename I>
    requires(Mutable(I) && ForwardIterator(I))
I rotate(I f, I m, I l)
{
    // Precondition: mutable_bounded_range(f, l) ∧ m ∈ [f, l]
    if (m == f) return l;
    if (m == l) return f;
    return rotate_nontrivial(f, m, l, IteratorConcept(I)());
}
```

The type function IteratorConcept returns a *concept tag type*, a type that encodes the strongest concept modeled by its argument. We then implement a procedure for each concept tag type:

```
template<typename I>
    requires(Mutable(I) && ForwardIterator(I))
```

```
I rotate_nontrivial(I f, I m, I l, forward_iterator_tag)
{
    // Precondition: mutable_bounded_range(f, l) ∧ f ≺ m ≺ l
    return rotate_forward_nontrivial(f, m, l);
}
```

```
template<typename I>
    requires(Mutable(I) && BidirectionalIterator(I))
I rotate_nontrivial(I f, I m, I l, bidirectional_iterator_tag)
{
    // Precondition: mutable_bounded_range(f, l) ∧ f ≺ m ≺ l
    return rotate_bidirectional_nontrivial(f, m, l);
}
```

```
template<typename I>
    requires(Mutable(I) && IndexedIterator(I))
I rotate_nontrivial(I f, I m, I l, indexed_iterator_tag)
{
    // Precondition: mutable_bounded_range(f, l) ∧ f ≺ m ≺ l
    return rotate_indexed_nontrivial(f, m, l);
}
```

```
template<typename I>
    requires(Mutable(I) && RandomAccessIterator(I))
I rotate_nontrivial(I f, I m, I l, random_access_iterator_tag)
{
    // Precondition: mutable_bounded_range(f, l) ∧ f ≺ m ≺ l
    return rotate_random_access_nontrivial(f, m, l);
}
```

Concept dispatch does not take into consideration factors other than type requirements. For example, as summarized in Table 10.1, we can rotate a range of random-access iterators by using three algorithms, each performing a different number of assignments. When the range fits into cache memory, the $n + \gcd(n, k)$ assignments performed by the random-access algorithm give us the best performance. But when the range does not fit into cache, the $3n$ assignments of the bidirectional algorithm or the $3(n - \gcd(n, k))$ assignments of the forward algorithm are faster. In this case additional factors are affecting whether the bidirectional or forward algorithm will be fastest, including the more regular loop structure of the bidirectional

Table 10.1 Number of Assignments Performed
by Rotate Algorithms

Algorithm	Assignments
indexed, random_access	$n + \gcd(n, k)$
bidirectional	$3n$ or $3(n - 2)$
forward	$3(n - \gcd(n, k))$
with_buffer	$n + (n - k)$
with_buffer_backward	$n + k$
partial	$3k$

Note: where $n = l - f$ and $k = l - m$

algorithm, which can make up for the additional assignments it performs, and details
of the processor architecture, such as its cache configuration and prefetch logic. It
should also be noted that the algorithms perform iterator operations in addition to
assignments of the value type; as the size of the value type gets smaller, the relative
cost of these other operations increases.

> **Project 10.1**   Design a benchmark comparing performance of all the algo-
> rithms for different array sizes, element sizes, and rotation amounts. Based
> on the results of the benchmark, design a composite algorithm that appro-
> priately uses one of the rotate algorithms depending on the iterator concept,
> size of the range, amount of rotation, element size, cache size, availability
> of temporary buffer, and other relevant considerations.

> **Project 10.2**   We have presented two kinds of position-based rearrange-
> ment algorithms: reverse and rotate. There are, however, other examples
> of such algorithms in the literature. Develop a taxonomy of position-based
> rearrangements, catalog existing algorithms, discover missing algorithms,
> and produce a library.

10.6 Conclusions

The structure of permutations allows us to design and analyze rearrangement algorithms. Even simple problems, such as reverse and rotate, lead to a variety of
useful algorithms. Selecting the appropriate one depends on iterator requirements
and system issues. Memory-adaptive algorithms provide a practical alternative to
the theoretical notion of in-place algorithms.

Chapter 11

Partition and Merging

*T*his chapter constructs predicate-based and ordering-based rearrangements from components from previous chapters. After presenting partition algorithms for forward and bidirectional iterators, we implement a stable partition algorithm. We then introduce a binary counter mechanism for transforming bottom-up divide-and-conquer algorithms, such as stable partition, into iterative form. We introduce a stable memory-adaptive merge algorithm and use it to construct an efficient memory-adaptive stable sort that works for forward iterators: the weakest concept that allows rearrangements.

11.1 Partition

In Chapter 6 we introduced the notion of a range partitioned by a predicate together with the fundamental algorithm partition_point on such a range. Now we look at algorithms for converting an arbitrary range into a partitioned range.

Exercise 11.1 Implement an algorithm partitioned_at_point that checks whether a given bounded range is partitioned at a specified iterator.

Exercise 11.2 Implement an algorithm potential_partition_point returning the iterator where the partition point would occur after partitioning.

Lemma 11.1 If m = potential_partition_point(f, l, p), then

$$\text{count\_if}(f, m, p) = \text{count\_if\_not}(m, l, p)$$

In other words, the number of misplaced elements on either side of m is the same.

The lemma gives the minimum number of assignments to partition a range, $2n + 1$, where n is the number of misplaced elements on either side of m: $2n$ assignments to misplaced elements and one assignment to a temporary variable.

Lemma 11.2 There are $u!v!$ permutations that partition a range with u false values and v true values.

A partition rearrangement is *stable* if the relative order of the elements not satisfying the predicate is preserved, as is the relative order of the elements satisfying the predicate.

Lemma 11.3 The result of stable partition is unique.

A partition rearrangement is *semistable* if the relative order of elements not satisfying the predicate is preserved. The following algorithm performs a semistable partition:[1]

```
template<typename I, typename P>
    requires(Mutable(I) && ForwardIterator(I) &&
        UnaryPredicate(P) && ValueType(I) == Domain(P))
I partition_semistable(I f, I l, P p)
{
    // Precondition: mutable_bounded_range(f, l)
    I i = find_if(f, l, p);
    if (i == l) return i;
    I j = successor(i);
    while (true) {
        j = find_if_not(j, l, p);
        if (j == l) return i;
        swap_step(i, j);
    }
}
```

The correctness of partition_semistable depends on the following three lemmas.

Lemma 11.4 Before the exit test, none(f, i, p) $\land$ all(i, j, p).

---

1. Bentley [1984, pages 287–291] attributes the algorithm to Nico Lomuto.

Lemma 11.5   After the exit test, $p(\mathsf{source}(i)) \wedge \neg p(\mathsf{source}(j))$.

Lemma 11.6   After the call of swap_step, $\mathsf{none}(f, i, p) \wedge \mathsf{all}(i, j, p)$.

Semistability follows from the fact that the swap_step call moves an element not satisfying the predicate before a range of elements satisfying the predicate, and therefore the order of elements not satisfying the predicate does not change.

partition_semistable uses only one temporary object, in swap_step.

Let $n = l - f$ be the number of elements in the range, and let w be the number of elements not satisfying the predicate that follow the first element satisfying the predicate. Then the predicate is applied n times, exchange_values is performed w times, and the number of iterator increments is $n + w$.

Exercise 11.3   Rewrite partition_semistable, expanding the call of find_if_not inline and eliminating the extra test against l.

Exercise 11.4   Give the postcondition of the algorithm that results from replacing swap_step(i, j) with copy_step(j, i) in partition_semistable, suggest an appropriate name, and compare its use with the use of partition_semistable.

Let n be the number of elements in a range to be partitioned.

Lemma 11.7   A partition rearrangement that returns the partition point requires n applications of the predicate.

Lemma 11.8   A partition rearrangement of a nonempty range that does not return the partition point requires $n - 1$ applications of the predicate.[2]

Exercise 11.5   Implement a partition rearrangement for nonempty ranges that performs $n - 1$ predicate applications.

Consider a range with one element satisfying the predicate, followed by n elements not satisfying the predicate. partition_semistable will perform n calls of exchange_values, while one suffices. If we combine a forward search for an element satisfying the predicate with a backward search for an element not satisfying the

---

2. This lemma and the following exercise were suggested to us by Jon Brandt.

predicate, we avoid unnecessary exchanges. The algorithm requires bidirectional
iterators:

```
template<typename I, typename P>
    requires(Mutable(I) && BidirectionalIterator(I) &&
        UnaryPredicate(P) && ValueType(I) == Domain(P))
I partition_bidirectional(I f, I l, P p)
{
    // Precondition: mutable_bounded_range(f, l)
    while (true) {
        f = find_if(f, l, p);
        l = find_backward_if_not(f, l, p);
        if (f == l) return f;
        reverse_swap_step(l, f);
    }
}
```

As with partition_semistable, partition_bidirectional uses only one temporary
object.

Lemma 11.9   The number of times exchange_values is performed, v, equals
the number of misplaced elements not satisfying the predicate. The total
number of assignments, therefore, is $3v$.

Exercise 11.6   Implement a partition rearrangement for forward iterators
that calls exchange_values the same number of times as partition_bidirectional
by first computing the potential partition point.

It is possible to accomplish partition with a different rearrangement that has
only a single cycle, resulting in $2v + 1$ assignments. The idea is to save the first
misplaced element, creating a "hole," then repeatedly find a misplaced element on
the opposite side of the potential partition point and move it into the hole, creating
a new hole, and finally move the saved element into the last hole.

Exercise 11.7   Using this technique, implement partition_single_cycle.

Exercise 11.8   Implement a partition rearrangement for bidirectional iterators that finds appropriate sentinel elements and then uses find_if_unguarded
and an unguarded version of find_backward_if_not.

Exercise 11.9 Repeat the previous exercise, incorporating the single-cycle technique.

The idea for a bidirectional partition algorithm, as well as the single-cycle and sentinel variations, are from C. A .R. Hoare.[3]

When stability is needed for both sides of the partition and enough memory is available for a buffer of the same size as the range, the following algorithm can be used:

```
template<typename I, typename B, typename P>
    requires(Mutable(I) && ForwardIterator(I) &&
        Mutable(B) && ForwardIterator(B) &&
        ValueType(I) == ValueType(B) &&
        UnaryPredicate(P) && ValueType(I) == Domain(P))
I partition_stable_with_buffer(I f, I l, B f_b, P p)
{
    // Precondition: mutable_bounded_range(f, l)
    // Precondition: mutable_counted_range(f_b, l − f)
    pair<I, B> x = partition_copy(f, l, f, f_b, p);
    copy(f_b, x.m1, x.m0);
    return x.m0;
}
```

When there is not enough memory for a full-size buffer, it is possible to implement stable partition by using a divide-and-conquer algorithm. If the range is a singleton range, it is already partitioned, and its partition point can be determined with one predicate application:

```
template<typename I, typename P>
    requires(Mutable(I) && ForwardIterator(I) &&
        UnaryPredicate(P) && ValueType(I) == Domain(P))
pair<I, I> partition_stable_singleton(I f, P p)
{
    // Precondition: readable_bounded_range(f, successor(f))
```

---

3. See Hoare [1962] on the Quicksort algorithm. Because of the requirements of Quicksort, Hoare's partition interchanges elements that are greater than or equal to a chosen element with elements that are less than or equal to the chosen element. A range of equal elements is divided in the middle. Observe that these two relations, $\leq$ and $\geq$, are not complements of each other.

```
    I l = successor(f);
    if (!p(source(f))) f = l;
    return pair<I, I>(f, l);
}
```

The returned value is the partition point and the limit of the range: in other words, the range of values satisfying the predicate.

Two adjacent partitioned ranges can be combined into a single partitioned range by rotating the range bounded by the first and second partition points around the middle:

```
template<typename I>
    requires(Mutable(I) && ForwardIterator(I))
pair<I, I> combine_ranges(const pair<I, I>& x,
                          const pair<I, I>& y)
{
    // Precondition: mutable_bounded_range(x.m0, y.m0)
    // Precondition: x.m1 ∈ [x.m0, y.m0]
    return pair<I, I>(rotate(x.m0, x.m1, y.m0), y.m1);
}
```

Lemma 11.10   combine_ranges is associative when applied to three nonoverlapping ranges.

Lemma 11.11   If, for some predicate p,

$$(\forall i \in [x.m0, x.m1)) \, p(i) \land$$
$$(\forall i \in [x.m1, y.m0)) \, \neg p(i) \land$$
$$(\forall i \in [y.m0, y.m1)) \, p(i)$$

then after

$$z \leftarrow \text{combine\_ranges}(x, y)$$

the following hold:

$$(\forall i \in [x.m0, z.m0)) \, \neg p(i)$$
$$(\forall i \in [z.m0, z.m1)) \, p(i)$$

The inputs are the ranges of values satisfying the predicate and so is the output; therefore a nonsingleton range is stably partitioned by dividing it in the middle, partitioning both halves recursively, and then combining the partitioned parts:

```
template<typename I, typename P>
    requires(Mutable(I) && ForwardIterator(I) &&
        UnaryPredicate(P) && ValueType(I) == Domain(P))
pair<I, I> partition_stable_n_nonempty(I f, DistanceType(I) n, P p)
{
    // Precondition: mutable_counted_range(f, n) ∧ n > 0
    if (one(n)) return partition_stable_singleton(f, p);
    DistanceType(I) h = half_nonnegative(n);
    pair<I, I> x = partition_stable_n_nonempty(f, h, p);
    pair<I, I> y = partition_stable_n_nonempty(x.m1, n - h, p);
    return combine_ranges(x, y);
}
```

Since empty ranges never result from subdividing a range of size greater than 1, we handle that case only at the top level:

```
template<typename I, typename P>
    requires(Mutable(I) && ForwardIterator(I) &&
        UnaryPredicate(P) && ValueType(I) == Domain(P))
pair<I, I> partition_stable_n(I f, DistanceType(I) n, P p)
{
    // Precondition: mutable_counted_range(f, n)
    if (zero(n)) return pair<I, I>(f, f);
    return partition_stable_n_nonempty(f, n, p);
}
```

Exactly n predicate applications are performed at the bottom level of recursion. The depth of the recursion for partition_stable_n_nonempty is $\lceil \log_2 n \rceil$. At every recursive level, we rotate $n/2$ elements on the average, requiring between $n/2$ and $3n/2$ assignments, depending on the iterator category. The total number of assignments is $n \log_2 n/2$ for random-access iterators and $3n \log_2 n/2$ for forward and bidirectional iterators.

Exercise 11.10 Use techniques from the previous chapter to produce a memory-adaptive version of partition_stable_n.

11.2 Balanced Reduction

Although the performance of partition_stable_n depends on subdividing the range in
the middle, its correctness does not. Since combine_ranges is a partially associative
operation, the subdivision could be performed at any point. We can take advantage
of this fact to produce an iterative algorithm with similar performance; such an
algorithm is useful, for example, when the size of the range is not known in advance
or to eliminate procedure call overhead. The basic idea is to use reduction, applying
partition_stable_singleton to each singleton range and combining the results with
combine_ranges:

```
reduce_nonempty(
    f, l,
    combine_ranges<I>,
    partition_trivial<I, P>(p));
```

where partition_trivial is a function object that binds the predicate parameter to
partition_stable_singleton:

```
template<typename I, typename P>
    requires(ForwardIterator(I) &&
    UnaryPredicate(P) && ValueType(I) == Domain(P))
struct partition_trivial
{
    P p;
    partition_trivial(const P & p) : p(p) { }
    pair<I, I> operator()(I i)
    {
        return partition_stable_singleton<I, P>(i, p);
    }
};
```

Using reduce_nonempty leads to quadratic complexity. We need to take advantage
of partial associativity to create a balanced reduction tree. We use a binary counter
technique to build the reduction tree bottom-up.[4] A hardware binary counter increments an n-bit binary integer by 1. A 1 in position i has a *weight* of 2^i; a carry

---

4. The technique is attributed to John McCarthy in Knuth [1998, Section 5.2.4 (Sorting by Merging),
Exercise 17, page 167].

from this position has a weight of 2^{i+1} and propagates to the next-higher position. Our counter uses the "bit" in position i to represent either empty or the result of reducing 2^i elements from the original range. When the carry propagates to the next higher position, it is either stored or is combined with another value of the same weight. The carry from the highest position is returned by the following procedure, which takes the identity element as an explicit parameter, as does reduce_nonzeroes:

```
template<typename I, typename Op>
    requires(Mutable(I) && ForwardIterator(I) &&
        BinaryOperation(Op) && ValueType(I) == Domain(Op))
Domain(Op) add_to_counter(I f, I l, Op op, Domain(Op) x,
                            const Domain(Op)& z)
{
    if (x == z) return z;
    while (f != l) {
        if (source(f) == z) {
            sink(f) = x;
            return z;
        }
        x = op(source(f), x);
        sink(f) = z;
        f = successor(f);
    }
    return x;
}
```

Storage for the counter is provided by the following type, which handles overflows from add_to_counter by extending the counter:

```
template<typename Op>
    requires(BinaryOperation(Op))
struct counter_machine
{
    typedef Domain(Op) T;
    Op op;
    T z;
    T f[64];
    pointer(T) l;
```

```
counter_machine(Op op, const Domain(Op)& z) :
    op(op), z(z), l(f) { }
void operator()(const T& x)
{
    // Precondition: must not be called more than 2^64 − 1 times
    T tmp = add_to_counter(f, l, op, x, z);
    if (tmp != z) {
        sink(l) = tmp;
        l = successor(l);
    }
}
};
```

This uses a built-in C++ array; alternative implementations are possible.[5]

After add_to_counter has been called for every element of a range, the nonempty positions in the counter are combined with leftmost reduction to produce the final result:

```
template<typename I, typename Op, typename F>
    requires(Iterator(I) && BinaryOperation(Op) &&
        UnaryFunction(F) && I == Domain(F) &&
        Codomain(F) == Domain(Op))
Domain(Op) reduce_balanced(I f, I l, Op op, F fun,
                           const Domain(Op)& z)
{
    // Precondition: bounded_range(f, l) ∧ l − f < 2^64
    // Precondition: partially_associative(op)
    // Precondition: (∀x ∈ [f, l)) fun(x) is defined
    counter_machine<Op> c(op, z);
    while (f != l) {
        c(fun(f));
        f = successor(f);
    }
    transpose_operation<Op> t_op(op);
    return reduce_nonzeroes(c.f, c.l, t_op, z);
}
```

---

5. The choice of 64 elements for the array handles any application on 64-bit architectures.

The values in higher positions of the counter correspond to earlier elements of the original range, and the operation is not necessarily commutative. Therefore we must use a transposed version of the operation, which we obtain by using the following function object:

```
template<typename Op>
    requires(BinaryOperation(Op))
struct transpose_operation
{
    Op op;
    transpose_operation(Op op) : op(op) { }
    typedef Domain(Op) T;
    T operator()(const T& x, const T& y)
    {
        return op(y, x);
    }
};
```

Now we can implement an iterative version of stable partition with the following procedure:

```
template<typename I, typename P>
    requires(ForwardIterator(I) && UnaryPredicate(P) &&
        ValueType(I) == Domain(P))
I partition_stable_iterative(I f, I l, P p)
{
    // Precondition: bounded_range(f, l) ∧ l − f < 2^64
    return reduce_balanced(
        f, l,
        combine_ranges<I>,
        partition_trivial<I, P>(p),
        pair<I, I>(f, f)
    ).m0;
}
```

$\text{pair}_{I,I}(f, f)$ is a good way to represent the identity element since it is never returned by partition_trivial or the combining operation.

The iterative algorithm constructs a different reduction tree than the recursive algorithm. When the size of the problem is equal to 2^k, the recursive and iterative versions perform the same sequence of combining operations; otherwise the iterative version may do up to a linear amount of extra work. For example, in some algorithms the complexity goes from $n \log_2 n$ to $n \log_2 n + \frac{n}{2}$.

Exercise 11.11   Implement an iterative version of sort_linked_nonempty_n from Chapter 8, using reduce_balanced.

Exercise 11.12   Implement an iterative version of reverse_n_adaptive from Chapter 10, using reduce_balanced.

Exercise 11.13   Use reduce_balanced to implement an iterative and memory-adaptive version of partition_stable_n.

11.3 Merging

In Chapter 9 we presented copying merge algorithms that combine two increasing ranges into a third increasing range. For sorting, it is useful to have a rearrangement that merges two adjacent increasing ranges into a single increasing range. With a buffer of size equal to that of the first range, we can use the following procedure:[6]

```
template<typename I, typename B, typename R>
    requires(Mutable(I) && ForwardIterator(I) &&
        Mutable(B) && ForwardIterator(B) &&
        ValueType(I) == ValueType(B) &&
        Relation(R) && ValueType(I) == Domain(R))
I merge_n_with_buffer(I f0, DistanceType(I) n0,
                    I f1, DistanceType(I) n1, B f_b, R r)
{
    // Precondition: mergeable(f0, n0, f1, n1, r)
    // Precondition: mutable_counted_range(f_b, n0)
    copy_n(f0, n0, f_b);
    return merge_copy_n(f_b, n0, f1, n1, f0, r).m2;
}
```

where mergeable is defined as follows:

    property(I : *ForwardIterator*, N : *Integer*, R : *Relation*)
      requires(*Mutable*(I) $\wedge$ ValueType(I) = Domain(R))

---

6. Solving Exercise 9.5 explains the need for extracting the member m2.

mergeable : $I \times N \times I \times N \times R$

$(f_0, n_0, f_1, n_1, r) \mapsto f_0 + n_0 = f_1 \wedge$
$ \text{mutable\_counted\_range}(f_0, n_0 + n_1) \wedge$
$ \text{weak\_ordering}(r) \wedge$
$ \text{increasing\_counted\_range}(f_0, n_0, r) \wedge$
$ \text{increasing\_counted\_range}(f_1, n_1, r)$

Lemma 11.12 The postcondition for merge_n_with_buffer is

$$\text{increasing\_counted\_range}(f_0, n_0 + n_1, r)$$

A merge is *stable* if the output range preserves the relative order of equivalent elements both within each input range and between the first and second input range.

Lemma 11.13 merge_n_with_buffer is stable.

Note that merge_linked_nonempty, merge_copy, and merge_copy_backward are also stable.

We can sort a range with a buffer of half of its size:[7]

```
template<typename I, typename B, typename R>
    requires(Mutable(I) && ForwardIterator(I) &&
        Mutable(B) && ForwardIterator(B) &&
        ValueType(I) == ValueType(B) &&
        Relation(R) && ValueType(I) == Domain(R))
I sort_n_with_buffer(I f, DistanceType(I) n, B f_b, R r)
{
    // Precondition: mutable_counted_range(f, n) ∧ weak_ordering(r)
    // Precondition: mutable_counted_range(f_b, n/2)
    DistanceType(I) h = half_nonnegative(n);
    if (zero(h)) return f + n;
    I m = sort_n_with_buffer(f, h,     f_b, r);
        sort_n_with_buffer(m, n - h, f_b, r);
    return merge_n_with_buffer(f, h, m, n - h, f_b, r);
}
```

---

7. A similar algorithm was first described in John W. Mauchly's lecture "Sorting and collating" [Mauchly, 1946].

Lemma 11.14   The postcondition for sort_n_with_buffer is

$$\text{increasing\_counted\_range}(f, n, r)$$

A sorting algorithm is *stable* if it preserves the relative order of elements with equivalent values.

Lemma 11.15   sort_n_with_buffer is stable.

The algorithm has $\lceil \log_2 n \rceil$ recursive levels. Each level performs at most $3n/2$ assignments, for a total bounded by $\frac{3}{2}n\lceil \log_2 n \rceil$. At the ith level from the bottom, the worst-case number of comparisons is $n - \frac{n}{2^i}$, giving us the following bound on the number of comparisons:

$$n\lceil \log_2 n \rceil - \sum_{i=1}^{\lceil \log_2 n \rceil} \frac{n}{2^i} \approx n\lceil \log_2 n \rceil - n$$

When a buffer of sufficient size is available, sort_n_with_buffer is an efficient algorithm. When less memory is available, a memory-adaptive merge algorithm can be used. Subdividing the first subrange in the middle and using the middle element to subdivide the second subrange at its lower bound point results in four subranges r_0, r_1, r_2, and r_3 such that the values in r_2 are strictly less than the values in r_1. Rotating the ranges r_2 and r_3 leads to two new merge subproblems (r_0 with r_2 and r_1 with r3):

```
template<typename I, typename R>
    requires(Mutable(I) && ForwardIterator(I) &&
        Relation(R) && ValueType(I) == Domain(R))
void merge_n_step_0(I f0, DistanceType(I) n0,
                    I f1, DistanceType(I) n1, R r,
                    I& f0_0, DistanceType(I)& n0_0,
                    I& f0_1, DistanceType(I)& n0_1,
                    I& f1_0, DistanceType(I)& n1_0,
                    I& f1_1, DistanceType(I)& n1_1)
{
    // Precondition: mergeable(f0, n0, f1, n1, r)
    f0_0 = f0;
    n0_0 = half_nonnegative(n0);
    f0_1 = f0_0 + n0_0;
    f1_1 = lower_bound_n(f1, n1, source(f0_1), r);
```

```
        f1_0 = rotate(f0_1, f1, f1_1);
        n0_1 = f1_0 - f0_1;
        f1_0 = successor(f1_0);
        n1_0 = predecessor(n0 - n0_0);
        n1_1 = n1 - n0_1;
}
```

Lemma 11.16   The rotate does not change the relative positions of elements with equivalent values.

An iterator i in a range is a *pivot* if its value is not smaller than any value preceding it and not larger than any value following it.

Lemma 11.17   After merge_n_step_0, f1_0 is a pivot.

We can perform an analogous subdivision from the right by using upper_bound:

```
template<typename I, typename R>
    requires(Mutable(I) && ForwardIterator(I) &&
        Relation(R) && ValueType(I) == Domain(R))
void merge_n_step_1(I f0, DistanceType(I) n0,
                    I f1, DistanceType(I) n1, R r,
                    I& f0_0, DistanceType(I)& n0_0,
                    I& f0_1, DistanceType(I)& n0_1,
                    I& f1_0, DistanceType(I)& n1_0,
                    I& f1_1, DistanceType(I)& n1_1)
{
    // Precondition: mergeable(f_0, n_0, f_1, n_1, r)
    f0_0 = f0;
    n0_1 = half_nonnegative(n1);
    f1_1 = f1 + n0_1;
    f0_1 = upper_bound_n(f0, n0, source(f1_1), r);
    f1_1 = successor(f1_1);
    f1_0 = rotate(f0_1, f1, f1_1);
    n0_0 = f0_1 - f0_0;
    n1_0 = n0 - n0_0;
    n1_1 = predecessor(n1 - n0_1);
}
```

This leads to the following algorithm from Dudziński and Dydek [1981]:

```
template<typename I, typename B, typename R>
    requires(Mutable(I) && ForwardIterator(I) &&
        Mutable(B) && ForwardIterator(B) &&
        ValueType(I) == ValueType(B) &&
        Relation(R) && ValueType(I) == Domain(R))
I merge_n_adaptive(I f0, DistanceType(I) n0,
                   I f1, DistanceType(I) n1,
                   B f_b, DistanceType(B) n_b, R r)
{
    // Precondition: mergeable(f0, n0, f1, n1, r)
    // Precondition: mutable_counted_range(f_b, n_b)
    typedef DistanceType(I) N;
    if (zero(n0) || zero(n1)) return f0 + n0 + n1;
    if (n0 <= N(n_b))
        return merge_n_with_buffer(f0, n0, f1, n1, f_b, r);
    I f0_0; I f0_1; I f1_0; I f1_1;
    N n0_0; N n0_1; N n1_0; N n1_1;
    if (n0 < n1) merge_n_step_0(
                        f0, n0, f1, n1, r,
                        f0_0, n0_0, f0_1, n0_1,
                        f1_0, n1_0, f1_1, n1_1);
    else         merge_n_step_1(
                        f0, n0, f1, n1, r,
                        f0_0, n0_0, f0_1, n0_1,
                        f1_0, n1_0, f1_1, n1_1);
    merge_n_adaptive(f0_0, n0_0, f0_1, n0_1,
                        f_b, n_b, r);
    return merge_n_adaptive(f1_0, n1_0, f1_1, n1_1,
                        f_b, n_b, r);
}
```

Lemma 11.18   merge_n_adaptive terminates with an increasing range.

Lemma 11.19   merge_n_adaptive is stable.

Lemma 11.20   There are at most $\lfloor \log_2(\min(n0, n1)) \rfloor + 1$ recursive levels.

Using merge_n_adaptive, we can implement the following sorting procedure:

```
template<typename I, typename B, typename R>
    requires(Mutable(I) && ForwardIterator(I) &&
        Mutable(B) && ForwardIterator(B) &&
        ValueType(I) == ValueType(B) &&
        Relation(R) && ValueType(I) == Domain(R))
I sort_n_adaptive(I f, DistanceType(I) n,
                  B f_b, DistanceType(B) n_b, R r)
{
    // Precondition: mutable_counted_range(f, n) ∧ weak_ordering(r)
    // Precondition: mutable_counted_range(f_b, n_b)
    DistanceType(I) h = half_nonnegative(n);
    if (zero(h)) return f + n;
    I m = sort_n_adaptive(f, h,       f_b, n_b, r);
            sort_n_adaptive(m, n - h, f_b, n_b, r);
    return merge_n_adaptive(f, h, m, n - h, f_b, n_b, r);
}
```

Exercise 11.14   Determine formulas for the number of assignments and the number of comparisons as functions of the size of the input and buffer ranges. Dudziński and Dydek [1981] contains a careful complexity analysis of the case in which there is no buffer.

We conclude with the following algorithm:

```
template<typename I, typename R>
    requires(Mutable(I) && ForwardIterator(I) &&
        Relation(R) && ValueType(I) == Domain(R))
I sort_n(I f, DistanceType(I) n, R r)
{
    // Precondition: mutable_counted_range(f, n) ∧ weak_ordering(r)
    temporary_buffer<ValueType(I)> b(half_nonnegative(n));
    return sort_n_adaptive(f, n, begin(b), size(b), r);
}
```

It works on ranges with minimal iterator requirements, is stable, and is efficient even when temporary_buffer is only able to allocate a few percent of the requested memory.

Project 11.1   Develop a library of sorting algorithms constructed from abstract components. Design a benchmark to analyze their performance for different array sizes, element sizes, and buffer sizes. Document the library with recommendations for the circumstances in which each algorithm is appropriate.

11.4 Conclusions

Complex algorithms are decomposable into simpler abstract components with carefully defined interfaces. The components so discovered are then used to implement other algorithms. The iterative process going from complex to simple and back is central to the discovery of a systematic catalog of efficient components.

Chapter 12

Composite Objects

C*hapters 6 through 11 presented algorithms working on collections of objects (data structures) through iterators or coordinate structures in isolation from construction, destruction, and structural mutation of these collections: Collections themselves were not viewed as objects. This chapter provides examples of composite objects, starting with pairs and constant-size arrays and ending with a taxonomy of implementations of dynamic sequences. We describe a general schema of a composite object containing other objects as its parts. We conclude by demonstrating the mechanism enabling efficient behavior of rearrangement algorithms on nested composite objects.*

12.1 Simple Composite Objects

To understand how to extend regularity to composite objects, let us start with some simple cases. In Chapter 1 we introduced the type constructor pair, which, given two types T_0 and T_1, returns the structure type $pair_{T_0, T_1}$. We implement pair with a structure template together with some global procedures:

```
template<typename T0, typename T1>
    requires(Regular(T0) && Regular(T1))
struct pair
{
    T0 m0;
    T1 m1;
    pair() { } // default constructor
    pair(const T0& m0, const T1& m1) : m0(m0), m1(m1) { }
};
```

C++ ensures that the default constructor performs a default construction of both members, guaranteeing that they are in partially formed states and can thus be assigned to or destroyed. C++ automatically generates a copy constructor and assignment that, respectively, copies or assigns each member and automatically generates a destructor that invokes the destructor for each member. We need to provide equality and ordering manually:

```
template<typename T0, typename T1>
    requires(Regular(T0) && Regular(T1))
bool operator==(const pair<T0, T1>& x, const pair<T0, T1>& y)
{
    return x.m0 == y.m0 && x.m1 == y.m1;
}

template<typename T0, typename T1>
    requires(TotallyOrdered(T0) && TotallyOrdered(T1))
bool operator<(const pair<T0, T1>& x, const pair<T0, T1>& y)
{
    return x.m0 < y.m0 || (!(y.m0 < x.m0) && x.m1 < y.m1);
}
```

Exercise 12.1 Implement the default ordering, less, for pair$_{T0, T1}$, using the default orderings for T0 and T1, for situations in which both member types are not totally ordered.

Exercise 12.2 Implement triple$_{T_0, T_1, T_2}$.

While pair is a heterogeneous type constructor, array_k is a homogeneous type constructor, which, given an integer k and a type T, returns the constant-size sequence type array_k$_{k, T}$:

```
template<int k, typename T>
    requires(0 < k && k <= MaximumValue(int) / sizeof(T) &&
        Regular(T))
struct array_k
{
    T a[k];
    T& operator[](int i)
    {
        // Precondition: 0 ≤ i < k
        return a[i];
    }
};
```

The requirement on k is defined in terms of type attributes. MaximumValue(N) returns the maximum value representable by the integer type N, and sizeof is the built-in type attribute that returns the size of a type. C++ generates the default constructor, copy constructor, assignment, and destructor for array_k with correct semantics. We implement the member function that allows reading or writing x[i].[1]

IteratorType(array_k$_{k,T}$) is defined to be pointer to T. We provide procedures to return the first and the limit of the array elements:[2]

```
template<int k, typename T>
    requires(Regular(T))
pointer(T) begin(array_k<k, T>& x)
{
    return addressof(x.a[0]);
}

template<int k, typename T>
    requires(Regular(T))
pointer(T) end(array_k<k, T>& x)
{
    return addressof(x.a[k]);
}
```

An object x of array_k$_{k,T}$ type can be initialized to a copy of the counted range ⟦f, k⟧ with code like

```
copy_n(f, k, begin(x));
```

We do not know how to implement a proper initializing constructor that avoids the automatically generated default construction of every element of the array. In addition, while copy_n takes any category of iterator and returns the limit iterator, there would be no way to return the limit iterator from a copy constructor.

Equality and ordering for arrays use the lexicographical extensions introduced in Chapter 7:

```
template<int k, typename T>
    requires(Regular(T))
bool operator==(const array_k<k, T>& x, const array_k<k, T>& y)
```

---

1. As with begin and end, overloading on constant is needed for a complete implementation.

2. A complete implementation will also provide a constant iterator type, as a constant pointer to T, together with versions of begin and end overloaded on constant array_k that return the constant iterator type.

```
{
    return lexicographical_equal(begin(x), end(x),
                                 begin(y), end(y));
}


template<int k, typename T>
    requires(Regular(T))
bool operator<(const array_k<k, T>& x, const array_k<k, T>& y)
{
    return lexicographical_less(begin(x), end(x),
                                begin(y), end(y));
}
```

Exercise 12.3   Implement versions of $=$ and $<$ for array_$k_{k, T}$ that generate inline unrolled code for small k.

Exercise 12.4   Implement the default ordering, less, for array_$k_{k, T}$.

We provide a procedure to return the number of elements in the array:

```
template<int k, typename T>
    requires(Regular(T))
int size(const array_k<k, T>& x)
{
    return k;
}
```

and one to determine whether the size is 0:

```
template<int k, typename T>
    requires(Regular(T))
bool empty(const array_k<k, T>& x)
{
    return false;
}
```

We took the trouble to define size and empty so that array_k would model *Sequence*, which we define later.

Exercise 12.5   Extend array_k to accept k = 0.

array_k models the concept *Linearizable*:

Linearizable(W) $\triangleq$
 Regular(W)
 $\land$ IteratorType : *Linearizable* $\rightarrow$ *Iterator*
 $\land$ ValueType : *Linearizable* $\rightarrow$ *Regular*
   W $\mapsto$ ValueType(IteratorType(W))
 $\land$ SizeType : *Linearizable* $\rightarrow$ *Integer*
   W $\mapsto$ DistanceType(IteratorType(W))
 $\land$ begin : W $\rightarrow$ IteratorType(W)
 $\land$ end : W $\rightarrow$ IteratorType(W)
 $\land$ size : W $\rightarrow$ SizeType(W)
   x $\mapsto$ end(x) $-$ begin(x)
 $\land$ empty : W $\rightarrow$ bool
   x $\mapsto$ begin(x) = end(x)
 $\land$ [ ] : W $\times$ SizeType(W) $\rightarrow$ ValueType(W)&
   (w, i) $\mapsto$ deref(begin(w) + i)

empty always takes constant time, even when size takes linear time. The precondition for w[i] is $0 \le i \le$ size(w); its complexity is determined by the iterator type specification of concepts refining *Linearizable:* linear for forward and bidirectional iterators and constant for indexed and random-access iterators.

A linearizable type describes a range of iterators via the standard functions begin and end, but unlike array_k, copying a linearizable does not need to copy the underlying objects; as we shall see later, it is not a *container*, a sequence that owns its elements. The following type, for example, models *Linearizable* and is not a container; it designates a bounded range of iterators residing in some data structure:

```
template<typename I>
    requires(Readable(I) && Iterator(I))
struct bounded_range {
    I f;
    I l;
    bounded_range() { }
    bounded_range(const I& f, const I& l) : f(f), l(l) { }
    const ValueType(I)& operator[](int i)
```

```
    {
        // Precondition: 0 ≤ i < l − f
        return source(f + i);
    }
};
```

C++ automatically generates the copy constructor, assignment, and destructor, with the same semantics as pair$_{I,I}$. If T is bounded_range$_I$, IteratorType(T) is defined to be I, and SizeType(T) is defined to be DistanceType(I).

It is straightforward to define the iterator-related procedures:

```
template<typename I>
    requires(Readable(I) && Iterator(I))
I begin(const bounded_range<I>& x) { return x.f; }

template<typename I>
    requires(Readable(I) && Iterator(I))
I end(const bounded_range<I>& x) { return x.l; }

template<typename I>
    requires(Readable(I) && Iterator(I))
DistanceType(I) size(const bounded_range<I>& x)
{
    return end(x) - begin(x);
}

template<typename I>
    requires(Readable(I) && Iterator(I))
bool empty(const bounded_range<I>& x)
{
    return begin(x) == end(x);
}
```

Unlike array_k, equality for bounded_range does not use lexicographic equality but instead effectively treats the object as a pair of iterators and compares the corresponding values:

```
template<typename I>
    requires(Readable(I) && Iterator(I))
```

```
bool operator==(const bounded_range<I>& x,
                const bounded_range<I>& y)
{
    return begin(x) == begin(y) && end(x) == end(y);
}
```

The equality so defined is consistent with the copy constructor generated by C++, which treats it just as a pair of iterators. Consider a type W that models *Linearizable*. If W is a container with linear coordinate structure, lexicographical_equal is its correct equality, as we defined for array_k. If W is a homogeneous container whose coordinate structure is not linear (e.g., a tree or a matrix), neither lexicographical_equal nor *range equality* (as we defined for bounded_range) is the correct equality, although lexicographical_equal may still be a useful algorithm. If W is not a container but just a description of a range owned by another data structure, range equality is its correct equality.

The default total ordering for bounded_range$_1$ is defined lexicographically on the pair of iterators, using the default total ordering for I:

```
template<typename I>
    requires(Readable(I) && Iterator(I))
struct less< bounded_range<I> >
{
    bool operator()(const bounded_range<I>& x,
                    const bounded_range<I>& y)
    {
        less<I> less_I;
        return less_I(begin(x), begin(y)) ||
                (!less_I(begin(y), begin(x)) &&
                 less_I(end(x), end(y)));
    }
};
```

Even when an iterator type has no natural total ordering, it should provide a default total ordering: for example, by treating the bit pattern as an unsigned integer.

pair and array_k are examples of a very broad class of *composite objects*. An object is a *composite object* if it is made up of other objects, called its *parts*. The whole–part relationship satisfies the four properties of *connectedness*, *noncircularity*, *disjointness*, and *ownership*. *Connectedness* means that an object has an affiliated coordinate structure that allows every part of the object to be reached from the object's starting address. *Noncircularity* means that an object is not a subpart of itself, where *subparts* of an object are its parts and subparts of its parts. (Noncircularity implies that no object is a part of itself.) *Disjointness* means that if two objects have a subpart in common, one of the two is a subpart of the other. *Ownership* means that copying an object copies its parts, and destroying the object destroys its parts. A composite object is *dynamic* if the set of its parts could change over its lifetime.

We refer to the type of a composite object as a composite object type and to a concept modeled by a composite object type as a composite object concept. No algorithms can be defined on composite objects as such, since composite object is a concept schema rather than a concept.

array_k is a model of the concept *Sequence:* a composite object concept that refines *Linearizable* and whose range of elements are its parts:

$Sequence(S) \triangleq$
    $Linearizable(S)$
    $\wedge$ ($\forall s \in S$) ($\forall i \in$ [begin(s), end(s))) deref(i) is a part of s
    $\wedge$ = : $S \times S \to$ bool
        $(s, s') \mapsto$ lexicographical_equal(
                begin(s), end(s), begin(s'), end(s'))
    $\wedge$ < : $S \times S \to$ bool
        $(s, s') \mapsto$ lexicographical_less(
                begin(s), end(s), begin(s'), end(s'))

If s and s' are equal but not identical sequences, begin(s) $\neq$ begin(s'), but source(begin(s)) = source(begin(s')). This is an example of *projection regularity*. Note that begin and end can be regular for a *Linearizable* that is not a *Sequence;* for example, they are regular for bounded_range.

Exercise 12.6 Define a property projection_regular_function.

12.2 Dynamic Sequences

array_k$_{k, T}$ is a *constant-size sequence:* The parameter k is determined at compile time and applies to all objects of the type. We do not define a corresponding concept for constant-size sequences, since we are not aware of other useful models. Similarly, we do not define a concept for a *fixed-size sequence*, whose size is determined at construction time. All the data structures we know that model a fixed-size sequence also model a *dynamic-size sequence*, whose size varies as elements are inserted or erased. (There are, however, fixed-size composite objects; for example, $n \times n$ square matrices.)

Regardless of the specific data structure, the requirements of regular types dictate standard behavior for a dynamic sequence. When it is destroyed, all its elements are destroyed, and their resources are freed. Equality and total ordering on dynamic sequences are defined lexicographically, just as for array_k. When a dynamic sequence is assigned to, it becomes equal to but disjoint from the right-hand side; similarly, a copy constructor creates an equal but disjoint sequence.

If s is a dynamic-size, or simply *dynamic*, sequence of size $n \geq 0$, *inserting* a range r of size k at *insertion index* i increases the size to $n + k$. The insertion index i may be any of the $n + 1$ values in the closed interval $[0, n]$. If s' is the value of the sequence after the insertion, then

$$s'[j] = \begin{cases} s[j] & \text{if } 0 \leq j < i \\ r[j - i] & \text{if } i \leq j < i + k \\ s[j - k] & \text{if } i + k \leq j < n + k \end{cases}$$

Similarly, if s is a sequence of size $n \geq k$, *erasing* k elements at *erasure index* i decreases the size to $n - k$. The erasure index i may be any of the $n - k$ values in the open interval $[0, n - k)$. If s' is the value of the sequence after the erasure, then

$$s'[j] = \begin{cases} s[j] & \text{if } 0 \leq j < i \\ s[j + k] & \text{if } i \leq j < n - k \end{cases}$$

The need to insert and erase elements introduces many varieties of sequential data structures with different complexity tradeoffs for insert and erase. All these categories depend on the presence of *remote* parts. A part is remote if it does not reside at a constant offset from the address of an object but must be reached via a traversal of the object's coordinate structure starting at its *header*. The header of a composite object is the collection of its *local* parts, that is, the parts residing at constant offsets from the starting address of the object. The number of local parts in an object is a constant determined by its type.

In this section we summarize the properties of sequential data structures falling into the fundamental categories: *linked* and *extent-based*.

Linked data structures connect data parts with pointers serving as links. Each element resides in a distinct *permanently placed* part: During the lifetime of an element, its address never changes. Along with the element, the part contains connectors to adjacent parts. The iterators are linked iterators; indexed iterators are not supported. Insert and erase operations taking constant time are possible, since they are implemented by relinking operations and, therefore, do not invalidate iterators. There are two main varieties of linked list: singly linked and doubly linked.

A *singly linked* list has a linked *ForwardIterator*. The cost of insert and erase after a specified iterator is constant, whereas the cost of insert before and erase at an arbitrary iterator is linear in the distance from the front of the list. Thus the cost of insert and erase at the front of the list is constant. There are several varieties of singly linked lists, differing in the structure of the header and the link of the last element. The header of a *basic* list consists of a link to the first element, or a special *null* value to indicate an empty list; the link of the last element is null. The header of a *circular* list consists of the link to the last element or null to indicate an empty list; the link of the last element points to the first element. The header of a *first-last* list consists of two parts: the header of a null-terminated basic list and a link to the last element of the list or null if the list is empty.

Several factors affect the choice of a singly linked list implementation. A smaller header is valuable in an application with a large number of lists, many of which are empty. The iterator for a circular list is larger, and its successor operation is slower because it is necessary to distinguish between the pointer to the first and the pointer to the limit. A data structure supporting constant-time insert at the back can be used as a queue or output-restricted deque. These implementation tradeoffs are summarized in the following table:

Variety	One-word header	Simple iterator	Back insert
basic	yes	yes	no
circular	yes	no	yes
first-last	no	yes	yes

A *doubly linked* list has a linked *BidirectionalIterator*. The cost of insert before or after an erase at an arbitrary iterator is constant. As with singly linked lists, there are several varieties of doubly linked lists. The header of a *circular* list consists of a pointer to the first element or null to indicate an empty list; the backward link of the first element points to the last element, and the forward link of the last element points to the first element. A *dummy node* list is similar to a circular list but has an additional dummy node between the last and first elements; the header consists of a link to the dummy node, which might omit the actual data object. A *two-pointer header* is similar to a dummy node list, but the header consists of two pointers corresponding to the links of the dummy node.

Two factors affecting the choice of a singly linked list implementation are relevant for doubly linked list implementations, namely, header size and iterator complexity. There are additional issues specific to doubly linked lists. Some algorithms may be simplified if a list has a permanent limit iterator, since the limit can then be used as a value distinguishable from any valid iterator over the entire lifetime of the list. As we will see later in this chapter, the presence of links from remote parts to local parts makes it more costly to perform a rearrangement on elements that are of the list type. These implementation tradeoffs are summarized in the following table:

Variety	One-word header	Simple iterator	No remote to local links	Permanent limit
circular	yes	no	yes	no
dummy node	yes	yes	yes	no[3]
two-pointer header	no	yes	no	yes

In Chapter 8 we introduced link rearrangements, which rearrange the connectivity of linked iterators in one or more linked ranges without creating or destroying iterators or changing the relationships between the iterators and the objects they designate. Link rearrangements can be restricted to one list, or they can involve multiple lists, in which case ownership of the elements changes. For example, split_linked can be used to move elements satisfying a predicate from one list to another, and combine_linked_nonempty can be used to move elements in one list to merged positions in another list. *Splicing* is a link rearrangement that erases a range from one list and reinserts it in another list.

Backward links in a linked structure are not used in algorithms like sorting. They do, however, allow constant-time erasure and insertion of elements at an arbitrary location, which are more expensive in a singly linked structure. Since the efficiency of insertion and deletion is often the reason for choosing linked structures in the first place, bidirectional linkage should be seriously considered.

Extent-based data structures group elements in one or more *extents*, or remote blocks of data parts, and provide random access to them. Insert and erase at an arbitrary position take time proportionate to the size of the sequence, whereas insert and erase at the back and possibly the front take amortized constant time.[4] Insert and erase invalidate certain iterators following specific rules for each implementation; in other words, no element is permanently placed. Some extent-based data structures

---

3. If the dummy node is allocated even when the list is empty, there is a permanent limit; unfortunately, this violates the desirable property of empty data structures having no remote parts and thus being constructable without any additional resources.

4. The *amortized* complexity of an operation is the complexity averaged over a worst-case sequence of operations. The notion of amortized complexity was introduced in Tarjan [1985].

use a *single extent*, whereas others are *segmented*, using multiple extents as well as additional index structures.

In a single-extent array the extent need only be present when the size is nonzero. To avoid reallocation at every insert, the extent contains a reserve area; when the reserve area is exhausted, the extent is reallocated. The header contains a pointer to the extent; additional pointers keeping track of the data and reserve areas normally reside in a prefix of the extent. Placing the additional pointers in the prefix and not in the header improves both space and time complexity when arrays are nested.

There are several varieties of single-extent arrays. In a *single-ended* array, the data starts at a fixed offset in the extent and is followed by the reserve area.[5] In a *double-ended* array, the data is in the middle of the extent, with reserve areas surrounding it at both ends; if growth at either end exhausts the corresponding reserve area, the extent is reallocated. In a *circular* array, the extent is treated as if the successor to its highest address is its lowest address; thus the single reserve area always logically precedes and follows the data, which can grow in both directions.

Several factors affect the choice of a single-extent array implementation. For single-ended and double-ended arrays, machine addresses are the most efficient implementation of iterators; the iterator for a circular array is larger, and its traversal functions are slower because of the need to keep track of whether the in-use area has wrapped around to the start of the extent. A data structure supporting constant-time insert/erase at the front allows a data structure to be used as a queue or an output-restricted deque. A double-ended array could require reallocation even when one of its two reserve areas has available space; a single-ended or circular array only requires reallocation when no reserve remains.

Variety	Simple iterator	Front insert/erase	Reallocation efficient
single-ended	yes	no	yes
double-ended	yes	yes	no
circular	no	yes	yes

When an insert occurs and the extent of a single-ended or circular array is full, *reallocation* occurs: A larger extent is allocated, and the existing elements are moved to the new extent. In the case of a double-ended array, an insertion exhausting the

---

5. Of course, it is possible to grow data from the back downward, but this does not appear to be practically useful.

reserve at one end of the array requires either reallocation or moving the elements toward the other end to redistribute the remaining reserve. Reallocation—and moving elements within a double-ended array—invalidates all the iterators pointing into the array.

When reallocation occurs, increasing the size of the extent by a multiplicative factor leads to an amortized constant number of constructions per element. Our experiments suggest a factor of 2 as a good tradeoff between minimizing the amortized number of constructions per element and the storage utilization.

Exercise 12.7   Derive expressions for the storage utilization and number of constructions per element for various multiplicative factors.

Project 12.1   Combine theoretical analysis with experimentation to determine optimal reallocation strategies for single-extent arrays under various realistic workloads.

For a single-ended or circular single-extent array a, there is a function capacity such that $size(a) \leq capacity(a)$, and insertion in a performs reallocation only when the size after the insertion is greater than the capacity before the insertion. There is also a procedure reserve that allows the capacity of an array to be increased to a specified amount.

Exercise 12.8   Design an interface for capacity and reserve for double-ended arrays.

A *segmented* array has one or more extents holding the elements and an *index* data structure managing pointers to the extents. Checking for the end of the extent makes the iterator traversal functions slower than for a single-extent array. The index must support the same behavior as the segmented array: It must support random access and insertion and erasure at the back and, if desired, at the front. Full reallocation is never needed, because another extent is added when an existing extent becomes full. Reserve space is only needed in the extents at one or both ends.

The main source of variety of segmented arrays is the structure of the index. A *single-extent* index is a single-extent array of pointers to data extents; such an index supports growth at the back, whereas a double-ended or circular index supports growth at either end. A *segmented* index is itself a segmented array, typically with a single-extent index, but potentially also with a segmented index. A *slanted* index has multiple levels. Its root is a single fixed-size extent; the first few elements are pointers to data extents; the next element points to an indirect index extent containing pointers to data extents; the next points to a doubly indirect extent containing pointers to indirect index extents; and so on.[6]

Project 12.2   Design a complete family of interfaces for dynamic sequences. It should include construction, insertion, erasure, and splicing. Ensure that there are variations to handle the special cases for different implementations. For example, it should be possible to insert after as well as before a specified iterator to handle singly linked lists.

Project 12.3   Implement a comprehensive library of dynamic sequences, providing various singly linked, doubly linked, single-extent, and segmented data structures.

Project 12.4   Design a benchmark for dynamic sequences based on realistic application workloads, measure the performance of various data structures, and provide a selection guide for the user, based on the results.

12.3 Underlying Type

In Chapters 2 through 5 we studied algorithms on mathematical values and saw how equational reasoning as enabled by regular types applies to algorithms as well as to proofs. In Chapters 6 through 11 we studied algorithms on memory and saw how equational reasoning remains useful in a world with changing state. We dealt with small objects, such as integers and pointers, which are cheaply assigned and copied. In this chapter we introduced composite objects that satisfy the requirements of regular types and can thus be used as elements of other composite objects. Dynamic sequences and other composite objects that separate the header from the remote parts allow for an efficient way to implement rearrangements: moving headers without moving the remote parts.

　　To understand the problem of an inefficient rearrangement involving composite objects, consider the swap_basic procedure defined as follows:

```
template<typename T>
    requires(Regular(T))
void swap_basic(T& x, T& y)
{
```

---

6. This is based on the original UNIX file system [see Thompson and Ritchie, 1974].

```
    T tmp = x;
    x = y;
    y = tmp;
}
```

Suppose that we call swap_basic(a, b) to interchange two dynamic sequences. The copy construction and the two assignments it performs take linear time. Furthermore, an out-of-memory exception could occur even though no net increase of memory is needed.

We could avoid this expensive copying by specializing swap_basic to swap the headers of the specific dynamic sequence type and, if necessary, update links from the remote parts to the header. There are, however, problems with specializing swap_basic. First, it needs to be repeated for each data structure. More important, many rearrangement algorithms are not based on swap_basic, including in-place permutations, such as cycle_from, and algorithms that use a buffer, such as merge_n_with_buffer. Finally, there are situations, such as reallocating a single-extent array, in which objects are moved from an old extent to a new one.

We want to generalize the idea of swapping headers to arbitrary rearrangements, to allow the use of buffer memory and reallocation, and to continue to write abstract algorithms that do not depend on the implementation of the objects they manipulate. To accomplish this, we associate every regular type T with its *underlying type*, U = UnderlyingType(T). The type U is identical to the type T when T has no remote parts or has remote parts with links back to the header.[7] Otherwise U is identical to type T in every respect except that it does not maintain ownership: Destruction does not affect the remote parts, and copy construction and assignment simply copy the header without copying the remote parts. When the underlying type is different from the original type, it has the same layout (bit pattern) as the header of the original type.

The fact that the same bit pattern could be interpreted as an object of a type and of its underlying type allows us to view the memory as one or the other, using the built-in reinterpret_cast function template. Objects of UnderlyingType(T) may only be used to hold temporary values while implementing a rearrangement of objects of type T. The complexity of copy construction and assignment for a *proper* underlying type—one that is not identical to the original type—are proportional to the size of the header of type T. An additional benefit in this case is that copy construction and assignment for UnderlyingType(T) never throw an exception.

---

7. This explains the warning against links from remote parts to the header in our discussion of doubly linked lists.

The implementation of the underlying type for an original type T is straightforward and could be automated. $U = \text{UnderlyingType}(T)$ always has the same layout as the header of T. The copy constructor and assignment for U just copy the bits; they do not construct a copy of the remote parts of T. For example, the underlying type of pair_{T_0, T_1} is a pair whose members are the underlying types of T_0 and T_1; similarly for other tuple types. The underlying type of $\text{array\_k}_{k, T}$ is an array_k_k whose elements are the underlying type of T.

Once UnderlyingType(T) has been defined, we can cast a reference to T into a reference to UnderlyingType(T), without performing any computation, with this procedure:

```
template<typename T>
    requires(Regular(T))
UnderlyingType(T)& underlying_ref(T& x)
{
    return reinterpret_cast<UnderlyingType(T)&>(x);
}
```

Now we can efficiently swap composite objects by rewriting swap_basic as follows:

```
template<typename T>
    requires(Regular(T))
void swap(T& x, T& y)
{
    UnderlyingType(T) tmp = underlying_ref(x);
    underlying_ref(x)     = underlying_ref(y);
    underlying_ref(y)     = tmp;
}
```

which could also be accomplished with:

```
swap_basic(underlying_ref(x), underlying_ref(y));
```

Many rearrangement algorithms can be modified for use with underlying type simply by reimplementing exchange_values and cycle_from the same way we reimplemented swap.

To handle other rearrangement algorithms, we use an iterator adapter. Such an adapter has the same traversal operations as the original iterator, but the value type is replaced by the underlying type of the original value type; source returns underlying_ref(source(x.i)), and sink returns underlying_ref(sink(x.i)), where x is the adapter object, and i is the original iterator object inside x.

Exercise 12.9   Implement such an adapter that works for all iterator concepts.

Now we can reimplement reverse_n_with_temporary_buffer as follows:

```
template<typename I>
    requires(Mutable(I) && ForwardIterator(I))
void reverse_n_with_temporary_buffer(I f, DistanceType(I) n)
{
    // Precondition: mutable_counted_range(f, n)
    temporary_buffer<UnderlyingType(ValueType(I))> b(n);
    reverse_n_adaptive(underlying_iterator<I>(f), n,
                       begin(b), size(b));
}
```

where underlying_iterator is the adapter from Exercise 12.9.

Project 12.5   Use underlying type systematically throughout a major C++ library, such as STL, or design a new library based on the ideas in this book.

12.4 Conclusions

We extended the structure types and constant-size array types of C++ to dynamic data structures with remote parts. The concepts of ownership and regularity determine treatment of parts by copy construction, assignment, equality, and total ordering. As we showed for the case of dynamic sequences, useful varieties of data structures should be carefully implemented, classified, and documented so that programmers can select the best one for each application. Rearrangements on nested data structures are efficiently implemented by temporarily relaxing the ownership invariant.

Afterword

W*e recap the main themes of the book: regularity, concepts, algorithms and their interfaces, programming techniques, and meanings of pointers. For each theme, we also discuss its particular limitations.*

Regularity

Regular types define copy construction and assignment in terms of equality. Regular functions return equal results when applied to equal arguments. For example, regularity of transformations allowed us to define and reason about algorithms for analyzing orbits. Regularity was in fact relied on throughout the book by ordering relations, the successor function for forward iterators, and many others.

When we work with built-in types, we usually treat the complexity of equality, copying, and assignment as constant. When we deal with composite objects, the complexity of these operations is expected to be linear in the *area* of objects: the total amount of memory, including remote as well as local parts. Our expectation, however, that equality is at worst linear in the area of its arguments cannot always be met in practice.

For example, consider representing a *multiset*, or unordered collection of potentially repeated elements, as an unsorted dynamic sequence. Although inserting a new element takes constant time, testing two multisets for equality takes $O(n \log n)$ time to sort them and then compare them lexicographically. If equality testing is infrequent, this is a good tradeoff; however, putting such multisets into a sequence to be searched with find could lead to unacceptable performance. For an extreme example, consider a situation in which the equality for a type must be implemented with graph isomorphism, a problem for which no polynomial-time algorithm is known.

We noted in Section 1.2 that when implementing behavioral equality on values is not feasible, we can often implement representational equality. For composite objects, we often implement representational equality with the techniques of Section 7.4. Such *structural* equality is often useful in giving the semantics of copy construction and assignment and may be useful for other purposes. Recall that representational equality implies behavioral equality. Similarly, while a natural total ordering is not always realizable, a default total ordering based on structure (e.g., lexicographical ordering for sequences) allows us to efficiently sort and search. There are, of course, objects for which neither copy construction nor assignment—nor even equality—makes sense, because they own a unique resource.

Concepts

We use concepts from abstract algebra—semigroups, monoids, and modules—to describe such algorithms as power, remainder, and gcd. In many cases we need to adapt standard mathematical concepts to fit algorithms. Sometimes, we introduce new concepts, such as *HalvableMonoid*, to strengthen requirements. Sometimes, we relax requirements, as with the partially_associative property. Often we deal with partial domains, as with the definition-space predicate passed to collision_point. Mathematical concepts are tools to be used and freely modified. It is the same with concepts originating in computer science. The iterator concepts describe fundamental properties of certain algorithms and data structures; however, there are other coordinate structures described by concepts yet to be discovered. It is a task of the programmer to determine whether a given concept is useful.

Algorithms and Their Interfaces

Bounded half-open ranges correspond naturally to the implementation of many data structures and provide a convenient way to represent inputs and outputs for such algorithms as find, rotate, partition, merge, and so on. However, with some algorithms, such as partition_point_n, a counted range is the natural interface. Even for algorithms for which bounded ranges are natural, there usually exist natural variations taking counted ranges. Limiting ourselves to a single variety of interface would be a false economy.

Three rotation algorithms, described in Chapter 10, correspond to three iterator concepts. For every algorithm, we need to discover its conceptual requirements, the preconditions on its input, and any other characteristics that make its use appropriate. It is rarely the case that a single algorithm is appropriate in all circumstances.

Programming Techniques

Using successor, a transformation that is strictly functional, allowed us to write a variety of clear and efficient programs. In Chapter 9, however, we chose to encapsulate calls of successor and predecessor into small mutative machines, such as copy_step, since it led to clearer code for a family of related algorithms. Similarly, it is appropriate to use goto in the state machines in Chapter 8 and to use reinterpret_cast for the underlying type mechanism in Chapter 12. Instead of restricting the expressive power of the underlying machine and the language, it is necessary to determine the appropriate use for each available construct. Good software results from the proper organization of components, not from syntactic or semantic restrictions.

Meanings of Pointers

The book demonstrates two ways of using pointers: (1) as iterators and other coordinates representing intermediate positions within an algorithm, and (2) as *connectors*, representing ownership of the remote parts of a composite object. For example, in Section 12.2, we discussed the use of pointers to connect nodes within a list and extents within an array.

These two roles for pointers determine different behavior when an object is copied, destroyed, or compared for equality. Copying an object follows its connectors to copy the remote parts, so the new object contains new connectors pointing to the copied parts. On the other hand, copying an object containing iterators (e.g., a bounded_range) simply copies the iterators without following them. Similarly, destroying an object follows its connectors to destroy the remote parts, while destroying an object containing iterators has no effect on the object to which the iterators point. Finally, equality on a container follows connectors to compare corresponding parts, while equality on a noncontainer (e.g., a bounded_range) simply tests for equality of corresponding iterators.

There is, however, a third way to use pointers: to represent a *relationship* between entities. A relationship between two or more objects is not a part owned by these objects; it has an existence of its own while maintaining mutual dependencies between the objects it relates. In general, a pointer representing a relationship does not participate in the regular operations. For example, copying an object does not follow or copy a relationship pointer, since the relationship exists for the object being copied but not for its copy. If a one-to-one relationship is represented as a pair of embedded pointers linking two objects, destroying either of the objects must clear the corresponding pointer in the other object.

Designing data structures as composite objects with ownership and remote parts leads to a programming style in which the primary objects—those that are not subparts of other objects—reside in static variables, with a lifetime of the entire program execution or, in local variables, with a lifetime of a block. Dynamically allocated memory is used only for remote parts. This extends the stack-based block structure of Algol 60 to handle arbitrary data structures. Such structure naturally fits many applications. However, there are circumstances in which reference counting, garbage collection, or other memory-management techniques are appropriate.

Conclusions

Programming is an iterative process: studying useful problems, finding efficient algorithms for them, distilling the concepts underlying the algorithms, and organizing the concepts and algorithms into a coherent mathematical theory. Each new discovery adds to the permanent body of knowledge, but each has its limitations.

Appendix A

Mathematical Notation

We use the symbol $\triangleq$ to mean "equals by definition."

If P and Q are propositions, so too are $\neg P$ (read as "not P"), $P \vee Q$ ("P or Q"), $P \wedge Q$ ("P and Q"), $P \Rightarrow Q$ ("P implies Q"), and $P \Leftrightarrow Q$ ("P is equivalent to Q"). For equivalence, we often write "P if and only if Q".

If P is a proposition and x is a variable, $(\exists x)P$ is a proposition (read as "there exists x such that P"). If P is a proposition and x is a variable, $(\forall x)P$ is a proposition (read as "for all x, P"); $(\forall x)P \Leftrightarrow (\neg(\exists x)\neg P)$.

We use this vocabulary from set theory:

$a \in X$ ("a is an *element* of X")

$X \subset Y$ ("X is a *subset* of Y")

$\{a_0, \ldots, a_n\}$ ("the *finite set* with elements $a_0, \ldots,$ and a_n")

$\{a \in X | P(a)\}$ ("the *subset* of X for which the predicate P holds")

$X \cup Y$ ("the *union* of X and Y")

$X \cap Y$ ("the *intersection* of X and Y")

$X \times Y$ ("the *direct product* of X and Y")

$f : X \to Y$ ("f is a *function* from X to Y")

$f : X_0 \times X_1 \to Y$ ("f is a function from the product of X_0 and X_1 to Y")

$x \mapsto \mathcal{E}(x)$ ("x maps to $\mathcal{E}(x)$", always given following a function signature)

A *closed interval* $[a, b]$ is the set of all elements x such that $a \le x \le b$. An *open interval* (a, b) is the set of all elements x such that $a < x < b$. A *half-open-on-right interval* $[a, b)$ is the set of all elements x such that $a \le x < b$. A *half-open-on-left interval* $(a, b]$ is the set of all elements x such that $a < x \le b$. A *half-open interval* is our shorthand for half-open on right. These definitions generalize to weak orderings.

We use this notation in specifications, where i and j are iterators and n is an integer:

$i \prec j$ ("i precedes j")

$i \preceq j$ ("i precedes or equals j")

$[i, j)$ ("half-open bounded range from i to j")

$[i, j]$ ("closed bounded range from i to j")

$[\![i, n)\!\!)$ ("half-open weak or counted range from i for $n \geq 0$")

$[\![i, n]\!]$ ("closed weak or counted range from i for $n \geq 0$")

We use this terminology when discussing concepts:

Weak refers to weakening, which includes dropping, an axiom. For example, a weak ordering replaces equality with equivalence.

Semi refers to dropping an operation. For example, a semigroup lacks the inverse operation.

Partial refers to restricting the definition space. For example, partial subtraction (cancellation) $a - b$ is defined when $a \geq b$.

Appendix B

Programming Language

Sean Parent and Bjarne Stroustrup

T*his appendix defines the subset of C++ used in the book. To simplify the syntax, we use a few library facilities as intrinsics. These intrinsics are not written in this subset but take advantage of other C++ features. Section B.1 defines this subset; Section B.2 specifies the implementation of the intrinsics.*

B.1 Language Definition

Syntax Notation

An Extended Backus-Naur Form designed by Niklaus Wirth is used. Wirth [1977, pages 822–823] describes it as follows:

> The word *identifier* is used to denote *nonterminal symbol*, and *literal* stands for *terminal symbol*. For brevity, *identifier* and *character* are not defined in further detail.

```
syntax     = {production}.
production = identifier "=" expression ".".
expression = term {"|" term}.
term       = factor {factor}.
factor     = identifier | literal
                 | "(" expression ")"
                 | "[" expression "]"
                 | "{" expression "}".
literal    = """" character {character} """".
```

Repetition is denoted by curly brackets, i.e., {a} stands for ϵ | a | aa | aaa | ... . Optionality is expressed by square brackets, i.e., [a] stands for a | ϵ . Parentheses merely serve for grouping, e.g., (a | b) c stands for ac | bc. Terminal symbols, i.e., literals, are enclosed in quote marks (and, if a quote mark appears as a literal itself, it is written twice).

Lexical Conventions

The following productions give the syntax for identifiers and literals:

```
identifer = (letter | "_") {letter | "_" | digit}.
literal   = boolean | integer | real.
boolean   = "false" | "true".
integer   = digit {digit}.
real      = integer "." [integer] | "." integer.
```

Comments extend from two slashes to the end of the line:

```
comment   = "//" {character} eol.
```

Basic Types

Three C++ types are used: `bool` has values `false` and `true`, `int` has signed integer values, and `double` has IEEE 64-bit floating-point values:

```
basic_type = "bool" | "int" | "double".
```

Expressions

Expressions may be either runtime or compile time. Compile-time expressions may evaluate to either a value or a type.

Expressions are defined by the following grammar. Operators in inner productions—those appearing lower in the grammar—have a higher order of precedence than those in outer productions:

```
expression     = conjunction {"||" conjunction}.
conjunction    = equality {"&&" equality}.
equality       = relational {("==" | "!=") relational}.
relational     = additive {("<" | ">" | "<=" | ">=") additive}.
additive       = multiplicative {("+" | "-") multiplicative}.
multiplicative = prefix {("*" | "/" | "%") prefix}.
prefix         = ["-" | "!" | "const"] postfix.
postfix        = primary {"." identifier
                        | "(" [expression_list] ")"
                        | "[" expression "]"
                        | "&"}.
```

```
primary              = literal | identifier | "(" expression ")"
                       | basic_type | template_name | "typename".

expression_list = expression {"," expression}.
```

The || and && operators designate ∨ (disjunction) and ∧ (conjunction), respectively. The operands must be Boolean values. The first operand is evaluated prior to the second operand. If the first operand determines the outcome of the expression (`true` for ||, or `false` for &&), the second operand is not evaluated, and the result is the value of the first operand. Prefix ! is ¬ (negation) and must be applied to a Boolean value.

== and != are, respectively, equality and inequality operators and return a Boolean value.

<, >, <=, and >= are, respectively, less than, greater than, less or equal, and greater or equal, also returning a Boolean value.

+ and − are, respectively, addition and subtraction; prefix − is additive inverse.

*, /, and % are, respectively, multiplication, division, and remainder.

Postfix . (dot) takes an object of structure type and returns the member corresponding to the identifier following the dot. Postfix () takes a procedure or object on which the apply operator is defined and returns the result of invoking the procedure or function object with the given arguments. When applied to a type, () performs a construction using the given arguments; when applied to a type function, it returns another type. Postfix [] takes an object on which the index operator is defined and returns the element whose position is determined by the value of the expression within the brackets.

Prefix const is a type operator returning a type that is a constant version of its operand.

Postfix & is a type operator returning a reference type of its operand.

Enumerations

An enumeration generates a type with a unique value corresponding to each identifier in the list. The only operations defined on enumerations are those of regular types: equality, relational operations, inequality, construction, destruction, and assignment:

```
enumeration     = "enum" identifier "{" identifer_list "}" ";".
identifer_list = identifier {"," identifier}.
```

Structures

A structure is a type consisting of a heterogeneous tuple of named, typed objects
called data members. Each data member is either an individual object or an array
of constant size. In addition, the structure may include definitions of constructors,
a destructor, member operators (assignment, application, and indexing), and local
typedefs. A structure with an apply operator member is known as a *function object*.
Omitting the structure body allows a forward declaration.

```
structure            = "struct" structure_name [structure_body] ";".
structure_name       = identifier.
structure_body       = "{" {member} "}".
member               = data_member
                         | constructor | destructor
                         | assign | apply | index
                         | typedef.
data_member          = expression identifier ["[" expression "]"] ";".
constructor          = structure_name "(" [parameter_list] ")"
                           [":" initializer_list] body.
destructor           = "~" structure_name "(" ")" body.
assign               = "void" "operator" "="
                           "(" parameter ")" body.
apply                = expression "operator" "(" ")"
                           "(" [parameter_list] ")" body.
index                = expression "operator" "[" "]"
                           "(" parameter ")" body.

initializer_list = initializer {"," initializer}.
initializer      = identifer "(" [expression_list] ")".
```

A constructor taking a constant reference to the type of the structure is a *copy
constructor*. If a copy constructor is not defined, a member-by-member copy constructor is generated. A constructor with no arguments is a *default constructor*. A
member-by-member default constructor is generated only if no other constructors
are defined. If an assignment operator is not defined, a member-by-member assignment operator is generated. If no destructor is supplied, a member-by-member
destructor is generated. Each identifier in an initializer list is the identifier of a data
member of the structure. If a constructor contains an initializer list, every data member of the structure is constructed with a constructor matching[1] the expression list

---

1. The matching mechanism performs overload resolution by exact matching without any implicit
conversions.

of the initializer; all these constructions occur before the body of the constructor is executed.

Procedures

A procedure consists of its return type or, when no value is returned, void, followed by its name and parameter list. The name may be an identifier or an operator. A parameter expression must yield a type. A procedure signature without a body allows a forward declaration.

```
procedure       = (expression | "void") procedure_name
                    "(" [parameter_list] ")" (body | ";").
procedure_name = identifier | operator.
operator        = "operator"
                    ("==" | "<" | "+" | "-" | "*" | "/" | "%").
parameter_list = parameter {"," parameter}.
parameter       = expression [identifier].
body            = compound.
```

Only the listed operators can be defined. A definition for the operator != is generated in terms of ==; definitions for the operators >, <=, and >= are generated in terms of <. When a procedure is called, the value of each argument expression is bound to the corresponding parameter, and the body of the procedure is executed.

Statements

Statements make up the body of procedures, constructors, destructors, and member operators:

```
statement          = [identifier ":"]
                       (simple_statement | assignment
                       | construction | control_statement
                       | typedef).
simple_statement  = expression ";".
assignment         = expression "=" expression ";".
construction       = expression identifier [initialization] ";".
initialization     = "(" expression_list ")" | "=" expression.
control_statement = return | conditional | switch | while | do
                       | compound | switch | break | goto.
return             = "return" [expression] ";".
conditional        = "if" "(" expression ")" statement
                       ["else" statement].
switch             = "switch" "(" expression ")" "{" {case} "}".
```

```
case                = "case" expression ":" {statement}.
while               = "while" "(" expression ")" statement.
do                  = "do" statement
                      "while" "(" expression ")" ";".
compound            = "{" {statement} "}".
break               = "break" ";".
goto                = "goto" identifier ";".
typedef             = "typedef" expression identifier ";".
```

A simple statement, which is often a procedure call, is evaluated for its side effects. An assignment applies the assignment operator for the type of the object on the left-hand side. The first expression for a construction is a type expression giving the type to be constructed. A construction without an initialization applies the default constructor. A construction with a parenthesized expression list applies the matching constructor. A construction with an equal sign followed by an expression applies the copy constructor; the expression must have the same type as the object being constructed.

The `return` statement returns control to the caller of the current function with the value of the expression as the function result. The expression must evaluate to a value of the return type of the function.

The conditional statement executes the first statement if the value of the expression is true; if the expression is false and there is an `else` clause, the second statement is executed. The expression must evaluate to a Boolean.

The `switch` statement evaluates the expression and then executes the first statement following a case label with matching value; subsequent statements are executed to the end of the `switch` statement or until a `break` statement is executed. The expression in a `switch` statement must evaluate to an integer or enumeration.

The `while` statement repeatedly evaluates the expression and executes the statement as long as the expression is true. The `do` statement repeatedly executes the statement and evaluates the expression until the expression is false. In either case, the expression must evaluate to a Boolean.

The compound statement executes the sequence of statements in order.

The `goto` statement transfers execution to the statement following the corresponding label in the current function.

The `break` statement terminates the execution of the smallest enclosing `switch`, `while`, or `do` statement; execution continues with the statement following the terminated statement.

The `typedef` statement defines an alias for a type.

Templates

A template allows a structure or procedure to be parameterized by one or more types or constants. Template definitions and template names use < and > as delimiters.[2]

```
template        = template_decl
                    (structure | procedure | specialization).
specialization  = "struct" structure_name "<" additive_list ">"
                    [structure_body] ";".
template_decl   = "template" "<" [parameter_list] ">" [constraint].
constraint      = "requires" "(" expression ")".

template_name   = (structure_name | procedure_name)
                    ["<" additive_list ">"].
additive_list   = additive {"," additive}.
```

When a template_name is used as a primary, the template definition is used to generate a structure or procedure with template parameters replaced by corresponding template arguments. These template arguments are either given explicitly as the delimited expression list in the template_name or, for procedures, may be deduced from the procedure argument types.

A template structure can be specialized, providing an alternative definition for the template that is considered when the arguments match before the unspecialized version of the template structure.

When the template definition includes a constraint, the template argument types and values must satisfy the Boolean expression following requires.

Intrinsics

pointer(T) is a type constructor that returns the type pointer to T. If x is an object of type T, addressof(x) returns a value of type pointer(T) referring to x. source, sink, and deref are unary functions defined on pointer types. source is defined for all pointer types and returns a corresponding constant reference; see Section 6.1. sink and deref are defined for pointer types to nonconstant objects and return corresponding nonconstant references; see Section 9.1. reinterpret_cast is a function template that takes a reference type and an object (passed by reference) and returns a reference of the reference type to the same object. The object must also have a valid interpretation with the reference type.

---

2. To disambiguate between the use of < and > as relations or as template name delimiters, once a structure_name or procedure_name is parsed as part of a template, it becomes a terminal symbol.

B.2 Macros and Trait Structures

To allow the language defined in Section B.1 to compile as a valid C++ program, a few macros and structure definitions are necessary.

Template Constraints

The `requires` clause is implemented with this macro:[3]

```
#define requires(...)
```

Intrinsics

`pointer(T)` and `addressof(x)` are introduced to give us a simple linear notation and allow simple top-down parsing. They are implemented as

```
#define pointer(T) T*

template<typename T>
pointer(T) addressof(T& x)
{
    return &x;
}
```

Type Functions

Type functions are implemented by using a C++ technique called a *trait class*. For each type function—say, ValueType—we define a corresponding structure template: say, `value_type<T>`. The structure template contains one typedef, named `type` by convention; if appropriate, a default can be provided in the base structure template:

```
template<typename T>
struct value_type
{
    typedef T type;
};
```

To provide a convenient notation, we define a macro[4] that extracts the typedef as the result of the type function:

---

3. This implementation treats requirements as documentation only.
4. Such a macro works only inside a template definition, because of the use of the keyword `typename`.

```
#define ValueType(T) typename value_type< T >::type
```

We refine the global definition for a particular type by specializing:

```
template<typename T>
struct value_type<pointer(T)>
{
    typedef T type;
};
```

Bibliography

Agarwal, Saurabh and Gudmund Skovbjerg Frandsen. 2004. Binary GCD like algorithms for some complex quadratic rings. In *Algorithmic Number Theory*, 6th International Symposium, Burlington, VT, USA, June 13–18, 2004. *Proceedings*, ed. Duncan A. Buell, vol. 3076 of *Lecture Notes in Computer Science*, pages 57–71. Springer.

Bentley, Jon. 1984. Programming pearls. *Communications of the ACM* 27(4): 287–291.

Bolzano, Bernard. 1817. *Rein analytischer Beweis des Lehrsatzes, daß zwischen je zwey Werthen, die ein entgegengesetztes Resultat gewhren, wenigstens eine reelle Wurzel der Gleichung liege*. Prague: Gottlieb Haase.

Boute, Raymond T. 1992. The Euclidean definition of the functions div and mod. *ACM Transactions on Programming Languages and Systems* 14(2): 127–144.

Boyer, Robert S. and J. Strother Moore. 1977. A fast string searching algorithm. *Communications of the ACM* 20(10): 762–772.

Brent, Richard P. 1980. An improved Monte Carlo factorization algorithm. *BIT* 20: 176–184.

Cauchy, Augustin-Louis. 1821. *Cours D'Analyse de L'Ecole Royale Polytechnique*. L'Académie des Sciences.

Chrystal, G. 1904. *Algebra: An Elementary Text-Book. Parts I and II*. Adam and Charles Black, 1904. Reprint, AMS Chelsea Publishing, 1964.

Dehnert, James C. and Alexander A. Stepanov. 2000. Fundamentals of generic programming. In *Generic Programming*, International Seminar on Generic Programming, Dagstuhl Castle, Germany, April/May 1998. *Selected Papers*, eds. Mehdi Jazayeri, Rüdiger G. K. Loos, and David R. Musser, vol. 1766 of *Lecture Notes in Computer Science*, pages 1–11. Springer.

Diaconis, Persi and Paul Erdös. 2004. On the distribution of the greatest common divisor. In *A Festschrift for Herman Rubin*, ed. Anirban DasGupta, vol. 45 of *Lecture Notes—Monograph Series*, pages 56–61. Institute of Mathematical Statistics.

Dijkstra, Edsger W. 1972. Notes on structured programming. In *Structured Programming*, eds. O.-J. Dahl, E. W. Dijkstra, and C. A. R. Hoare, pages 1–82. London and New York: Academic Press.

Dirichlet, P. G. L. 1863. *Forlesungen über Zahlentheorie*. Vieweg und Sohn, 1863. With supplements by Richard Dedekind. English translation by John Stillwell. *Lectures on Number Theory*, American Mathematical Society and London Mathematical Society, 1999.

Dudziński, Krzysztof and Andrzej Dydek. 1981. On a stable minimum storage merging algorithm. *Information Processing Letters* 12(1): 5–8.

Dwyer, Barry. 1974. Simple algorithms for traversing a tree without an auxiliary stack. *Information Processing Letters* 2: 143–145.

Fiduccia, Charles M. 1985. An efficient formula for linear recurrences. *SIAM Journal on Computing* 14(1): 106–112.

Fletcher, William and Roland Silver. 1966. Algorithm 284: Interchange of two blocks of data. *Communications of the ACM* 9(5): 326.

Floyd, Robert W. and Donald E. Knuth. 1990. Addition Machines. *SIAM Journal on Computing* 19(2): 329–340.

Frobenius, Georg Ferdinand. 1895. Über endliche gruppen. In *Sitzungesberichte der Königlich Preussischen Akademie der Wissenschaften zu Berlin*, Phys.-math. Classe, pages 163–194. Berlin.

Grassmann, Hermann Günther. 1861. *Lehrbuch der Mathematik für höhere Lehranstalten*, vol. 1. Berlin: Enslin.

Gries, David and Harlan Mills. 1981. Swapping sections. Tech. Rep. 81-452, Department of Computer Science, Cornell University.

Heath, Sir Thomas L. 1925. *The Thirteen Books of Euclid's Elements*. Cambridge University Press, 1925. Reprint, Dover, 1956.

Heath, T. L. 1912. *The Works of Archimedes*. Cambridge University Press, 1912. Reprint, Dover, 2002.

Hoare, C. A. R. 1962. Quicksort. *The Computer Journal* 5(1): 10–16.

Iverson, Kenneth. 1962. *A Programming Language*. Wiley.

Knuth, Donald E. 1997. *The Art of Computer Programming* Volume 2: *Seminumerical Algorithms* (3rd edition). Reading, MA: Addison-Wesley.

Knuth, Donald E. 1998. *The Art of Computer Programming* Volume 3: *Sorting and Searching* (2nd edition). Reading, MA: Addison Wesley.

Knuth, Donald E. 2005. *The Art of Computer Programming* Volume 1, fascicle 1: *MMIX: A RISC Computer for the New Millenium*. Boston: Addison-Wesley.

Knuth, Donald E., J. Morris, and V. Pratt. 1977. Fast pattern matching in strings. *SIAM Journal on Computing* 6: 323–350.

Kwak, Jin Ho and Sungpyo Hong. 2004. *Linear Algebra*. Birkhäuser.

Lagrange, J.-L. 1795. *Leçons élémentaires sur les mathématiques, données à l'école normale en 1795*. 1795. Reprinted: *Oeuvres*, vol. VII, pages 181–288. Paris: Gauthier-Villars, 1877.

Levy, Leon S. 1982. An improved list-searching algorithm. *Information Processing Letters* 15(1): 43–45.

Lindstrom, Gary. 1973. Scanning list structures without stack or tag bits. *Information Processing Letters* 2: 47–51.

Mauchly, John W. 1946. Sorting and collating. In *Theory and Techniques for Design of Electronic Digital Computers*. Moore School of Electrical Engineering, University of Pennsylvania, 1946. Reprinted in: *The Moore School Lectures*, eds. Martin Campbell-Kelly and Michael R. Williams, pages 271–287. Cambridge, Massachusetts: MIT Press, 1985.

McCarthy, D. P. 1986. Effect of improved multiplication efficiency on exponentiation algorithms derived from addition chains. *Mathematics of Computation* 46(174): 603–608.

Miller, J. C. P. and D. J. Spencer Brown. 1966. An algorithm for evaluation of remote terms in a linear recurrence sequence. *The Computer Journal* 9(2): 188–190.

Morris, Joseph M. 1979. Traversing binary trees simply and cheaply. *Information Processing Letters* 9(5): 197–200.

Musser, David R. 1975. Multivariate polynomial factorization. *Journal of the ACM* 22(2): 291–308.

Musser, David R. and Gor V. Nishanov. 1997. A fast generic sequence matching algorithm. Tech. Rep., Computer Science Department, Rensselaer Polytechnic Institute. Archived as http://arxiv.org/abs/0810.0264v1.

Patterson, David A. and John L. Hennessy. 2007. *Computer Organization and Design: The Hardware/Software Interface* (3rd revised edition). Morgan Kaufmann.

Peano, Giuseppe. 1908. *Formulario Mathematico, Editio V*. Torino: Fratres Bocca Editores, 1908. Reprinted: Roma: Edizioni Cremonese, 1960.

Rivest, R., A. Shamir, and L. Adleman. 1978. A method for obtaining digital signatures and public-key cryptosystems. *Communications of the ACM* 21(2): 120–126.

Robins, Gay and Charles Shute. 1987. *The Rhind Mathematical Papyrus*. British Museum Publications.

Robson, J. M. 1973. An improved algorithm for traversing binary trees without auxiliary stack. *Information Processing Letters* 2: 12–14.

Schorr, H. and W. M. Waite. 1967. An efficient and machine-independent procedure for garbage collection in various list structures. *Communications of the ACM* 10(8): 501–506.

Sedgewick, R. T., T. G. Szymanski, and A. C. Yao. 1979. The complexity of finding cycles in periodic functions. In *Proc. 11th SIGACT Meeting*, ed. Michael J. Fischer, pages 376–390.

Sigler, Laurence E. 2002. *Fibonacci's Liber Abaci: Leonardo Pisano's Book of Calculation*. Springer-Verlag.

Stein, Josef. 1967. Computational problems associated with Racah algebra. *J. Comput. Phys.* 1: 397–405.

Stepanov, Alexander and Meng Lee. 1995. The Standard Template Library. Technical Report 95-11(R.1), HP Laboratories.

Stroustrup, Bjarne. 2000. *The C++ Programming Language: Special Edition* (3rd edition). Boston: Addison-Wesley.

Tarjan, Robert Endre. 1983. *Data Structures and Network Algorithms*. SIAM.

Tarjan, Robert Endre. 1985. Amortized computational complexity. *SIAM Journal on Algebraic and Discrete Methods* 6(2): 306–318.

Thompson, Ken and Dennis Ritchie. 1974. The UNIX time-sharing system. *Communications of the ACM* 17(7): 365–375.

van der Waerden, Bartel Leenert. 1930. *Moderne Algebra* Erster Teil. Julius Springer, 1930. English translation by Fred Blum. *Modern Algebra*, New York: Frederic Ungar Publishing, 1949.

Weilert, André. 2000. (1+i)-ary GCD computation in $\mathbb{Z}[i]$ as an analogue of the binary GCD algorithm. *J. Symb. Comput.* 30(5): 605–617.

Wirth, Niklaus. 1977. What can we do about the unnecessary diversity of notation for syntactic definitions? *Communications of the ACM* 20(11): 822–823.

Index

→ (function), 231
− (additive inverse), in additive group, 67
∧ (and), 231
− (difference)
 in additive group, 67
 in cancellable monoid, 72
 of integers, 18
 of iterator and integer, 111
 of iterators, 93
× (direct product), 231
∈ (element), 231
= (equality), 7
 for array_k, 212
 for pair, 210
≜ (equals by definition), 12, 231
⇔ (equivalent), 231
∃ (exists), 231
∀ (for all), 231
> (greater), 62
≥ (greater or equal), 62
⇒ (implies), 231
[ ] (index)
 for array_k, 211
 for bounded_range, 214
≠ (inequality), 7, 62
∩ (intersection), 231
< (less), 62
 for array_k, 212
 natural total ordering, 61
 for pair, 210
≤ (less or equal), 62
↦ (maps to), 231
¬ (not), 231
∨ (or), 231
a^n (power of associative operation), 32
f^n (power of transformation), 17
≺ (precedes), 95

≼ (precedes or equal), 95
· (product)
 of integers, 18
 in multiplicative semigroup, 66
 in semimodule, 69
/ (quotient), of integers, 18
[f, l] (range, closed bounded), 94
⟦f, n⟧ (range, closed weak or counted), 94
[f, l) (range, half-open bounded), 94
⟦f, n) (range, half-open weak or
  counted), 94
⊂ (subset), 231
+ (sum)
 in additive semigroup, 66
 of integers, 18
 of iterator and integer, 92
∪ (union), 231

A
abs algorithm, 16, 71
absolute value, properties, 71
abstract entity, 1
abstract genus, 2
abstract procedure, 13
 overloading, 43
abstract species, 2
accumulation procedure, 46
accumulation variable
 elimination, 39
 introduction, 35
action, 28
acyclic descendants of bifurcate coordinate,
  116
additive inverse (−), in additive group, 67
AdditiveGroup concept, 67
AdditiveMonoid concept, 67
AdditiveSemigroup concept, 66

address, 4
    abstracted by iterator, 89
add_to_counter algorithm, 199
advance_tail machine, 135
algorithm. *See* machine
    abs, 16, 71
    add_to_counter, 199
    all, 97
    bifurcate_compare, 131
    bifurcate_compare_nonempty, 130
    bifurcate_equivalent, 129
    bifurcate_equivalent_nonempty, 128
    bifurcate_isomorphic, 126
    bifurcate_isomorphic_nonempty, 125
    circular, 25
    circular_nonterminating_orbit, 25
    collision_point, 22
    collision_point_nonterminating_orbit, 23
    combine_copy, 160
    combine_copy_backward, 162
    combine_linked_nonempty, 138
    combine_ranges, 196
    compare_strict_or_reflexive, 57–58
    complement, 50
    complement_of_converse, 50
    connection_point, 26
    connection_point_nonterminating_orbit, 26
    convergent_point, 26
    converse, 50
    copy, 152
    copy_backward, 155
    copy_bounded, 153
    copy_if, 158
    copy_n, 154
    copy_select, 158
    count_if, 97, 98
    cycle_from, 173
    cycle_to, 173
    distance, 19
    euclidean_norm, 16
    exchange_values, 164
    fast_subtractive_gcd, 78
    fibonacci, 46
    find, 96
    find_adjacent_mismatch, 103
    find_adjacent_mismatch_forward, 106, 135
    find_backward_if, 112
    find_if, 97

find_if_not_unguarded, 102
find_if_unguarded, 101
find_last, 136
find_mismatch, 102
find_n, 101
find_not, 97
for_each, 96
for_each_n, 101
gcd, 80
height, 122
height_recursive, 118
increment, 91
is_left_successor, 119
is_right_successor, 120
k_rotate_from_permutation_indexed, 180
k_rotate_from_permutation_random_
    access, 180
largest_doubling, 75
lexicographical_compare, 129
lexicographical_equal, 127
lexicographical_equivalent, 127
lexicographical_less, 130
lower_bound_n, 109
lower_bound_predicate, 108
median_5, 61
memory-adaptive, 177
merge_copy, 163
merge_copy_backward, 163
merge_linked_nonempty, 141
merge_n_adaptive, 206
merge_n_with_buffer, 202
none, 97
not_all, 97
orbit_structure, 28
orbit_structure_nonterminating_orbit, 27
partitioned_at_point, 191
partition_bidirectional, 194
partition_copy, 160
partition_copy_n, 160
partition_linked, 140
partition_point, 107
partition_point_n, 107
partition_semistable, 192
partition_single_cycle, 194
partition_stable_iterative, 201
partition_stable_n, 197
partition_stable_n_adaptive, 197
partition_stable_n_nonempty, 197

algorithm. *See* machine (*cont.*)
  partition_stable_singleton, 196
  partition_stable_with_buffer, 195
  partition_trivial, 198
  phased_applicator, 147
  potential_partition_point, 191
  power, 42
  power_accumulate, 41
  power_accumulate_positive, 41
  power_left_associated vs. power_0, 34
  power_right_associated, 33
  power_unary, 18
  predicate_source, 140
  quotient_remainder, 85
  quotient_remainder_nonnegative, 82
  quotient_remainder_nonnegative_iterative,
    83
  reachable, 121
  reduce, 99
  reduce_balanced, 200
  reduce_nonempty, 99
  reduce_nonzeroes, 100
  relation_source, 141
  remainder, 84
  remainder_nonnegative, 74
  remainder_nonnegative_iterative, 75
  reverse_append, 139, 140
  reverse_bidirectional, 175
  reverse_copy, 156
  reverse_copy_backward, 156
  reverse_indexed, 186
  reverse_n_adaptive, 178
  reverse_n_bidirectional, 175
  reverse_n_forward, 177
  reverse_n_indexed, 175
  reverse_n_with_buffer, 176
  reverse_swap_ranges, 167
  reverse_swap_ranges_bounded, 167
  reverse_swap_ranges_n, 168
  reverse_with_temporary_buffer, 187, 225
  rotate, 187
  rotate_bidirectional_nontrivial, 182
  rotate_cycles, 181
  rotate_forward_annotated, 183
  rotate_forward_nontrivial, 184
  rotate_forward_step, 184
  rotate_indexed_nontrivial, 181
  rotate_nontrivial, 188

  rotate_partial_nontrivial, 185
  rotate_random_access_nontrivial, 181
  rotate_with_buffer_backward_nontrivial,
    186
  rotate_with_buffer_nontrivial, 185
  select_0_2, 53, 63
  select_0_3, 54
  select_1_2, 54
  select_1_3, 55
  select_1_3_ab, 55
  select_1_4, 56, 59
  select_1_4_ab, 56, 59
  select_1_4_ab_cd, 56, 58
  select_2_3, 54
  select_2_5, 60
  select_2_5_ab, 60
  select_2_5_ab_cd, 59
  slow_quotient, 73
  slow_remainder, 72
  some, 97
  sort_linked_nonempty_n, 142
  sort_n, 207
  sort_n_adaptive, 207
  sort_n_with_buffer, 203
  split_copy, 158
  split_linked, 137
  subtractive_gcd, 78
  subtractive_gcd_nonzero, 77
  swap, 224
  swap_basic, 223
  swap_ranges, 165
  swap_ranges_bounded, 166
  swap_ranges_n, 166
  terminating, 23
  transpose_operation, 201
  traverse, 123
  traverse_nonempty, 118
  traverse_phased_rotating, 148
  traverse_rotating, 146
  underlying_ref, 224
  upper_bound_n, 109
  upper_bound_predicate, 109
  weight, 122
  weight_recursive, 117
  weight_rotating, 147
aliased property, 150
aliased write-read, 150
aliased write-write, 159

all algorithm, 97
ambiguous value type, 3
amortized complexity, 219
and ($\wedge$), 231
annihilation property, 68
annotation variable, 183
ArchimedeanGroup concept, 83
ArchimedeanMonoid concept, 72
area of object, 227
Aristotle, 77
Arity type attribute, 11
array, varieties, 220–221
array_k type, 210
Artin, Emil, 13
assignment, 7
    for array_k, 211
    for pair, 210
associative operation, 31, 98
    power of (a^n), 32
associative property, 31
    exploited by power, 33
    partially_associative, 98
    of permutation composition, 170
asymmetric property, 50
attribute, 1
auxiliary computation during recursion, 176
Axiom of Archimedes, 72, 73

B
backward movement in range, 112
BackwardLinker concept, 134
backward_offset property, 161
basic singly linked list, 218
begin
    for array_k, 211
    for bounded_range, 214
    for *Linearizable*, 213
behavioral equality, 3, 228
BidirectionalBifurcateCoordinate concept,
    119–120
BidirectionalIterator concept, 111
BidirectionalLinker concept, 134
BifurcateCoordinate concept, 115
bifurcate_compare algorithm, 131
bifurcate_compare_nonempty algorithm, 130
bifurcate_equivalent algorithm, 129
bifurcate_equivalent_nonempty algorithm,
    128

bifurcate_isomorphic algorithm, 126
bifurcate_isomorphic_nonempty algorithm,
    125
BinaryOperation concept, 31
binary_scale_down_nonnegative, 40
binary_scale_up_nonnegative, 40
bisection technique, 107
Bolzano, Bernard, 107
bounded integer type, 87
bounded range, 93
bounded_range property, 93
bounded_range type, 214
Brandt, Jon, 193

C
CancellableMonoid concept, 72
cancellation in monoid, 72
categories of ideas, 1
Cauchy, Augustin Louis, 107
circular algorithm, 25
circular array, 220
circular doubly linked list, 218
circular singly linked list, 218
circular_nonterminating_orbit algorithm, 25
closed bounded range ($[f, l]$), 94
closed interval, 231
closed weak or counted range ($[\![f, n]\!]$), 94
clusters of derived procedures, 62
codomain, 10
Codomain type function, 11
Collins, George, 13
collision point of orbit, 21
collision_point algorithm, 22
collision_point_nonterminating_orbit
    algorithm, 23
combine_copy algorithm, 160
combine_copy_backward algorithm, 162
combine_linked_nonempty algorithm, 138
combine_ranges algorithm, 196
common-subexpression elimination, 35
commutative property, 66
CommutativeRing concept, 69
CommutativeSemiring concept, 68
compare_strict_or_reflexive algorithm,
    57–58
complement algorithm, 50
complement of converse of relation, 50
complement of relation, 50

complement_of_converse algorithm, 50
complement_of_converse property, 104
complexity
    amortized, 219
    of empty, 213
    of indexing of a sequence, 213
    of regular operations, 227
    of source, 90
    of successor, 92
composite object, 215
composition
    of permutations, 170
    of transformations, 17, 32
computational basis, 6
concept, 11
    AdditiveGroup, 67
    AdditiveMonoid, 67
    AdditiveSemigroup, 66
    ArchimedeanGroup, 83
    ArchimedeanMonoid, 72
    BackwardLinker, 134
    BidirectionalBifurcateCoordinate, 119–120
    BidirectionalIterator, 111
    BidirectionalLinker, 134
    BifurcateCoordinate, 115
    BinaryOperation, 31
    CancellableMonoid, 72
    CommutativeRing, 69
    CommutativeSemiring, 68
    consistent, 87
    DiscreteArchimedeanRing, 86
    DiscreteArchimedeanSemiring, 85
    EmptyLinkedBifurcateCoordinate, 144
    EuclideanMonoid, 77
    EuclideanSemimodule, 80
    EuclideanSemiring, 79
    examples from C++ and STL, 11
    ForwardIterator, 106
    ForwardLinker, 133
    FunctionalProcedure, 11
    HalvableMonoid, 74
    HomogeneousFunction, 12
    HomogeneousPredicate, 16
    IndexedIterator, 110
    Integer, 18, 40
    Iterator, 91
    Linearizable, 213
    LinkedBifurcateCoordinate, 144

modeled by type, 11
Module, 70
MultiplicativeGroup, 68
MultiplicativeMonoid, 67
MultiplicativeSemigroup, 66
NonnegativeDiscreteArchimedeanSemiring,
    86
Operation, 16
OrderedAdditiveGroup, 70
OrderedAdditiveMonoid, 70
OrderedAdditiveSemigroup, 70
Predicate, 15
RandomAccessIterator, 113
refinement, 11
Regular, 11
Relation, 49
relational concept, 69
Ring, 69
Semimodule, 69
Semiring, 68
Sequence, 216
TotallyOrdered, 62
Transformation, 17
type concept, 11
UnaryFunction, 12
UnaryPredicate, 16
univalent, 86
useful, 87
weakening, 11
concept dispatch, 106, 187
concept schema
    composite object, 216
    coordinate structure, 124
concept tag type, 187
concrete entity, 1
concrete genus, 2
concrete species, 2
connectedness of composite object, 215
connection point of orbit, 20
connection_point algorithm, 26
connection_point_nonterminating_orbit
    algorithm, 26
connectors, 229
consistency of concept's axioms, 87
constant-size sequence, 216
constructor, 7
container, 213
convergent_point algorithm, 26

converse algorithm, 50
converse of relation, 50
coordinate structure
     bifurcate coordinate, 115
     of composite object, 215
     concept schema, 124
     iterator, 89
copy algorithm, 152
copy constructor, 8
     for array_k, 211
     for pair, 210
copy of object, 5
copying rearrangement, 172
copy_backward algorithm, 155
copy_backward_step machine, 154
copy_bounded algorithm, 153
copy_if algorithm, 158
copy_n algorithm, 154
copy_select algorithm, 158
copy_step machine, 152
counted_range property, 93
counter_machine type, 200
count_down machine, 153
count_if algorithm, 97, 98
cycle detection intuition, 21
cycle in a permutation, 171
cycle of orbit, 20
cycle size, 20
cycle_from algorithm, 173
cycle_to algorithm, 173
cyclic element under transformation, 18
cyclic permutation, 171

D
DAG (directed acyclic graph), 116
datum, 2
de Bruijn, N. G., 74
default constructor, 8
     for array_k, 211
     for pair, 209
default ordering, 62
default total ordering, 62
     importance of, 228
definition space, 9
definition-space predicate, 17
dependence of axiom, 86
deref, 150
derived relation, 50

descendant of bifurcate
          coordinate, 116
destructor, 7
     for pair, 210
difference ($-$)
     in additive group, 67
     in cancellable monoid, 72
     of integers, 18
     of iterator and integer, 111
     of iterators, 93
DifferenceType type function, 113
direct product ($\times$), 231
directed acyclic graph, 116
DiscreteArchimedeanRing concept, 86
DiscreteArchimedeanSemiring concept, 85
discreteness property, 85
disjoint property, 134
disjointness of composite object, 216
distance algorithm, 19
distance in orbit, 19
DistanceType type function, 17, 91
distributive property, holds for semiring,
          68
divisibility on an Archimedean monoid,
          76
division, 68
domain, 10
Domain type function, 12
double-ended array, 220
doubly linked list, 218–219
Dudziński, Krzysztof, 206
dummy node doubly linked list, 218
Dydek, Andrzej, 206
dynamic-size sequence, 216

E
efficient computational basis, 6
element ($\in$), 231
eliminating common subexpression, 35
empty
     for array_k, 212
     for bounded_range, 214
     for *Linearizable*, 213
empty coordinate, 144
empty range, 95
EmptyLinkedBifurcateCoordinate
          concept, 144
end

for array_k, 211
for bounded_range, 214
for *Linearizable*, 213
entity, 1
equality
=, 7
≠, 62
for array_k, 212
behavioral, 3, 228
equal for *Regular*, 127
for objects, 5
for pair, 210
for regular type, 7
representational, 3, 228
structural, 228
for uniquely represented type, 3
for value type, 3
equals by definition (≜), 12, 231
equational reasoning:, 4
equivalence class, 51
equivalence property, 51
equivalent (⇔), 231
equivalent coordinate collections, 126
erasure in a sequence, 217
Euclidean function, 79
EuclideanMonoid concept, 77
EuclideanSemimodule concept, 80
EuclideanSemiring concept, 79
euclidean_norm algorithm, 16
even, 40
exchange_values algorithm, 164
exists (∃), 231
expressive computational basis, 6

F
fast_subtractive_gcd algorithm, 78
fibonacci algorithm, 46
Fibonacci sequence, 45
find algorithm, 96
find_adjacent_mismatch algorithm, 103
find_adjacent_mismatch_forward algorithm, 106, 135
find_backward_if algorithm, 112
find_if algorithm, 97
find_if_not, 97
find_if_not_unguarded algorithm, 102
find_if_unguarded algorithm, 101
find_last algorithm, 136

find_mismatch algorithm, 102
find_n algorithm, 101
find_not algorithm, 97
finite order, under associative operation, 32
finite set, 171
first-last singly linked list, 218
fixed point of transformation, 170
fixed-size sequence, 216
Floyd, Robert W., 21
for all (∀), 231
ForwardIterator concept, 106
ForwardLinker concept, 133
forward_offset property, 162
for_each algorithm, 96
for_each_n algorithm, 101
Frobenius, Georg Ferdinand, 32
from-permutation, 172
function, 2
→, 231
on abstract entities, 2
on values, 3
function object, 9, 96, 236
functional procedure, 9
FunctionalProcedure concept, 11

G
garbage collection, 230
Gaussian integers, 40
Stein's algorithm, 81
gcd, 76
Stein, 81
subtractive, 76
gcd algorithm, 80
genus, 2
global state, 6
goto statement, 148
greater (>), 62
greater or equal (≥), 62
greatest common divisor (gcd), 76
group, 67
of permutations, 170

H
half_nonnegative, 40
half-open bounded range ([f, l)), 94
half-open interval, 231
half-open weak or counted range (⟦f, n⟧), 94
HalvableMonoid concept, 74

handle of orbit, 20
handle size, 20
header of composite object, 217
height algorithm, 122
height of bifurcate coordinate (DAG), 116
height_recursive algorithm, 118
Ho, Wilson, 182
Hoare, C. A. R., 195
homogeneous functional procedure, 10
HomogeneousFunction concept, 12
HomogeneousPredicate concept, 16

I

ideas, categories of, 1
identity
    of concrete entity, 1
    of object, 5
identity element, 65
identity token, 5
identity transformation, 170
identity_element property, 65
implies ($\Rightarrow$), 231
inconsistency of concept, 87
increasing range, 103
increasing_counted_range property, 105
increasing_range property, 105
increment algorithm, 91
independence of proposition, 86
index ([ ])
    for **array_k**, 211
    for **bounded_range**, 214
index permutation, 172
index of segmented array, 221
indexed iterator
    equivalent to random-access iterator, 113
IndexedIterator concept, 110
inequality ($\neq$), 7
    standard definition, 62
inorder, 118
input object, 6
input/output object, 6
InputType type function, 11
insertion in a sequence, 217
Integer concept, 18, 40
interpretation, 2
intersection ($\cap$), 231
interval, 231
into transformation, 169

invariant, 148
    loop, 37
    recursion, 36
inverse of permutation, 170, 171
inverse_operation property, 66
isomorphic coordinate sets, 124
isomorphic types, 86
is_left_successor algorithm, 119
is_right_successor algorithm, 120
iterator adapter
    for bidirectional bifurcate coordinates,
        project, 124
    random access from indexed, 114
    reverse from bidirectional, 112
    underlying type, 224
Iterator concept, 91
iterator invalidation in array, 221
IteratorConcept type function, 187
IteratorType type function, 133, 134, 213

K

Kislitsyn, Sergei, 55
k_rotate_from_permutation_indexed
        algorithm, 180
k_rotate_from_permutation_random_access
        algorithm, 180

L

Lagrange, J.-L., 107
Lakshman, T. K., 159
largest_doubling algorithm, 75
less ($<$), 62
    for **array_k**, 212
    for **bounded_range**, 215
    less for *TotallyOrdered*, 130
    natural total ordering, 61
    for **pair**, 210
less or equal ($\leq$), 62
lexicographical_compare algorithm, 129
lexicographical_equal algorithm, 127
lexicographical_equivalent algorithm, 127
lexicographical_less algorithm, 130
limit in a range, 95
linear ordering, 52
Linearizable concept, 213
link rearrangement, 134
    on lists, 219
linked iterator, 133

linked structures, forward vs. bidirectional, 219
LinkedBifurcateCoordinate concept, 144
linker object, 133
linker_to_head machine, 139
linker_to_tail machine, 135
links, reversing, 145
list
   doubly linked, 218
   singly linked, 218
Lo, Raymond, 182
load, 4
local part of composite object, 217
local state, 6
locality of reference, 143
loop invariant, 37
lower bound, 107
lower_bound_n algorithm, 109
lower_bound_predicate algorithm, 108

M
machine, 120
   advance_tail, 135
   copy_backward_step, 154
   copy_step, 152
   count_down, 153
   linker_to_head, 139
   linker_to_tail, 135
   merge_n_step_0, 205
   merge_n_step_1, 205
   reverse_copy_backward_step, 156
   reverse_copy_step, 155
   reverse_swap_step, 166
   swap_step, 165
   traverse_step, 121
   tree_rotate, 145
maps to ($\mapsto$), 231
marking, 118
Mauchly, John W., 107
median_5 algorithm, 61
memory, 4
memory-adaptive algorithm, 177
merge, stability, 203
mergeable property, 203
merge_copy algorithm, 163
merge_copy_backward algorithm, 163
merge_linked_nonempty algorithm, 141
merge_n_adaptive algorithm, 206

merge_n_step_0 machine, 205
merge_n_step_1 machine, 205
merge_n_with_buffer algorithm, 202
mod (remainder), 18
model, partial, 70
models, 11
Module concept, 70
monoid, 67
multipass traversal, 106
MultiplicativeGroup concept, 68
MultiplicativeMonoid concept, 67
MultiplicativeSemigroup concept, 66
multiset, 227
Musser, David, 13
mutable range, 151
mutable_bounded_range property, 151
mutable_counted_range property, 151
mutable_weak_range property, 151
mutative rearrangement, 172

N
natural total ordering, < reserved for, 61
negative, 40
nil, 134
Noether, Emmy, 13
noncircularity of composite object, 216
none algorithm, 97
NonnegativeDiscreteArchimedeanSemiring
   concept, 86
nontotal procedure, 17
not ($\neg$), 231
not_all algorithm, 97
not_overlapped property, 157
not_overlapped_backward property, 155
not_overlapped_forward property, 153
not_write_overlapped property, 159
null link, 218

O
object, 4
   area, 227
   equality, 5
   starting address, 216
   state, 4
object type, 4
odd, 40
one, 40
one-to-one transformation, 169

onto transformation, 169
open interval, 231
Operation concept, 16
or ($\vee$), 231
orbit, 18–20
orbit_structure algorithm, 28
orbit_structure_nonterminating_orbit
 algorithm, 27
OrderedAdditiveGroup concept, 70
OrderedAdditiveMonoid concept, 70
OrderedAdditiveSemigroup concept, 70
ordering, linear, 52
ordering-based rearrangement, 172
output object, 6
overloading, 43, 133, 144
own state, 6
ownership, of parts by composite
 object, 216

P

pair type, 11, 209
parameter passing, 9
part of composite object, 215–219
partial model, 70
partial procedure, 17
partial (usage convention), 232
partially formed object state, 7
partially_associative property, 98
partition algorithm, origin of, 195
partition point, 105
 lower and upper bounds, 107
partition rearrangement, semistable, 192
partitioned property, 105
partitioned range, 105
partitioned_at_point algorithm, 191
partition_bidirectional algorithm, 194
partition_copy algorithm, 160
partition_copy_n algorithm, 160
partition_linked algorithm, 140
partition_point algorithm, 107
partition_point_n algorithm, 107
partition_semistable algorithm, 192
partition_single_cycle algorithm, 194
partition_stable_iterative algorithm, 201
partition_stable_n algorithm, 197
partition_stable_n_adaptive algorithm, 197
partition_stable_n_nonempty
 algorithm, 197

partition_stable_singleton algorithm, 196
partition_stable_with_buffer algorithm, 195
partition_trivial algorithm, 198
permanently placed part of composite object,
 217
permutation, 170
 composition, 170
 cycle, 171
 cyclic, 171
 from, 172
 index, 172
 inverse, 170, 171
 product of its cycles, 171
 reverse, 174
 rotation, 178
 to, 172
 transposition, 171
permutation group, 170
phased_applicator algorithm, 147
pivot, 205
position-based rearrangement, 172
positive, 40
postorder, 118
potential_partition_point algorithm, 191
power
 of associative operation (a^n), 32
 powers of same element commute, 32
 of transformation (f^n), 17
power algorithm, 42
 operation count, 34
power_accumulate algorithm, 41
power_accumulate_positive algorithm, 41
power_right_associated algorithm, 33
power_unary algorithm, 18
precedence preserving link rearrangement,
 135
precedes ($\prec$), 95
precedes or equal ($\preceq$), 95
precondition, 13
predecessor
 of integer, 40
 of iterator, 111
Predicate concept, 15
predicate-based rearrangement, 172
predicate_source algorithm, 140
prefix of extent, 220
preorder, 118
prime property, 14

procedure, 6
   abstract, 13
   functional, 9
   nontotal, 17
   partial, 17
   total, 17
product (·)
   of integers, 18
   in multiplicative semigroup, 66
   in semimodule, 69
program transformation
   accumulation-variable elimination, 39
   accumulation-variable introduction, 35
   common-subexpression elimination, 35
   enabled by regular types, 35
   forward to backward iterators, 112
   relaxing precondition, 38
   strengthening precondition, 38
   strict tail-recursive, 37
   tail-recursive form, 35
project
   abstracting platform-specific copy
      algorithms, 164
   algorithms for bidirectional bifurcate
      algorithms, 123
   axioms for random-access iterator, 113
   benchmark and composite algorithm for
      rotate, 189
   concepts for bounded binary
      integers, 87
   coordinate structure concept, 131
   cross-type operations, 14
   cycle-detection algorithms, 29
   dynamic-sequences benchmark, 222
   dynamic-sequences implementation, 222
   dynamic-sequences interfaces, 222
   floating-point nonassociativity, 42
   isomorphism, equivalence, and ordering
      using tree_rotate, 148
   iterator adapter for bidirectional bifurcate
      coordinates, 124
   linear recurrence sequences, 47
   minimum-comparison stable sorting and
      merging, 61
   nonhalvable Archimedean monoids, 75
   order-selection stability, 61
   reallocation strategy for single-extent
      arrays, 221

   searching for a subsequence within a
      sequence, 114
   setting for Stein gcd, 81
   sorting library, 208
   underlying type used in major library, 225
projection regularity, 216
proper underlying type, 223
properly partial object state, 5
properly partial value type, 2
property
   aliased, 150
   annihilation, 68
   associative, 31
   asymmetric, 50
   backward_offset, 161
   bounded_range, 93
   commutative, 66
   complement_of_converse, 104
   counted_range, 93
   discreteness, 85
   disjoint, 134
   distributive, 68
   equivalence, 51
   forward_offset, 162
   identity element, 65
   identity_element, 65
   increasing_counted_range, 105
   increasing_range, 105
   inverse_operation, 66
   mergeable, 203
   mutable_bounded_range, 151
   mutable_counted_range, 151
   mutable_weak_range, 151
   notation, 14
   not_overlapped, 157
   not_overlapped_backward, 155
   not_overlapped_forward, 153
   not_write_overlapped, 159
   partially_associative, 98
   partitioned, 105
   prime, 14
   readable_bounded_range, 95
   readable_counted_range, 96
   readable_tree, 123
   readable_weak_range, 96
   reflexive, 50
   regular_unary_function, 14
   relation_preserving, 103

property (*cont.*)
  strict, 50
  strictly_increasing_counted_range, 105
  strictly_increasing_range, 104
  symmetric, 50
  total_ordering, 51
  transitive, 49
  tree, 117
  trichotomy, 51
  weak trichotomy, 51
  weak_ordering, 52
  weak_range, 92
  writable_bounded_range, 150
  writable_counted_range, 150
  writable_weak_range, 150
  write_aliased, 159
proposition, independence of, 86
pseudopredicate, 136
pseudorelation, 137
pseudotransformation, 91

Q

quotient (/), of integers, 18
quotient
  in Euclidean semimodule, 80
  in Euclidean semiring, 79
QuotientType type function, 72
quotient_remainder algorithm, 85
quotient_remainder_nonnegative algorithm,
    82
quotient_remainder_nonnegative_iterative
    algorithm, 83

R

random-access iterator, equivalent to indexed
    iterator, 113
RandomAccessIterator concept, 113
range
  backward movement, 112
  closed bounded ([f, l]), 94
  closed weak or counted ([[f, n]]), 94
  empty, 95
  half-open bounded ([f, l)), 94
  half-open weak or counted ([[f, n)), 94
  increasing, 103
  limit, 95
  lower bound, 107

  mutable, 151
  partition point, 105
  partitioned, 105
  readable, 95
  size, 94
  strictly increasing, 103
  upper bound, 107
  writable, 150
reachability
  of bifurcate coordinate, 116
  in orbit, 18
reachable algorithm, 121
readable range, 95
readable_bounded_range property, 95
readable_counted_range property, 96
readable_tree property, 123
readable_weak_range property, 96
rearrangement, 172
  bin-based, 172
  copying, 172
  link, 134
  mutative, 172
  ordering-based, 172
  position-based, 172
  reverse, 174
  rotation, 179
recursion invariant, 36
reduce algorithm, 99
reduce_balanced algorithm, 200
reduce_nonempty algorithm, 99
reduce_nonzeroes algorithm, 100
reduction, 98
reference counting, 230
refinement of concept, 11
reflexive property, 50
Regular concept, 11
  and program transformation, 35
regular function on value type, 3
regular type, 6–8
regularity, 216, 217
regular_unary_function property, 14
Relation concept, 49
relational concept, 69
relationship, 229
relation_preserving property, 103
relation_source algorithm, 141
relaxing precondition, 38
remainder

algorithm, 84
in Euclidean semimodule, 80
in Euclidean semiring, 79
remainder (mod), of integers, 18
remainder_nonnegative algorithm, 74
remainder_nonnegative_iterative algorithm,
    75
remote part of composite object, 217
representation, 2
representational equality, 3, 228
requires clause, 13
    syntax, 240
resources, 4
result space, 10
returning useful information, 87, 96, 97,
    101–103, 106, 112, 152, 153, 159,
    163, 174, 179, 182, 211
reverse rearrangement, 174
reverse_append algorithm, 139, 140
reverse_bidirectional algorithm, 175
reverse_copy algorithm, 156
reverse_copy_backward algorithm, 156
reverse_copy_backward_step machine, 156
reverse_copy_step machine, 155
reverse_indexed algorithm, 186
reverse_n_adaptive algorithm, 178
reverse_n_bidirectional algorithm, 175
reverse_n_forward algorithm, 177
reverse_n_indexed algorithm, 175
reverse_n_with_buffer algorithm, 176
reverse_swap_ranges algorithm, 167
reverse_swap_ranges_bounded
    algorithm, 167
reverse_swap_ranges_n algorithm, 168
reverse_swap_step machine, 166
reverse_with_temporary_buffer algorithm,
    187, 225
reversing links, 145
Rhind Mathematical Papyrus
    division, 73
    power, 33
Ring concept, 69
rotate algorithm, 187
rotate_bidirectional_nontrivial
    algorithm, 182
rotate_cycles algorithm, 181
rotate_forward_annotated algorithm,
    183

rotate_forward_nontrivial algorithm, 184
rotate_forward_step algorithm, 184
rotate_indexed_nontrivial algorithm, 181
rotate_nontrivial algorithm, 188
rotate_partial_nontrivial algorithm, 185
rotate_random_access_nontrivial algorithm,
    181
rotate_with_buffer_backward_nontrivial
    algorithm, 186
rotate_with_buffer_nontrivial algorithm, 185
rotation
    permutation, 178
    rearrangement, 179

S

schema, concept, 124
Schreier, Jozef, 55
Schwarz, Jerry, 150
segmented array, 221
segmented index, 221
select_0_2 algorithm, 53, 63
select_0_3 algorithm, 54
select_1_2 algorithm, 54
select_1_3 algorithm, 55
select_1_3_ab algorithm, 55
select_1_4 algorithm, 56, 59
select_1_4_ab algorithm, 56, 59
select_1_4_ab_cd algorithm, 56, 58
select_2_3 algorithm, 54
select_2_5 algorithm, 60
select_2_5_ab algorithm, 60
select_2_5_ab_cd algorithm, 59
semi (usage convention), 232
semigroup, 66
Semimodule concept, 69
Semiring concept, 68
semistable partition rearrangement, 192
sentinel, 101
Sequence concept, 216
    extent-based models, 219
    linked models, 219
set, 231
single-ended array, 220
single-extent array, 220
single-extent index, 221
single-pass traversal, 91
singly linked list, 218
sink, 149

size
   for array_k, 212
   for bounded_range, 214
   for *Linearizable*, 213
size of an orbit, 20
size of a range, 94
SizeType type function, 213
slanted index, 221
slow_quotient algorithm, 73
slow_remainder algorithm, 72
snapshot, 1
some algorithm, 97
sort_linked_nonempty_n algorithm, 142
sort_n algorithm, 207
sort_n_adaptive algorithm, 207
sort_n_with_buffer algorithm, 203
source, 90
space complexity, memory adaptive,
      177
species
   abstract, 2
   concrete, 2
splicing link rearrangement, 219
split_copy algorithm, 158
split_linked algorithm, 137
stability, 52
   of merge, 203
   of partition, 192
   of sort, 204
   of sort on linked range, 142
stability index, 53
Standard Template Library, x
starting address, 4, 216
state of object, 4
Stein, Josef, 81
Stein gcd, 81
STL, x
store, 4
strengthened relation, 53
strengthening precondition, 38
strict property, 50
strict tail-recursive, 37
strictly increasing range, 103
strictly_increasing_counted_range property,
      105
strictly_increasing_range property, 104
structural equality, 228
subpart of composite object, 216

subset ($\subset$), 231
subtraction, in additive group, 67
subtractive_gcd algorithm, 78
subtractive_gcd_nonzero algorithm, 77
successor
   definition space on range, 94
   of integer, 40
   of iterator, 91
sum (+)
   in additive semigroup, 66
   of integers, 18
   of iterator and integer, 92
swap algorithm, 224
swap_basic algorithm, 223
swap_ranges algorithm, 165
swap_ranges_bounded algorithm, 166
swap_ranges_n algorithm, 166
swap_step machine, 165
symmetric complement of a relation, 52
symmetric property, 50

T
tail-recursive form, 35
technique. *See* program transformation
   auxiliary computation during recursion, 176
   memory-adaptive algorithm, 177
   operation–accumulation procedure duality,
      47
   reduction to constrained subproblem, 54
   returning useful information, 87, 96, 97,
      101–103, 106, 112, 152, 153, 159, 163,
      174, 179, 182, 211
   transformation–action duality, 28
   useful variations of an interface, 38
temporary_buffer type, 187
terminal element under transformation, 18
terminating algorithm, 23
three-valued compare, 63
Tighe, Joseph, 179
to-permutation, 172
total object state, 5
total procedure, 17
total value type, 2
TotallyOrdered concept, 62
total_ordering property, 51
trait class, 240
transformation, 17
   composing, 17, 32

cyclic element, 18
  fixed point of, 170
  identity, 170
  into, 169
  of program. *See* program transformation
  one-to-one, 169
  onto, 169
  orbit, 18
  power of (f^n), 17
  terminal element, 18
Transformation concept, 17
transitive property, 49
transpose_operation algorithm, 201
transposition, 171
traversal
  multipass, 106
  single-pass, 91
  of tree, recursive, 119
traverse algorithm, 123
traverse_nonempty algorithm, 118
traverse_phased_rotating algorithm, 148
traverse_rotating algorithm, 146
traverse_step machine, 121
tree property, 117
tree_rotate machine, 145
trichotomy law, 51
triple type, 11
trivial cycle, 171
twice, 40
two-pointer header doubly linked list, 218
type
  array_k, 210
  bounded_range, 214
  computational basis, 6
  counter_machine, 200
  isomorphism, 86
  models concept, 11
  pair, 11, 209
  regular, 6
  temporary_buffer, 187
  triple, 11
  underlying_iterator, 225
  visit, 118
type attribute, 10
  Arity, 11
type concept, 11
type constructor, 11
type function, 11

Codomain, 11
DifferenceType, 113
DistanceType, 17, 91
Domain, 12
  implemented via trait class, 240
InputType, 11
IteratorConcept, 187
IteratorType, 133, 134, 213
QuotientType, 72
SizeType, 213
UnderlyingType, 223
ValueType, 90, 149, 213
WeightType, 115

U
unambiguous value type, 3
UnaryFunction concept, 12
UnaryPredicate concept, 16
underlying type, 164, 223
  iterator adapters, 224
  proper, 223
UnderlyingType type function, 223
underlying_iterator type, 225
underlying_ref algorithm, 224
union (∪), 231
uniquely represented object type, 5
uniquely represented value type, 2
univalent concept, 86
upper bound, 107
upper_bound_n algorithm, 109
upper_bound_predicate algorithm, 109
useful variations of an interface, 38
usefulness of concept, 87

V
value, 2
value type, 2
  ambiguous, 3
  properly partial, 2
  regular function on, 3
  total, 2
  uniquely represented, 2
ValueType type function, 90, 149, 213
visit type, 118

W
weak (usage convention), 232
weak-trichotomy law, 51

weakening of concept, 11
weak_ordering property, 52
weak_range property, 92
weight algorithm, 122
WeightType type function, 115
weight_recursive algorithm, 117
weight_rotating algorithm, 147
well-formed object, 5
well-formed value, 2

words in memory, 4
writable range, 150
writable_bounded_range property, 150
writable_counted_range property, 150
writable_weak_range property, 150
write_aliased property, 159

Z
zero, 40

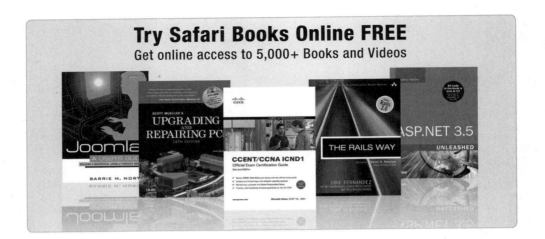